# Tabloiding the Truth

Steve Buckledee

# Tabloiding the Truth

## It's the Pun Wot Won It

Steve Buckledee
Faculty of Humanities
University of Cagliari
Cagliari, Italy

ISBN 978-3-030-47275-7     ISBN 978-3-030-47276-4  (eBook)
https://doi.org/10.1007/978-3-030-47276-4

© The Editor(s) (if applicable) and The Author(s) 2020
This work is subject to copyright. All rights are solely and exclusively licensed by the Publisher, whether the whole or part of the material is concerned, specifically the rights of translation, reprinting, reuse of illustrations, recitation, broadcasting, reproduction on microfilms or in any other physical way, and transmission or information storage and retrieval, electronic adaptation, computer software, or by similar or dissimilar methodology now known or hereafter developed.
The use of general descriptive names, registered names, trademarks, service marks, etc. in this publication does not imply, even in the absence of a specific statement, that such names are exempt from the relevant protective laws and regulations and therefore free for general use.
The publisher, the authors and the editors are safe to assume that the advice and information in this book are believed to be true and accurate at the date of publication. Neither the publisher nor the authors or the editors give a warranty, expressed or implied, with respect to the material contained herein or for any errors or omissions that may have been made. The publisher remains neutral with regard to jurisdictional claims in published maps and institutional affiliations.

Cover illustration: Lenscap/Alamy Stock Photo

This Palgrave Macmillan imprint is published by the registered company Springer Nature Switzerland AG
The registered company address is: Gewerbestrasse 11, 6330 Cham, Switzerland

# Acknowledgements

I am grateful to Cathy Scott, who first put the idea of writing this book in my head, and my editor, Alice Green. My gratitude extends to family, friends and colleagues who have had to put up with me over the years, chief among them Maria, who has somehow resisted the temptation to simulate a domestic accident. Thanks also to Reach PLC for permission to reproduce a substantial part of an article covered by copyright.

# Contents

| | | |
|---|---|---|
| 1 | Introduction: A Uniquely British Phenomenon? | 1 |
| 2 | From 'Horse Dope' to 'Saucy Soap' Sensations: The Making of the Modern Tabloid | 11 |
| 3 | From 'Gotcha' to 'Shocking and Awful': How the Tabloids Report Britain's Military Conflicts | 19 |
| 4 | From 'Rivers of Blood' to 'Migrants Are Like Cockroaches': The Tabloids and Race | 51 |
| 5 | Totties, Time Warps and Traitors to the Sisterhood: The Tabloids and Sex | 77 |
| 6 | 'Ve vill Occupy ze Sunbeds Here at Precisely 5 a.m....!': National Stereotypes and Britain's Relationship with Europe | 93 |

7 'Drug Trial Moment of Horror' to 'European Health Tourist Scam': Investigative Journalism and Other Merits of the Tabloids     111

8 From 'Zip Me Up Before You Go Go' to 'Boring Old Gits to Wed': The Tabloids and Celebrities     131

9 'Bonkers Bruno Locked Up' and 'Under the Carapace of Glittering, Hedonistic Celebrity': When the Tabloids Misread the Public Mood     151

10 'Parents' Car Hid a Corpse' and 'Terror as Plane Hits Ash Cloud': Lies and Distortions in the Tabloids     163

11 Conclusions     181

Index     191

# 1

# Introduction: A Uniquely British Phenomenon?

Thirteen days after News International closed *The News of the World* in the wake of the phone-hacking scandal, Charlie Beckett (2011a) used the headline 'Why does Britain have such a popular, political and aggressive tabloid press?' in an article published on the website of the London School of Economics. As founding director of *Polis*, a think tank for research and debate on international journalism, he had regular contact with media professionals in other countries who expressed their perplexity as the full extent of *The News of the World*'s shenanigans emerged. What they all wanted to know was why Britain seemed to be alone in having such unpleasant downmarket newspapers that promulgated odious political views, delighted in revealing the sordid details of celebrities' sex lives and employed journalists who were apparently willing to break the law in order to secure a scoop. Although Beckett could answer their multifaceted question with reference to historical, political and cultural factors, he felt the need to consult other Britons via Twitter.

The consensus was that while other countries had lowbrow tabloids, celebrity gossip magazines and trash TV, Britain was indeed 'the odd one out in combining the sensationalism, politics and real investigative reporting in a small newspaper format'. Tabloid-style journalism exists in many societies but the various elements that coexist in a UK red-top or black-top are found on separate platforms in other countries.

Feedback on Beckett's article included contributions by professionals in the field. The award-winning investigative journalist, Iain Overton, offered a number of aspects that explain the uniqueness of the British tabloids: a newspaper-reading tradition that has been passed from generation to generation since Victorian times, the prurience of our Protestant culture, the class system and a national impulse to attack the great and the good, and the fact that in Britain 'we blood-let in print not on pavements'. The right-wing blogger Paul Staines, better known by his *nom de clavier* Guido Fawkes, argued that Britain's 'boisterous tabloid culture' is a positive thing. No one commenting upon the article denied that the UK tabloids were in various ways different from popular newspapers in other countries.

Ten days later, Beckett (2011b) had a longer version of his article published in the *Guardian*. The headline was more explicit in indicating the uniqueness of Britain's best-selling newspapers: 'The tabloids – a particularly British beast'. While not denying the UK tabloids' many vices, he also expressed the view that the tabloid mindset is an important component of Britain's tradition of press freedom, and for his foreign contacts, he had his explanations ready:

> I patiently point out to them the virtues of a robust, unregulated press that is tough enough to take on those in authority. I remind them that many agenda-setting revelations of corruption or deceit are broken by the tabloids. These tabloids care about the less grandiose affairs that impact on most people's lives. I point out that they are also read by expensively educated folk who hold down important jobs and pay high rates of tax. I emphasise how competitive our newspaper market is and that the tabloids are very popular, so they must be doing something right.

This second article stimulated more than a hundred readers' comments on the *Guardian Online*, many of which were highly critical of Beckett's defence of the tabloids. None, however, took issue with his claim that the beast was of British pedigree.

Roy Greenslade (2015), *Guardian* columnist and Emeritus Professor of Journalism at City University London, also believes that the British tabloids feature peculiarities that have no direct equivalents elsewhere: 'No other nation fostered newspapers that combined information and entertainment in such appealing packages that they were able to command, at their height, a collective audience that accounted for about 85% of the entire population'. Greenslade joined the *Sun* in 1969 when it had just been acquired by Rupert Murdoch, later became assistant editor and then in 1990 answered Robert Maxwell's call to become editor of the *Daily Mirror*. Having worked in the newspaper business for more than half a century, he can state—to use his own word 'advisedly'—that Britain is the only country 'to have created a nationwide tabloid culture'.

The paradox is that while the British tabloids have been phenomenally successful, they are routinely reviled as vulgar, reactionary, culturally retrograde, sexist, homophobic, racist and often downright cruel in their gleeful destruction of careers and reputations. The expression *Sun reader* has come to mean a bigoted ignoramus. Tabloid reporters and editors are portrayed as unprincipled individuals who respect no code of professional ethics, are obsessed with the salacious, pry into people's private lives, are insensitive to those who have suffered distressing experiences and are disturbingly willing to bend the truth to suit their ideological agenda. A superior education (real or imagined) seems to be incompatible with a tolerant attitude towards Britain's best-selling newspapers, and when an academic such as Charlie Beckett argues that the tabloids sometimes do a good job, and points out that a significant percentage of their readers are well educated, he invites vitriol. A small sample of readers' comments on his *Guardian* article is given below.

> harbinger posted: This is such a rambling, incoherent and superficial piece of writing that I can hardly believe that Beckett actually runs the media department at LSE.
> Lairdlardy posted: do not dress a Turd up in fancy apologetics and then tell us its hygeine (*sic*)
> jekylnhyde posted: Don't try to pretend that educated people read the tabloids. Ignoring the trash that's in them the patronising, untalented writing would offend anyone who has learnt English to any level.

> LittleRichardjohn posted: This isn't a defence of the rights of the press, more a defence of the right to crap on anyone's doorstep on the way home from the pub.
> Barrier posted: Unfucking believable

The ease with which one can post online feedback facilitates knee-jerk reactions based upon mere anecdotal evidence, or perhaps just prejudice, rather than statistical data and detailed investigation. Academics who have studied circulation and readership figures and have conducted serious research into the tabloids' content and language over the decades tend to agree with Beckett. Bingham and Conboy (2015: 22) write:

> [...] we can find instances when tabloids were progressive and generous, when they provided a powerful voice for ordinary people against elitism and vested interests, and when they challenged the entrenched majority view. They offered a platform for a wide range of voices and contributors. Love them or loathe them, we need to take the tabloids seriously and understand how they contributed to the unfolding of British life over the last century.

It should be noted that Bingham and Conboy refer to instances when the tabloids *were*, not *have been*, progressive and generous. Their choice of the past simple rather than the present perfect is significant since in British English the latter 'locates the situation within a period of time beginning in the past and extending forward to include the present' while the former is used 'where the time of the situation is identified as wholly in the past' (Huddleston 1984: 158). Similarly, subsequent past simple verbs—*provided, challenged, offered, contributed*—underscore the idea that the tabloids no longer have the power and/or desire to make the positive contribution to British life that they once did. It is hardly a revelation that the same newspapers that saw off the threat posed by television have struggled with the challenge of the internet and smartphones, and many observers believe that all newspapers, but most of all the downmarket titles, will eventually be swept away by the new media. However, it would be unwise to write obituaries for the tabloids just yet because they are adaptable animals.

## 1 Introduction: A Uniquely British Phenomenon?

Circulation figures for print editions have dropped significantly since the start of the century, and although all the national dailies have embraced the new technology and have gone online, that has not been enough to recoup the lost advertising revenue. Different papers have adopted different strategies to meet the economic challenge. In 2016, *The Independent* dispensed with its print edition and is now a freely accessible online newspaper. The *Times*, *Financial Times* and the *Telegraph* have put up paywalls for access to their online editions, which allows them to continue to appear on newsstands. The *Guardian* has no paywall but invites visitors to its website to make regular or one-off donations. The only tabloid to experiment with a paywall is the *Sun* which, on Rupert Murdoch's insistence, introduced a monthly subscription for online access in 2013, but two years later was forced to make most of its content free once again after losing vast numbers of users to rivals like *MailOnline*. At the time of writing, all the tabloids' online editions are freely accessible.

The need to adapt to changing circumstances has also led to a merger that would once have been unthinkable. In 2018, Trinity Mirror (publisher of the *Daily Mirror, Sunday Mirror* and *The Sunday People*) acquired Northern & Shell (*Daily Express, Sunday Express, Daily Star*) and formed Reach plc, one of the UK's biggest newspaper groups which also publishes some 240 regional papers. The notion of the Labour-supporting, anti-Brexit *Mirror* teaming up with the right-wing, fiercely pro-Brexit *Express* caused some consternation, and the deal was held up for several weeks until the Competition and Markets Authority was convinced that the merger did not represent a threat to media plurality. Since the marriage of convenience took place, the distinct styles and editorial stances of the *Express* and the *Mirror* have not changed in the slightest.

Despite the difficulties newspapers have in remaining viable in the digital age, nearly all the titles that existed in 2000 are still available. Indeed, there is a new kid on the block: in 2010, *The i* was launched as a sister paper to *The Independent*. The extraordinary success of *Metro* has also created food for thought in the industry. Founded in 1999 and distributed free in city centres and railway, bus and tube stations, by 2018 *Metro* had overtaken the *Sun* as Britain's most-read daily paper and was generating enough advertising revenue to make profits of around £1 m a month. What *The i* and *Metro* have in common is that both present news stories in succinct bite-size articles suitable for busy people who want their news in condensed form and commuters who only have a few underground stops in which to find out what is going on in the world.

Statistics released by PAMCo (Audience Measurement for Publishers, the governing body that oversees audience measurement for the media industry) show that in 2018 around 25 million people still read a UK newspaper or its website every day (Ponsford 2019). Of the nineteen titles investigated, all but two had digital editions that attracted more readers than their print editions, the exceptions being the Scottish weekly newspaper, the *Sunday Post*, and the *Times*, which, as noted above, has a paywall for access to its website. Total digital readership—primarily smartphone but also tablet and desktop—was up 12% on the previous year. The market leader was the *Sun* with a monthly reach of 29,286 million readers (including 8250 million for the print edition), closely followed by the *Mail* with a monthly reach of 29,280 million (7821 million for the print edition). Interestingly, the third best performer was not a tabloid but the *Guardian*, which suggests that the decision to solicit donations instead of imposing a paywall was a wise choice. Indeed, 2018 marked a turning point for the Guardian Media Group in that for the first time digital revenues (advertising income plus readers' contributions) slightly exceeded those from the printed newspaper (Waterson 2018).

Since the tabloids allow free access to their websites, they attract a huge number of visitors, so it is possible—indeed likely—that they too will soon see their digital editions generating more revenue than their inexorably declining print editions. Addison (2017: position 6072) notes that the success of the *MailOnline* website has had consequences that go far beyond the mere survival of the *Daily Mail* title:

> [...] it is starting to generate cash to cover the costs of the decline in profits from the company's newspaper. *Daily Mail* content is now read by more people – more *young* people – than ever before. And it's always hiring: the old newspaper has a shrinking editorial staff of around 330, fewer than half *MailOnline*'s ever-expanding total staff of over 800.

It is interesting that in referring to current readers of *Daily Mail* content, Addison italicises the adjective *young*. The typical reader of the newspaper has traditionally been assumed to be white, lower-middle or middle class, conservative in behaviour and conservative in politics, patriotic, suspicious of anything arty-farty, and either middle-aged or elderly. With the switch from paid print to free digital, the tabloids now have much more heterogeneous readerships. In the pre-internet days, most people bought just one national daily and generally chose one that reflected their own values, beliefs and prejudices. We all had mental schemata of the typical *Express* reader and the typical *Mirror* reader and it was difficult to imagine either parting with a few coins to buy a copy of the other's abominable paper. Today people who have time to spare can look at the websites of a number of newspapers, including those whose stance on political and social issues they find odious. Their identities hidden behind a nickname, they often post extremely hostile, sometimes offensive, comments on what they read. They might decide to share selected content on social media, not because they approve of it, but because they want others to know how obnoxious they find it. Those of a creative bent even post parodies in the style of a particular newspaper or a specific journalist.

By now, no one really doubts that in 2016 Russian trolls used Twitter to meddle in both the US presidential election and the Brexit referendum in the UK. Much of the so-called news on social media comes from sources that are difficult, sometimes impossible, to trace. Fact checking before posting is inconceivable. People can publish whatever they like secure in the knowledge that the risk of being called to account is negligible. In short, social media are repositories of fake news. Except when a news story is accessed via a link to the online edition of a long-established news provider. You may not like what you read on thesun.co.uk but at least it will be something written by a named journalist or columnist for a newspaper whose editor, owner, London office and telephone number can be traced. As regards the veracity of news items on the tabloids' websites, we take it for granted that the facts have been sensationalised and that a bit of spin has been put on anything of a political nature. Unambiguous falsehoods are relatively rare but they do occur, and when they do it is a simple matter to register a complaint with the Independent

Press Standards Organisation (IPSO). Those who scoff at Charlie Beckett's defence of the tabloids' role in maintaining press freedom in Britain would do well to consider that the increasingly common alternative is to read pieces posted anonymously by people whose paymasters, vested interests and political aims are similarly unknown.

As Oscar Wilde observed well over a century ago, 'The truth is rarely pure, and never simple' Tabloided truths are far from pure and simple, but neither are they lies as such. They need to be interpreted rather than accepted at face value, and as I hope to demonstrate in this book, the process of interpretation need not be a chore.

## References

Addison, Adrian. 2017. *Mail Men: The Unauthorized Story of the Daily Mail*, Kindle edition. London: Atlantic Books.
Beckett, Charlie. 2011a. Why does Britain have such a popular, political and aggressive tabloid press? *Polis Journalism and Society at the LSE*, July 20. https://www.theguardian.com/commentisfree/2011/jul/30/tabloids-british-phone-hacking. Accessed 9 April 2019.
Beckett, Charlie. 2011b. The tabloids—A particularly British beast. *Guardian*, July 30. https://www.theguardian.com/commentisfree/2011/jul/30/tabloids-british-phone-hacking. Accessed 9 April 2019.
Bingham, Adrian, and Martin Conboy. 2015. *Tabloid Century: The Popular Press in Britain, 1896 to the Present*. Oxford: Peter Lang.
Greenslade, Roy. 2015. The tabloid century: How tabloid papers helped to define Britain. *Guardian*, May 18. https://www.theguardian.com/media/greenslade/2015/may/18/the-tabloid-century-how-popular-papers-helped-to-define-britain. Accessed 9 April 2019.
Huddleston, Rodney. 1984. *Introduction to the Grammar of English*. Cambridge: Cambridge University Press.
Ponsford, Dominic. 2019. Pamco figures show 25m reading a UK newspaper (or its website) every day. *Press Gazette*, March 20. https://www.pressgazette.co.uk/uk-newspaper-and-website-readership-2018-pamco/. Accessed 16 April 2019.

Waterson, Jim. 2018. Guardian Media Group digital revenues outstrip print for first time. *Guardian*, July 24. https://www.theguardian.com/media/2018/jul/24/guardian-media-group-digital-revenues-outstrip-print-for-first-time. Accessed 16 April 2019.

# 2

# From 'Horse Dope' to 'Saucy Soap' Sensations: The Making of the Modern Tabloid

The first quote in the title refers to the *Sun* headline of 17 November 1969, the date of the first issue of that newspaper following its acquisition by Rupert Murdoch. The second comes from a 21 April 2017 headline in the digital edition of the *Daily Star*, the tabloid that since its inception has tried unsuccessfully to out-Sun the *Sun*.

Murdoch's takeover of the *Sun* can be seen as the key event that transformed the popular press in Britain. Although no one could imagine the extent to which he would revolutionise the paper—at first it continued to support the Labour Party, as befits a newspaper that began life in 1964 as a relaunch of the left-wing *Daily Herald*—certain changes came in immediately, including the switch from broadsheet to tabloid format. In language and style, the *Sun* under Murdoch's editor, Larry Lamb, set out to appeal to younger readers; although the Swinging Sixties were beginning to get decidedly creaky, the zeitgeist was still that of the taboo-busting Permissive Society and the *Sun* aimed to combine audacious content with linguistic dare-devilry. The early emphasis on stories with a sexual content and photographs of attractive young women was in tune with the social climate of a decade that had seen the arrival of the contraceptive pill, the legalisation of abortion, the decriminalisation of homosexuality and the abolition of censorship in the theatre. The first fully topless Page 3 Girl appeared in November 1970, a year after the Murdoch takeover.

Although the other popular newspapers initially criticised the *Sun*'s brash and raunchy style, its headlines featuring not particularly subtle sexual innuendo and, most of all, its photos of (semi-)naked women, they were soon forced by the newcomer's commercial success to adopt a not dissimilar approach themselves if they were to remain economically competitive. In 1978, the *Daily Star* was launched in an obvious attempt to beat the *Sun* at its own game by focusing on sex, celebrities, sport, gossip, UFOs and the supernatural while largely ignoring politics and serious news. It has never been close to matching the *Sun*'s circulation figures, however, which suggests that most readers still want a paper that has a clear editorial line on the main political issues of the day (something they get with the *Mail*, the *Express*, the *Mirror* and the *Sun* itself).

The *Sun*'s first ever front-page headline—'HORSE DOPE SENSATION'—introduced an exclusive story in which a racehorse trainer, Roy Pettitt, confessed to having doped his animals to condition their performance (the Sun 1969). It had long been widely suspected that this practice went on but the *Sun*'s report was the first admission from a horseracing insider that drugs were used to fix the results of races. The story provoked outrage from racing fans who had laid bets on races that had been fixed but also angry denials from people within the sport, plus, according to Chippindale and Horrie (2013: position 697), an unsuccessful attempt to get the *Sun*'s racing correspondent banned from racecourses in Britain. The ensuing controversy represented mission accomplished for Larry Lamb. He could not have imagined, however, that in 2019 that first ever front page of the Murdoch-era *Sun* would feature on a T-shirt sold on something called the internet for approximately 45% of the average weekly wage in 1969.[1]

If the lead story established Lamb's commitment to the traditional scoop, ideally one that provoked heated debate, it was other pieces that signalled the *Sun*'s strategy of exploiting the climate of permissiveness far more than its rivals had so far done and testing the limits of taste and acceptability. The photograph everyone talked about showed the Rolling Stones by a swimming pool as a near-naked young woman just happened to be passing, an image that combined celebrity with semi-nudity and was a taste of things to come. At the time the 21-year-old Prince Charles was arguably the most eligible bachelor in the world, and the other front-page story that day concerned a certain Lady Leonora Grosvenor, who was rumoured to be the future king's girlfriend. From day one, Murdoch's *Sun* made it clear that no one was out of bounds and the royal family could not expect to be treated with deference. There was also the serialisation of the novel *The Love Machine* by the American actress-turned-writer Jacqueline Susann, an author who had acquired a reputation for telling sexually charged stories about the wealthy and glamorous. The characteristics of Murdoch's vision of the popular press were established in that first edition: sensationalism, sex (in both text and images), celebrity gossip, popular culture, sport, colloquial language and self-confidence bordering on cockiness. It proved to be a winning formula for a newspaper that had been losing readers for years. Someone who had played a minor part in the production of the first issue of the rebranded *Sun* notes that: 'Within three days the *Sun* had doubled its pre-Murdoch sale' (Greenslade 1999).

The *Sun* is nothing if not unapologetic. When, exactly a year later, Stephanie Rahn became the first naked Page 3 Girl, the picture caption pre-empted the inevitable criticism: 'From time to time some self-appointed critic stamps his tiny foot and declares that the *Sun* is obsessed with sex. It is not the *Sun*, but the critics, who are obsessed. The *Sun*, like most of its readers, likes pretty girls' (the Sun 1970). Ever since the Murdoch takeover, the policy has been not to defend its photos of sexy young women but to counter-attack. Critics are dismissed as strait-laced killjoys, humourless prudes and self-righteous moaners who don't like to see others having a bit of innocent fun. In the lines quoted above, the critic is 'self-appointed' and therefore lacks authority and credibility. He 'stamps his tiny foot', like Rumpelstiltskin, a gesture indicative of a petulant nature. Finally, given that the foot-stamping critic is depicted as male, the observation that the *Sun* and most of its readers like pretty girls generates an inferred meaning, or an *implicature* (Grice 1968): *Sun*-bashers are men who don't like photos of pretty girls, so they must be homosexual. In 1970, just three years after the decriminalisation of homosexuality, the word *gay* as a positive synonym for homosexual had entered mainstream English but a whole series of derogatory terms had wider circulation. For stand-up comics and tabloid newspapers, poofs were still fair game.

The Sunification of the other popular papers began in November 1969 and continued apace. In many respects, the relaunched *Sun* was a spiced-up and sexier version of the *Daily Mirror*, and it was the *Mirror* that had to adapt fastest to meet the challenge of the brash new competitor. Even so, in 1978 the *Sun*'s circulation overtook the *Mirror*'s. For as long as the *Sun* supported the Labour Party, the *Daily Mail* and the *Daily Express* could rely on the loyalty of their conservative readers, but both nevertheless had to respond to the Murdoch/Lamb innovations. On 3 May 1971, exactly seventy years after it was founded, the *Mail* switched to tabloid format, and during the 1970s and 1980s, under the astute editorship of David English, appealed to new readers with the introduction of its *Femail* section as well as improved sports coverage and far more celebrity gossip. The *Daily Express* resisted the switch to tabloid format until 1977, did not adapt quickly enough or radically enough, and as a consequence saw its circulation plummet until, as noted in the Introduction, an unlikely merger with the Labour-supporting *Mirror* became necessary.

If imitation is the sincerest form of flattery, the launch of the *Daily Star* on 2 November 1978 was an exercise in sycophancy in its most unvarnished form. Quite simply, the aim was to out-Sun the *Sun* with even more sex, even more sport, even more celebrity gossip, even more stories about the weird or the supernatural and even less hard news. At the time, Britain had a minority government led by Jim Callaghan and whether it could survive until the new year was a much-discussed topic, but the *Star* ignored the political speculation and introduced its first issue with the headline 'MODEL'S MYSTERY PLUNGE' (Nicholson 1978) and a report about a 'millionaire playboy' denying that he had pushed his beautiful girlfriend out of the window of his flat. Indications of the content of the inside pages were given in the right-hand column, including the footballer Jimmy Greaves on 'My life on the booze' and a picture special with the intriguing title 'The Nude and the Priest'.

The *Daily Star* quickly established itself as the most tabloid of the tabloids. For all their love of gossip and show business, the *Sun* and the

*Mirror* know when a news story is big enough to push the triviality off the front page. Not so the *Daily Star*. In July 2005, terrorism left Londoners feeling more insecure than at any time since the end of the Second World War. On the 7th of the month, there was a bomb attack on the London underground, followed by a failed attack on the 21st, and then, the next day, the shooting of a Brazilian citizen wrongly identified by the police as a suspected terrorist. On the 25th, 26th and 28th of July, the lead stories in both the *Sun* and the *Mirror* were about the ongoing investigations and the search for those terrorists who had not yet been apprehended. On the same days, the *Star* led with the following stories: a participant on the reality show *Big Brother* who had vowed to be sexier, the most haunted house in the UK and a séance involving the cast of the soap opera *Coronation Street*.

The second half of the chapter title refers to an article ostensibly written by Simon Green (2017) although it mainly consists of images and text lifted from social media. It was published on the *Daily Star*'s website on 21 April 2017 but it is about an episode of the Brazilian soap opera *Em Família* aired in 2014. The pertinent scene shows the actress Bruna Marquezine, girlfriend of the footballer Neymar, as she accidentally drops her bath towel, briefly revealing all to millions of viewers. Simon Green evidently found a clip of the scene on social media and used it for a short piece entitled 'Neymar's sexy girlfriend gets fully naked in saucy soap opera throwback scene'. It consists of three judiciously selected stills from the soap opera, two photographs of Neymar on the field of play, a third photo of the footballer and Bruna Marquezine together, and fewer than 200 words of text, including three comments posted by appreciative social media users. A naked actress plus a famous footballer are a tabloid journalist's dream, especially when he can find all the material he needs with a few clicks of the mouse. The adjective *saucy* sounds rather dated, an odd choice for an article assembled using modern technology, but in tabloid headlines an alliterative adjective + noun collocation is highly valued.

The *Star* probably gave Rupert Murdoch some slight cause for concern during the 1980s when its daily sales rose to about 1.5 million, but it has never come close to rivalling the *Sun*'s circulation figures. In

March 2019, its circulation was down to 326,000, a whopping year-on-year drop of 17 per cent (Tobitt 2019). The problem is that it has never had a clear identity of its own: it began life by stealing the *Sun*'s clothes but has never worn them as well as their original owner does; it has always had a lower cover price than its competitors, which has not brought the success enjoyed by the freely distributed *Metro*; it has a vaguely right-wing feel to it while neither enthusing nor disgusting readers the way the ideologically committed *Mail* and *Express* routinely do.

In the Introduction to this book, it is argued that Britain has a tabloid culture that has no parallel elsewhere. Nowhere is this more evident than in the language of the tabloids. It is not at all unusual for a headline to be incomprehensible to a native speaker of English from an anglophone community other than the British Isles. An unsigned piece in the *Sunday People* (Mirror Online 2009) used a headline that would surely have baffled an American reader: 'CARLY'S A £2M MAG WAG'. It might be deduced that *mag* is an abbreviation of magazine (although in Australia to mag means to talk too much), but neither of the usual denotations of *wag*—a verb to indicate how tails or tongues move, or a noun for a person, generally male, who is something of a joker—seem to make sense in the context. WAG, usually written in upper case, is actually an acronym for the **W**ives **A**nd **G**irlfriends of high-earning footballers. The term was coined in Germany during the summer of 2006 when the behaviour of the partners of England's World Cup team made a considerable impression on media observers. It has not entered the English of anglophone communities outside Britain. For the lexicographer Tony Thorne (2014: 465), the expression now refers to 'a spendthrift, vacuous, glamorous young female', although it should be noted that WAGs are viewed more positively by the owners of expensive boutiques, jeweller's shops and private clinics specialising in cosmetic surgery.

When the significance of WAG is known, the meaning of '£2M MAG WAG' is still not clear. The Carly of the headline refers to Carly Zucker, who was a contestant in the reality TV show *I'm a Celebrity… Get Me out of Here* in 2008, and like Bruna Marquezine allowed millions of viewers to see her naked body. Shortly afterwards, she became a WAG when she met the Chelsea and England footballer Joe Cole, and the couple acquired a degree of celebrity status in Britain while remaining unknown in other countries. In normal circumstances, if a young couple wish to have a lavish wedding ceremony, one or both of the respective families will have to foot the bill, but when the betrothed are both public figures, a celebrity magazine might offer them a very large sum of money for exclusive rights to cover their happy day.

Much of the content of the UK tabloids is related to sport, pop music, TV soaps and sitcoms, and consumer products, which means that there are references to football and cricketing terminology, entertainers' catchphrases, song lyrics, real people and fictional characters, and brand names and advertising slogans that mean nothing to people unfamiliar with British popular culture. Idioms abound, as do nicknames, puns and slang, including ephemeral slang that does not last long enough to be included in revised editions of dictionaries. The conventional wisdom is that newspapers such as the *Guardian* or the *Telegraph* are more difficult to read since they employ complex, multi-clause sentences and formal, polysyllabic and often low-frequency lexis, but for many readers, especially those whose mother tongue is not English, but also native speakers who know little about British society, it is the informal language of the tabloids that they struggle to understand. I teach English language and linguistics at an Italian university and on several occasions I have asked my students to consider the ways in which the *Guardian* and the *Sun* report precisely the same news story. Each time they found the formal, Latinate vocabulary and conventional grammar of the quality paper much easier to read than the colloquial language of the tabloid. The 'nationwide tabloid culture' (Greenslade 2015) discussed in the Introduction is, from a linguistic point of view, problematic for people born outside Britain's national borders.

In the following chapters, the tabloids' treatment of various themes will be investigated, beginning with the subject of Britain's involvement in armed conflicts. Changes over time will be considered, as will the sometimes radically divergent attitudes and approaches adopted by different papers. In each case, linguistic strategies will be analysed and evaluated.

## Note

1. Horse Dope Sensation T-shirt, https://shop.spreadshirt.co.uk/sunheadlines/horse+dope+sensation-A11120471.

## References

Chippindale, Peter, and Chris Horrie. 2013. *Stick It Up Your Punter!: The Uncut Story of the "Sun" Newspaper*, Kindle edition. London: Faber and Faber.

Green, Simon. 2017. Neymar's sexy girlfriend gets fully naked in saucy soap opera throwback scene. *Daily Star*, April 21. https://www.dailystar.co.uk/showbiz-tv/hot-tv/607639/Neymar-girlfriend-naked-video-bruna-Marquezine-model-soap-opera-brazil. Accessed 26 April 2019.

Greenslade, Roy. 1999. Night the Sun came up. *Guardian Online*, November 15. https://www.theguardian.com/media/1999/nov/15/mondaymediasection.comment1. Accessed 27 April 2019.

Greenslade, Roy. 2015. The tabloid century: How tabloid papers helped to define Britain. *Guardian Online*, May 18. https://www.theguardian.com/media/greenslade/2015/may/18/the-tabloid-century-how-popular-papers-helped-to-define-britain. Accessed 27 April 2019.

Grice, Paul. 1968. Utterer's meaning, sentence-meaning, and word-meaning. *Foundations of Language* 4: 1–18.

Nicholson, James. 1978. Model's mystery plunge. *Daily Star*, November 2.

Sunday People. 2009, updated 2013. Carly's a £2m Mag Wag. *Mirror Online*, February 10. https://www.mirror.co.uk/news/world-news/carlys-a-2m-mag-wag-1662508. Accessed 27 April 2019.

The Sun. 1969. Horse dope scandal. *Sun*, November 17.

The Sun. 1970. Caption to first page-3 nude model image. *Sun*, November 17.

Thorne, Tony. 2014. *Dictionary of Contemporary Slang*. London: Bloomsbury.

Tobitt, Charlotte. 2019. National newsbrand ABCs: Full figures for March 2019. *Press Gazette Online*, April 18. https://www.pressgazette.co.uk/national-newsbrand-abcs-full-circulation-figures-for-march-2019/. Accessed 27 April 2019.

# 3

# From 'Gotcha' to 'Shocking and Awful': How the Tabloids Report Britain's Military Conflicts

The 'Gotcha' of the chapter title refers to the Falklands War and the *Sun*'s infamous headline of 4 May 1982 when a Royal Navy submarine torpedoed the Argentinian cruiser the *General Belgrano*. The second quote, clearly a parody of the Pentagon's *shock and awe* strategy, is a *Daily Mirror* headline of 22 March 2003 as that newspaper campaigned vigorously against Britain's involvement in the Iraq War. In addition to the Falklands and Iraq Wars, this chapter investigates the tabloids' treatment of the Troubles in Northern Ireland from the late 1960s to the Good Friday Agreement of 1998.

In the general election campaign of 1979, the *Sun* switched its allegiances to the Conservative Party. At the time, both Rupert Murdoch and Larry Lamb were frequently exasperated by Society of Lithographic Artists, Designers and Engravers (SLADE), the trade union that could, and sometimes did, prevent the newspaper from being produced. Margaret Thatcher's pledge to get tough with the unions had a certain appeal, but it is probable that both men sensed that the public were getting fed up with consensus politics and were ready for a more adversarial approach. Thatcher duly won the election with a majority of 43 and the following year Lamb was rewarded when he became Sir Larry. Murdoch, fair dinkum Aussie that he is, had no time for pomposity and the

British class system, and was less than impressed when his editor actually expected people to use his title, so Lamb's days were numbered. In 1981, Kelvin MacKenzie became editor, and the new man immediately brought a very different managerial style to the editorial floor. He referred to the newspaper by the Cockney rhyming slang expression *Currant Bun*, tolerated no criticism of the *Boss* (Murdoch) and in laying down the law to his staff made liberal use of monosyllabic lexemes that denote genitalia, sexual acts or excreta.

Mrs. Thatcher's economic medicine had a bitter taste, especially for people in traditional industries in the North and Midlands, and by early 1982, few would have bet on her remaining in office for eleven and a half years. On two occasions, however, the perfect adversary came along to allow her to demonstrate her combative nature and win over public support. In 1984, it was Arthur Scargill, leader of the National Union of Mineworkers (NUM). In 1982, the enemy was an ocean away.

> Margaret Thatcher was a lucky Prime Minister. On 19 March 1982 the fortune that favoured her for so long provided an ideal dragon for the Prime Minister to slay. It breathed fire and smoke in the South Atlantic. In December of the previous year, General Leopoldo Galtieri had seized control of the military Junta that governed Argentina. In order to bolster up his dubious authority he first made bellicose claims about the imminent expulsion of the British from the Malvinas and then, as a token of his serious intent, landed a party of scrap merchants on South Georgia – an isolated outpost of the Empire – where they scavenged for metal and ran up the Argentine flag. The Falklands War had begun in farce. It was to end with over 650 Argentine and 255 British servicemen and women killed in the battle for those inhospitable islands. (Hattersley 1997: 287–288)

It was not immediately obvious that Argentina's territorial claim to the Falklands would lead to war. Many people hoped that a diplomatic solution could be found, with a joint sovereignty agreement suggested as a way to avoid bloodshed. Kelvin MacKenzie, however, could not wait for the shooting to begin. When his political editor, Walter Terry, and Christopher Potter (1982) reported on the Cabinet rejecting Argentina's proposal for a peaceful compromise, MacKenzie approved the front-page splash 'STICK IT UP YOUR JUNTA' with the subhead '1am: Maggie No to deal – then Argentina invokes war treaty'. That headline immediately became a slogan and appeared on T-shirts as the nation prepared for war and the *Sun* launched a jingoistic campaign to raise public support for the British servicemen, who were usually referred to as 'our brave boys' (the women serving in the armed forces were overlooked). When the *Sun* comes up with a good headline, the policy is to recycle it, or variations upon it, over the years and decades; thirty-two years after the Falklands War, the Euro-sceptical *Sun*'s message for the then President of the EU Commission was 'STICK IT UP YOUR JUNCKER' (Ashton 2014), a headline that was re-used repeatedly two years later during the Brexit referendum campaign. Others have also made use of the *Sun*'s best-known headlines, as we see in the title of Chippindale and Horrie's lively history of the paper: *Stick It Up Your Punter!* (2013[2]).

Tabloids do not try to compete with television when it comes to reporting international news, so do not have a large team of foreign correspondents, but before the hostilities began MacKenzie took the unusual step of sending a reporter to the South Atlantic. The only British journalists already in Port Stanley when the action started were reporters from the prestigious *Sunday Times, Financial Times* and *Daily Telegraph*, plus David Graves of the *Currant Bun*. When Argentine troops occupied the island, the four journalists were relieved to discover that they were not going to get first-hand experience of the Junta's torture techniques, but they were not allowed to make telephone calls, and therefore could not file copy to their London offices. However, they were permitted to fly to the Patagonian city of Comodoro, where they were largely confined to their hotel and had to rely on Argentinian television and newspapers to find out what was happening. Of course, experienced journalists know how to read between the lines of regime-controlled media reports, but they nevertheless had to be circumspect about what they reported to their editors given that their hosts were surely listening in. For the *Sun*'s reporter, the problem was that the copy he filed was embellished by MacKenzie and an inner circle of trusted staff. Basically, they omitted what did not fit in with their patriotic, triumphalist agenda and added elements for which they had no evidence whatsoever, and in so doing were putting David Graves' life at risk.

The enemy troops were not Argentinians or Argentines but *Argies*, and 'The Paper that Supports Our Boys' constructed a relentless, xenophobic campaign of vilifying the adversaries and lauding the mettle of our brave lads. Chippindale and Horrie (2013: positions 2152–2177) describe the *Sun*'s marketing of patriotic products: panties for the wives and girlfriends of servicemen embroidered with the name of the ship transporting their partners to the war zone, 'The *Sun* says Good Luck' badges, a game for the British-made Sinclair computer based on torpedo attacks on Argie ships, the '*Sun*-sational' T-shirt bearing the 'STICK IT UP YOUR JUNTA' headline and even cans of Fray Bentos corned beef guaranteed not to contain Argentinian meat.

Roy Greenslade (2002), at the time assistant editor to MacKenzie, returned from his holidays to find the *Sun*'s Bouverie Street office transformed into a grotesque parody of a military operations centre.

> News editor Tom Petrie was wearing some sort of naval officer's cap and told me he now wished to be known as Commander Petrie. A map of the south Atlantic was pinned on the board behind him under a picture of Winston Churchill. Reporter Muriel Burden, who ran a pen pals service, was christened the "Darling of the Fleet". I soon realised that Bouverie Street was the unofficial war office with MacKenzie playing chief of staff and Petrie as his aide-de-camp.

Grown men and women were playing at soldiers, while their infantile behaviour was matched by the puerility of their language in articles that reduced the deadly serious business of war to a trivial game. Not even the death of 368 Argentinian sailors made MacKenzie reflect a little on the reality of war. On 4 May, the *General Belgrano* was torpedoed by the British submarine HMS *Conqueror* and the *Sun* rushed out an article ostensibly written by Tony Snow (1982) 'aboard HMS Invincible', although it is likely that his original report was modified just as much as David Graves' copy was routinely sensationalised. The one-word headline was 'Gotcha', which reduced the dramatic event to the level of a children's comic strip. The drophead 'Our lads sink gunboat and hole cruiser' featured a first-person possessive pronoun that negated any pretence of impartial reporting. The cartoonish style was maintained in the opening sentences of the article:

> **THE NAVY had the Argies on their knees last night after devastating double blow.**
> **WALLOP:** They torpedoed the 14,000-ton Argentinian cruiser General Belgrano and left it a useless wreck.
> **WALLOP:** Task Force helicopters sank one Argentine patrol boat and severely damaged another.

In the opening sentence, the disparaging neologism 'Argies' contrasts with the 'Our lads' of the drophead as the conflict is presented as a simple clash between good guys and bad guys with none of the moral ambiguity that characterises the reality of war. Then, the double use of 'WALLOP' in bold upper case calls to mind the onomatopoeic 'sound effects' that accompany images of violence in comic strips. The 'Gotcha' edition was put together when fundamental details of the attack were not yet known, and it was only after it had gone to press that MacKenzie began to wonder about the great number of casualties that the torpedo strike must have caused. The headline was later changed to 'Did 1,200 Argies drown?' (Greenslade 2002), which was somewhat less vulgar but the editor evidently drew the line at calling the crew of the *General Belgrano* Argentinians. That version has never appeared on a T-shirt, however, and to this day, it is 'Gotcha' that the public associate with the *Sun*'s coverage of war. In later conflicts, the other tabloids were to varying degrees influenced by the jingoistic and sometimes ghoulish approach of the *Sun*, but in 1982 none had anything remotely similar to that infamous one-word headline.

The patriotic credentials of the *Daily Express* are not in doubt, but the first word of its headline on 4 May 1982 immediately places the focus on the victims of the torpedo attack: 'Fear for 700 on Argentine warship SUNK!' (Evans and Warden 1982). The subhead is 'Junta: Our cruiser is lost', and the sixth paragraph of the article cites an official statement released by the Joint Chiefs of Staff in Buenos Aires, which indicates a willingness to report the Argentine (never 'Argie') view of events. Concern about the number of deaths is maintained with the Pentagon quoted as saying that a man could not survive for more than thirty minutes in the icy waters of the South Atlantic, while it is stressed in italics that the *General Belgrano*'s two escort ships were left unharmed so that they could rescue survivors. Even-handedness is evident in the reporting of both Argentina's claim that the cruiser was attacked when it was fifty miles outside the war zone and Britain's counterclaim that it was only 'just outside' and represented a real threat to the Task Force. Similarly, Defence Secretary John Nott's warning that Britain would 'continue to tighten the screw' is balanced by the Junta's threat to retaliate with an attack on a British vessel (which it duly carried out 48 hours later with a missile strike on the Royal Navy destroyer *Sheffield*). The attack is described as 'a sledgehammer blow' but in general hyperbole and comic strip slang are avoided, while throughout the article British military personnel are referred to in the third person.

The *Daily Mirror*'s front-page headline also acknowledges the Argentinian authorities as the source of the initial news about the *General Belgrano*: 'ATTACKED CRUISER 'SUNK'—says Argentina' (Plaice 1982). Above the headline, concern over the victims is expressed—'Fears over 1,200 crew'—and Ellis Plaice's article also addresses the question that was to be hotly debated in the following days, i.e. whether the attack was justified given that the cruiser was outside the war zone. Indeed, twenty-nine years were to pass before intelligence reports were released that proved that the *General Belgrano* had been ordered to attack the British Task Force and was therefore a legitimate target (Walters 2011).

The *Mirror*'s coverage of the Falklands War did not just differ from the *Sun*'s in terms of language and style. Its editorial line was to favour a negotiated compromise, in stark contrast with the amateur dramatics at Bouverie Street and Kelvin MacKenzie's gung-ho enthusiasm for a proper shooting war. The two papers attacked each other: the *Mirror* was accused of being lily-livered and lacking in patriotism, while the *Sun* was portrayed as vulgar, irresponsible and trigger-happy. They were, of course, fighting a private war of their own, not over some windswept islands, but over circulation. They were the two best-selling newspapers in Britain, but both wanted the undisputed number one spot. Kelvin MacKenzie calculated that with the country getting behind the war effort, and with Mrs. Thatcher in the role of warrior queen, nationalism and triumphalism would be a winning combination. For Chris Horrie (2002), the *Sun* won the circulation war as quickly as the Task Force won the real war:

> Until 1980 the Sun and the Mirror had been neck and neck in circulation terms. In 1981 the Sun had 'bought' half a million extra readers by unleashing its ruinously expensive £1 million prize bingo competition. But as the Union flag was unfurled over Port Stanley a year later, the champagne flowed at the Sun to celebrate a crushing 1 million sales victory over its rival, the Mirror. The conflict had cost the lives of 1,000 men. But the corresponding victory in the circulation stakes had not cost the Sun – or the owner Rupert Murdoch – a penny.

Horrie, possibly writing from memory, gives a rounded-up figure for the total number of war casualties and is less than 100% accurate over the impact of the conflict on circulation. Boyce (2005: 167) notes that in the short term it was the *Mirror* that improved its sales by 95,000 copies while the *Sun* lost 40,000. Things changed once the hostilities ceased: in the aftermath of war, as the nation savoured its morale-boosting military victory and Mrs. Thatcher's lead in the polls grew by the day, the *Sun* pulled ahead of its great rival and has retained its advantage ever since. Twelve months after the end of the Falklands War, Margaret Thatcher was re-elected with a massive majority of 144, and the paper that backed her every word and action was at the apex of its influence.

Many critics rounded on the *Sun* for its coverage of the Falklands War but the increase in sales meant that MacKenzie's gamble had paid off. This was not lost on his competitors when it came to reporting subsequent wars, although the Sunification effect was not comparable with the exploitation of sex and nudity described in the previous chapter. Indeed, the Iraq War that started in 2003 was covered in widely diverse ways by the popular newspapers.

Always unrepentant, the *Sun* has remained convinced that its 'Gotcha' headline is 'a classic'. In 2015 and again a year later, it was reported that Britain had reinforced its South Atlantic garrison to send a signal to an Argentinian government thought to be contemplating an invasion. The headline of both the original and the updated article was 'We've gotcha backs' with the subhead 'EXCLUSIVE: Argie invasion alert as we send troops to Falklands' (Newton Dunn 2016a).

Finally, let us return to David Graves, the *Sun* journalist on Argentine territory who on a daily basis saw the truth he sent to Bouverie Street tabloided in a manner unlikely to please the Junta by men pretending to be soldiers. Chippindale and Horrie (2013[2]: position 2287) describe the moment he thought he was about to be arrested:

> One evening shortly after 'GOTCHA' Graves was having dinner in a restaurant when an Argentinian admiral approached his table. His heart sank as the imposing uniformed figure asked: 'Mr Graves, may I speak to you?' Graves assented and the admiral went on: 'We have been looking at your reports to London.' This was it, thought Graves – at the very least the boot out of the country, if not torture in one of the junta's dungeons. And then he saw the admiral was smiling gently. 'And these reports of yours, they don't always appear in quite the same way in the paper as you have written them, do they?' The admiral smiled again and walked off.

The Junta's senior military officers, routinely depicted as thuggish and ruthless, evidently had among their number at least one man with a sense of humour and an appreciation of irony.

\* \* \*

The armed conflict that claimed more than 3500 lives in the British Isles was never defined as a war. The Troubles in Northern Island were re-awakened in the 1960s when the Catholic/Republican minority, frustrated at discrimination in both the allocation of public housing and access to jobs in the shipyards, formed the Northern Ireland Civil Rights Association (NICRA) as an instrument of peaceful, law-abiding protest. Initially, the newspapers on the British mainland were sympathetic to NICRA's perfectly reasonable demands for greater democracy in local government, an end to discriminatory practices and the abolition of the Ulster Special Constabulary (commonly known as the B-Specials), a unit of the police force that recruited almost exclusively from the Protestant Unionist community and was seen by Catholics as an instrument of repression.

Protestant Unionists loyal to the British Crown were also getting organised. The Ulster Constitution Defence Committee (UCDC) was formed, including the paramilitary wing the Ulster Protestant Volunteers (UPV), while in the Shankill neighbourhood of Belfast the Ulster Volunteer Force (UVF) was founded. In 1968 and 1969, there were violent clashes in the streets of Belfast and Derry between Catholic and Protestant marchers, as well as arson attacks on houses in Catholic neighbourhoods. The predominantly Protestant police force, the Royal Ulster Constabulary (RUC), stood accused of complicity in Loyalist aggression. Things came to a head in August 1969 with two days of continuous fighting between Loyalists and the Catholic residents of the Bogside neighbourhood of Derry while the RUC openly sided with the former. TV coverage of the violence horrified the entire nation, and Home Secretary Jim Callaghan finally bowed to the inevitable and sent in troops to restore order. Sandbrook (2007: 755) reports that their impact was immediate: 'Almost as soon as they had arrived the fighting died down: the very sight of heavily armed British personnel patrolling the streets was enough to douse the passions of the last week, and a fragile peace descended'.

Initially, even Irish Nationalists cautiously welcomed the presence of British troops since they were not the RUC and would not merely look on while Catholics' homes were torched. For the Army, the honeymoon was short-lived, however. The Irish Republican Army had been dormant for decades but in the late 1960s it began to reorganise, and in December 1969 split into the Official IRA, a Marxist group that tended to limit its military operations to attacks on British soldiers and RUC officers, and the much more trigger-happy Provisional IRA (or *Provos*), which had no qualms about targeting civilians. Over the next three decades, it was the Provos that conducted a guerilla war in both Northern Ireland and the British mainland.

Arguably, the most audacious of the IRA's attacks on symbols of British authority was the bomb that exploded at 2.54 a.m. on 12 October 1984 at the Grand Hotel in Brighton. The Conservative Party Conference was in progress and the aim of the attack was nothing less than to kill Margaret Thatcher and as many members of her Cabinet as possible. Five people died in the blast and 34 were seriously injured, including the wife of the Trade and Industry Secretary, Norman Tebbit, who was left permanently disabled. As the IRA openly admitted, however, the carnage had not been on the scale they had hoped to see. The next day two of the tabloids focused on the lucky escape Mrs. Thatcher had had: the *Daily Star*'s headline (1984) was 'MIRACLE' with the drophead 'Top Tories in amazing escape at bomb hotel', while the *Daily Mail* (1984) went for 'THEY MISSED HER BY TWO MINUTES' followed by opening sentences explaining that Margaret Thatcher's bathroom had been totally destroyed by the bomb, and that the prime minister had been in that bathroom until moments before the explosion (her husband, Denis, had a separate room).

Perhaps the keywords on the *Daily Mail*'s front page were placed above the headline: 'Margaret Thatcher – defiant, resolute – and alive'. The *Daily Express* (1984) foregrounded the prime minister's defiance and resolution with the one-word headline: 'UNBOWED!', and what all the newspapers agreed on was that Mrs. Thatcher's decision to carry on with the conference turned the attack into a propaganda triumph for her and her government and a disaster for the IRA. The editorial in the *Express* (1984) was entitled 'Democracy will prevail!', a sentiment that was unanimously endorsed in both the tabloids and the broadsheets, while a sentence from the IRA's announcement claiming responsibility for the attack—'Today we were unlucky, but remember we only have to be lucky once'—was universally condemned as callous and cynical.

There was no need to tabloid the truth since the plain facts were sensational enough, and it was similarly unnecessary to demonise the enemy given that fifteen years of Provisional IRA attacks on civilian targets had left that organisation with very few defenders on the British mainland (although rather more people, particularly on the Left, were prepared to talk to *Sinn Fein*, the IRA's political wing). If the Falklands War revived Margaret Thatcher's fortunes when her poll ratings were not particularly good, the Brighton bombing strengthened her position still further. Her courage and her business-as-usual attitude were widely acclaimed and were applauded by the leader of the Labour Party, Neil Kinnock, and his predecessor, Michael Foot.

Thirty years later, when the Margaret Thatcher Foundation released some of her private papers, it emerged that she had been doubly fortunate on 12 October 1984: not only had she got out of the bathroom two minutes before it was destroyed, but the terrorist attack also persuaded her to radically modify her address to the party conference, and as a consequence she did not deliver the speech that undoubtedly would not have earned her universal acclaim and effusive plaudits from her parliamentary adversaries. She had planned to make a blistering attack on 'the enemy within', which consisted of striking miners on picket lines, the leader of the NUM, Arthur Scargill, the Labour Party and, most of all, Neil Kinnock, whom she intended to depict as a mere puppet at the service of Trotskyite extremists and undemocratic trade unions. In the aftermath of the explosion, her speech was hastily rewritten, the attack on the Labour leader was greatly toned down and the expression 'enemy within' omitted entirely. Travis (2014) quotes Neil Kinnock, now Lord Kinnock, former Vice-President of the European Commission, questioning whether her change of heart was entirely due to the shock of the bombing: 'In the end, she might not have used that passage, because people around her would have told her how absurdly counterproductive it would be'.

Uniformity in the newspapers' treatment of the Troubles was still evident sixteen years after the Good Friday Agreement. After eleven weeks of talks between the British and Irish governments plus the majority of parties represented in the Northern Ireland Assembly, on 23 December 2014 the Stormont House Agreement was published. The aim of this accord was to bring closure after decades of bloodshed and allow all concerned to move on, and a key feature of the agreement was the proposal to set up an Implementation and Reconciliation Group (IRG) along broadly similar lines to the Truth and Reconciliation Commission in post-apartheid South Africa. The purpose of the IRG was to grant immunity from prosecution to Loyalist and Republican terrorists, RUC officers and British soldiers who confessed to having committed crimes before the Good Friday Agreement. The most contentious aspect of the amnesty was the fact that the identities of those who confessed would not be revealed, thus denying relatives of people killed during the

Troubles the opportunity to direct their wrath at specific individuals. The *Daily Mail* during Paul Dacre's 26-year editorship was rarely in agreement with the Labour-supporting *Daily Mirror*, but on the issue of the IRG *MailOnline*'s report was a rehash of an article by Nick Sommerlad and Jilly Beattie (2015) published the day before in the *Daily Mirror* and on the *Mirror Online*. The headline, drophead and opening sentences of the *Mirror*'s report are:

> **Terrorists and soldiers accused of horrific murders in Northern Ireland's Troubles can confess and walk free**
> While hundreds of suspects will avoid prosecution in exchange for confessions to their crimes, relatives of the victims will still be kept in the dark
> Terrorists, British soldiers and RUC officers accused of horrific murders during the Troubles are being given the chance to wipe the slate clean on their violent pasts.
> But while hundreds of suspects will avoid prosecution in exchange for confessions to their crimes, relatives of the victims will still be kept in the dark about who killed their loved ones.

The headline, drophead and opening sentence of Anthony Joseph's piece for *MailOnline* (2015) are:

> **Outrage over 'shameful' plot to allow killers from the Northern Ireland Troubles to get away with murder if they confess – without telling victims' relatives**
>
> - **Hundreds of suspects will avoid prosecution if they confess**
> - **Relatives won't be told about who killed their loved ones or if it's solved**
> - **The plan bids to close a chapter on the three decades of the Troubles**
> - **Families of victims are outraged by the plot and described it as 'shameful'**
>
> Those accused of some of the most horrific murders during the Troubles in Northern Ireland have the chance to confess to their crimes without facing further consequences.

Both articles employ informal and figurative language that has more of an impact on readers than the formal, passionless terminology used in official reports: 'get away with murder' (*Mail*) and 'walk free' (*Mirror*) rather than *avoid prosecution*, 'wipe the slate clean' (*Mirror*) instead of *be granted immunity*, 'plot' (*Mail*)—a word that implies secrecy—for a plan that has been made public knowledge, 'kept in the dark' (*Mirror*) rather than *denied access to information*. The two articles also feature the emotive language that is a typical characteristic of tabloided truth: the expressions 'horrific murders' and 'loved ones' appear in both pieces.

Reports in online editions include far more photographs than can reasonably appear in a traditional newspaper, and the *Mirror* and the *Mail* feature similar images. The former has a photo of dead horses (covered) after a bomb attack on the Household Cavalry in Hyde Park in 1982, and the latter shows floral tributes to the victims of the same attack. The *Mirror* has three images of the Brighton bombing including one of the injured Norman Tebbit before he was rescued from the rubble. The *Mail* opts for a photo of the damaged exterior of the Grand Hotel, its own front page of 13 October 1984 and a 1994 shot of the ennobled Lord Tebbit with his wife, Margaret, in her wheelchair. Both show precisely the same photograph of the rehabilitated Martin McGuinness, the former IRA leader who in 2007 became deputy First Minister of Northern Ireland, with Gerry Adams, president of Sinn Fein.

Sommerlad and Beattie quote a number of people who are opposed to the amnesty: Eugene Reavey, whose three brothers were shot by Loyalists in 1976; Lord Tebbit; Jim Allister of the Traditional Unionist Voice party; Michael Gallagher, whose son was killed in 1998 by the Real IRA (who split from the Provisional IRA in 1997 and never accepted the peace process that led to the Good Friday Agreement); and Vincent Coyle, who lost a nephew, again to the Real IRA, in 2011. They also quote an unnamed Stormont source expressing the confident view that the agreement reached by Westminster, Dublin and Belfast would not be blocked by protests from victims' groups: 'It works for the governments, it tidies things up for them and they plan to move forward regardless'. There are no direct quotes in favour of the Stormont House Agreement, although it is pointed out the Northern Ireland Secretary in the previous Labour government, Peter Hain, had been strongly in favour of an amnesty.

That Anthony Joseph for *MailOnline* effectively lifted his article is explicitly acknowledged as the precise words Lord Tebbit said to Sommerlad and Beattie follow the reporting clause 'He told the *Daily Mirror*'. The same people cited in the *Mirror* follow, but not in the same order: Jim Allister, the 'Stormont source', Michael Gallagher, Vincent Coyle and Eugene Reavey. Peter Hain's belief in the need for an amnesty is mentioned; then, as in the *Mirror*, it is reported that the prime minister at the time, David Cameron, did not support the idea. As we saw in the previous chapter, in the digital age a journalist can produce an article without leaving his/her desk by simply making a pastiche using content available on social media. Joseph demonstrates that a similar trick can be performed by reordering and repackaging elements of an article from the online edition of a politically antithetical rival.

Someone reading the two pieces without knowing their sources would have difficulty telling which was from the pro-Labour *Mirror* and which from the pro-Tory and ostentatiously patriotic *Mail.* There is really only one clue to help us: in one article the fact that the amnesty would apply not just to terrorists but also to British soldiers is made clear immediately in the headline; in the other, this information is only given in the second paragraph of the text and is not repeated. Those familiar with the *Daily Mail* during Paul Dacre's editorship could imagine the paper being strongly in favour of an amnesty for ex-servicemen but firmly against similar treatment for IRA and UVF activists.

Two years later, it was the *Mail* and the *Sun* that spoke with one voice. When Martin McGuinness died in 2017, his metamorphosis from IRA commander to pragmatic politician willing to negotiate was seen by many—including Bill Clinton and Tony Blair—as a fundamental development in the peace process that led to the Good Friday Agreement. The *Sun* and the *Mail,* however, were having no truck with what they perceived as the hypocritical sanctification of a man with blood on his hands (or at least, not in their UK editions). On 22 March 2017, the *Sun*'s front-page headline was 'UNFORGIVEN' and the drophead read 'IRA killer can go to hell, say families' (Willetts 2017), while in the body content an editorial attributed to 'Sun Reporter' (2017) began: 'The Sun will not join in the revolting orgy of pious praise for Martin McGuinness.

It sickens us to hear so many people casually downplaying the psychopathic evil of his campaign of murder, to talk up the good he belatedly did'.

On the same day, the front page of the *Daily Mail* featured two photographs: one of a blood-strewn man being led away from a bomb attack in Guildford in 1974, and another of men, women and children fleeing the scene of a blast in Enniskillen in 1987. Evaluation of McGuinness's legacy was described in two long articles written by historians. Ruth Dudley Edwards' assessment (2017) was posted on *MailOnline* on 21 March, the day McGuinness died, which, given the length of the piece, suggests that it had been written in advance. She refers to him as 'the Bogside Butcher' and considers his apparent conversion to the role of peacemaker a mere sham based on cynical calculation: 'Although it suits the self-deluding to claim he opted for peace rather than war in the Nineties for entirely admiral motives, in fact, by then, the IRA had been defeated by a combination of the British Army, the Royal Irish Constabulary and MI5, and its leaders knew the game was up'. Four days later, Dominic Sandbrook (2017) attacked 'the liberal elite' and 'the bienpensant Left' who had eulogised the former IRA leader at his funeral in Derry, and like Dudley Edwards doubted the sincerity of McGuinness's transfiguration as a man of peace:

> Even after he had put aside the gun and transformed himself into a power-sharing politician – not because of some Damascene conversion, but because the IRA was close to defeat, and because funds from America were drying up – he never showed the slightest contrition. Not once did he even pretend to feel guilty about his crimes.

It was a different story—literally—in those papers' Irish editions. The front page of the *Irish Daily Mail* on 22 March 2017 only had one photograph, and it was not of an IRA bomb attack but a full-page black-and-white portrait with the simple caption 'Martin McGuinness, 1950–2017'. The body content included no fewer than nine pages of reactions to McGuinness's death and analysis of his life, plus a special 12-page pullout. On the same day, the *Irish Sun*'s front page featured four photographs of McGuinness at different stages of his eventful life, including one from 1972 of the young IRA activist in paramilitary uniform and another showing the highly symbolic moment in 2012 when the democratically elected politician shook hands with Queen Elizabeth. The headline—'IT'S NOT HOW YOU BEGIN… IT'S HOW YOU END'—is a quote from Eileen Paisley, widow of the hardline Protestant leader Ian Paisley, in recognition of the fact that although her late husband and McGuinness had been bitter foes for much of their lives, they ended up as colleagues in government and friends in private. The lead article begins: 'Peacemaker Martin McGuinness's body was carried through the streets of Derry on his final journey home' (Johnson 2017). The next day coverage of the funeral on the *Irish Sun*'s online edition (Kearns 2017) read like a roll call of past and present leaders in Eire and Northern Ireland who had gone to Derry to pay their respects: President Michael D. Higgins, Taoiseach Enda Kenny, former Taoiseach Bertie Ahern, leader of the Democratic Unionist Party, Arlene Foster (reported as having been applauded as she entered the Catholic church) plus Bill Clinton. Nine photographs depicted the better-known mourners and the very long cortège following the coffin draped in the Irish tricolour. David Kearns' report contained no mention of McGuinness's activities in the 1970s and 1980s.

The Irish editions of the *Mail* and the *Sun* have their own editors, so the respective owners of the two papers could argue that the wide divergence from versions offered to UK readers was merely a question of respecting editorial independence. It is probably not overly cynical, however, to suspect that concern about circulation figures also came into the equation.

As noted in the Introduction to this volume, the tabloids' online editions are read by people who do not agree at all with a paper's editorial line or with a specific writer's views. Dominic Sandbrook's long article condemning the so-called liberal elite's praise for McGuinness the peacemaker generated no fewer than 493 readers' comments. Many took issue with Sandbrook, pointing out inaccuracies in his article or accusing him of bias. In a few cases, pairs or small groups of readers got into an online dialogue about matters not directly pertinent to the original article.

\* \* \*

What the Falklands War and the deployment of troops in Northern Ireland had in common was that the majority of the British people backed the military intervention. Argentina had invaded and occupied a British Overseas Territory and could hardly expect the UK government to do nothing, while in the case of the Troubles London had little choice but to take action to protect Catholics who were being driven from their homes. It was a different story in the early weeks of 2003 when George W. Bush and Tony Blair were planning to invade Iraq and topple President Saddam Hussein. Although Saddam was every bit as unlikeable as the Argentine Junta and the Provisional IRA, many people were unconvinced that he still represented a serious threat: his military capability had been greatly reduced by his crushing defeat in the Gulf War of 1990–91 at the hands of a coalition led by George Bush Senior. That war liberated Kuwait from its Iraqi invaders but there had never been a mandate to bring about regime change, and Saddam was allowed to continue to rule his country. Twelve years later, the justification for overthrowing him centred on allegations that Iraq was stockpiling proscribed weapons, including weapons of mass destruction, a conjecture for which there was no hard evidence (although Saddam drew suspicion on himself by refusing to cooperate with UN weapons inspectors).

In 1990, Bush *père* had been astute enough to put together a coalition of 34 nations, including a number of Arab states, but the more impetuous Bush *fils* had just one ally: the UK. Tony Blair's eagerness to do the president's bidding was seen by many Britons as fawning obsequiousness unworthy of a British prime minister, and the moniker 'Bush's poodle' was one that he had to live with for the remaining four years of his premiership. Reporting on an opinion poll commissioned by the *Mail on Sunday*, Oliver (2003) noted that British voters were 'adamant' that Britain should not take part in George W. Bush's planned invasion of Iraq, two-thirds of women opposed British involvement and 57% of those questioned thought that Blair was behaving like Bush's poodle.

Days before the invasion began, Greenslade (2003) noted with approval that various polls suggested that the public was not falling for the spin emanating from both sides of the Atlantic: 'There is a genuine scepticism about the existence of Iraq's weapons of mass destruction, a readiness to question America's warmongering leadership and an obvious unease at Tony Blair's zealous push for war'. However, he also noted that while a majority of the people were against the Bush/Blair plan, the newspapers were not representative of public opinion: six titles with a combined circulation of 9.4 million supported the imminent war (*Telegraph, Times, Mail, Sun, Express* and *Star*) while just three with a combined circulation of 2.7 million opposed military action (*Guardian, Independent* and *Mirror*). Not for the first time, and certainly not for the last time, the *Mirror* took a different path from that chosen by its tabloid cousins.

The war officially began before dawn on 20 March 2003 but hostilities actually started some hours earlier. The *Daily Star*'s headline on 20 March was 'FIRST BLOOD', along with a photo of a soldier apparently aiming an assault rifle directly at the camera (which must have been an unnerving experience for the photographer). The opening sentences of the accompanying report (McJannet 2003a) gave the impression that it was the UK that was the dominant partner in the Anglo-American coalition: 'British troops yesterday fired the first shots in the war against the evil tyrant Saddam Hussein. Men from the SAS and Special Boat Section were involved in a ferocious exchange of fire inside Iraq'.

One does not have to be an expert Pentagon observer to find it difficult to believe that the British were allowed to have the privilege of firing the first shots, and it is still less likely that British officers ordered their men to open fire without waiting for the go-ahead from the Americans. In the 136 words printed on the first page (the report continued on page six), US warplanes and President Bush each got a single mention but the real heroics were performed by 'crack SBS commandos' on a 'high-risk mission' behind enemy lines. Their courage is contrasted with claims that Iraqi troops surrendered as soon as the fighting began, while would-be deserters rushed to the Kuwaiti border only to be told by frontier guards that they would have to wait for the official start of hostilities. By tabloiding the truth, a clear dichotomy was established: a bunch of undisciplined cowards led by an evil tyrant versus well-trained and utterly fearless professionals. There is, of course, a contradiction between the 'ferocious exchange of fire' described in the second sentence, a choice of words that implies that the Iraqis fought bravely, and the subsequent claims that Saddam's men were primarily concerned with making a run for it.

The *Star* got its priorities right, however. Everything described above was relegated to the bottom third of the front page. Major prominence was given to two photographs of good-looking young ladies wearing very little and the somewhat contentious claim that Australian women have the most attractive posteriors ('OZ BOTS ARE TOPS'). A war that was to throw Iraq into chaos and claim hundreds of thousands of civilian deaths and injuries was thus trivialised, given second billing to a model's buttocks.

On page six, the report gives further instances of desertions, and a second article by John McJannet (2003b), 'Time to chuck evil Saddam out of the Last Chance Saloon', again begins in a way that suggests that the military operation was led by the UK: 'British troops were ready to rid the world of evil Saddam Hussein last night as they took up final battle positions for an invasion of Iraq'. If the *Sun*'s 'Gotcha' report treated the sinking of the Belgrano as a comic strip, for the *Daily Star* the Iraq War was like a western in which the good guys in white hats hunted down the thoroughly bad guy with the black hat and bushy moustache.

On the same page, a cartoon by Bill Caldwell was unlikely to amuse Muslims since it depicted Saddam and his military henchmen kneeling on prayer mats. An officer asks the president, 'Do you really believe they have smart bombs with pin-point accuracy, oh Great One?' as a smart bomb makes a 90-degree turn to enter the mosque and hurtle towards Saddam's raised backside, a thinks bubble revealing its cogitation as 'Left a bit… That's him'. The subtext appears to be that faced with overwhelming technological superiority, the Iraqis' only hope is to have recourse to prayer. Still on page six, a short piece by Tony Leonard (2003) warned that Saddam Hussein was planning to attack his own citizens with chemical weapons, 'then blame the carnage on British and US forces'. The collocation 'British and US' is used three more times to modify the nouns *uniforms*, *bombing* and *troops*, the word order again reversing the true power relationship in the coalition.

On pages eight and nine, a third article by John McJannet (2003c), 'WE'LL TRY THE TYRANT FOR MASS MURDER', cited Tony Blair's statement in the Commons that Saddam Hussein would be 'held accountable' for his crimes against humanity, as well as his appeal for the country to 'unite behind its Armed Forces'. While McJannet noted with approval that the 139 Labour MPs who had voted against going to war nevertheless 'rallied behind their leader' once it became clear that British troops would be going into battle, the *Star* was less forgiving of others who did not back the Bush/Blair plan. France refused to join the coalition, and a very short piece on page eight reported on French troops from the 1st Regiment of Tirailleurs that had been sent to Catterick in North Yorkshire to cover for British soldiers who had left for Iraq; for the *Star*, they were enjoying a holiday in England while their infinitely more courageous British counterparts were risking their lives in the desert (Daily Star 2003a). On page nine, a photo showed two police officers physically removing a young female anti-war protester from Parliament Square, the lack of comment suggesting approval of the degree of force employed.

In 2003, the *Daily Star* did not yet have a digital edition but readers could send instant feedback via text messages. On page nine, seven messages were published, six of which wholeheartedly supported the war but the seventh was the only tiny voice of dissent to be found in the *Star*'s coverage of the conflict. A reader identifying himself as 'stuart' texted: 'i think george bush should worry bout his own country instead of stickin his big nose in other people's' (Daily Star 2003b). However poorly expressed it may have been, stuart's view was in line with those of Jacques Chirac, Gerhard Schröder, Vladimir Putin and many other heads of government.

In its reporting of the Iraq War, the *Daily Star*'s aping of the *Sun*'s war coverage was perfectly honed. All the *Sun*'s characteristics were present: the simplification of complex issues to black-or-white divisions, the demonisation and/or ridicule of the enemy, patriotism so exaggerated as to become laughable, trivialisation of armed conflict and indifference to the suffering of both enemy troops and the civilian population.

On the same day (20 March 2003), an unsigned editorial in the *Daily Express* strongly backed the war, was predictably critical of France and Germany and, rather less predictably, appreciative of Britain's Labour prime minister:

Unlike the French and Germans, who yesterday used the forum of the UN to once again condemn the war, Tony Blair has ensured that we are not running away from our responsibilities at home and in the Middle East. The best the French policy of appeasement could have achieved would have been a dangerous stalemate in which the people of Iraq would be condemned to yet more repression and suffering.

All Britons with some knowledge of their own history associate the word *appeasement* with Prime Minister Neville Chamberlain's signing of the Munich Agreement of 1938 which conceded the German-speaking Sudetenland region of Czechoslovakia to Nazi Germany, and to this day, the term has connotations of political cowardice. The reference to 'the French policy of appeasement' indicates that in the view of the *Daily Express* President Chirac's refusal to commit troops to the war was not merely a mistake, but was also symptomatic of a lack of courage. The accusation was implied rather than explicitly stated, unlike the policy of the *Sun*, which launched ferocious personal attacks on opponents of the Iraq War. The most infamous was aimed at Charles Kennedy, leader of the Liberal Democrats and an outspoken critic of Bush and Blair's claims that Saddam had a mighty arsenal of weapons of mass destruction: on 21 September 2004, when the short war had turned into a protracted endeavour to police the post-war chaos, the *Sun*'s front page featured photos of Kennedy and a cobra with the headline 'SPOT THE DIFFERENCE' and the zoologically erroneous subhead 'One's a spineless reptile that spits venom… the other's a poisonous snake' (Assinder 2004). As noted earlier, the *Sun* rarely admits that it was wrong, but in 2016, when the Chilcot Inquiry concluded that there was no justification for war since Saddam Hussein did not have secret weapons, the article was removed from the paper's online archive. There was no apology to Charles Kennedy's family (Kennedy himself had died a year earlier), nor indeed to snakes, which are vertebrates.

Although the *Express* fully backed the war, its actual reporting of the conflict contrasted markedly with the *Star*'s approach. When the fighting began its headline 'IN FOR THE KILL' was similar in tone to the *Star*'s

'FIRST BLOOD' but while John McJannet's front-page summary began with the words 'British troops', Tim Shipman's opening sentence (2003) did not exaggerate Britain's role in the coalition: 'Allied jets launched the first strikes in a war against Iraq last night'.

It was on pages two and three that the *Express* diverged most radically from the *Star*. While the latter avoided any reference to likely casualties among the American and British servicemen—indeed, its focus on Iraqi surrenders and desertions implied that Allied troops would not encounter much opposition—the *Express* used a headline stretching across two pages that disabused any readers tempted to see the war as a Western movie shoot-out that would be a low-risk operation for the overwhelmingly superior good guys: 'We won't all come back'.

The opening paragraphs of Shipman and Oliver's accompanying article (2003) left no one in doubt about the awful reality of war:

> British troops preparing for battle last night were warned that Saddam Hussein has already ordered his junior commanders to use chemical weapons and that it is "a case of when not if" they will be attacked with nerve and mustard gas.
> As time ran out for Saddam to flee and avert war, Lieutenant Colonel Tim Collins gave an emotionally-charged rallying address which reduced many of our toughest infantry troops to tears.
> The man leading the battle group of the 1st Battalion the Royal Irish Regiment told his soldiers: "It is my foremost intention to bring every single one of you out alive but there may be people among us who will not see the end of this campaign. We will put them in their sleeping bags and send them back. There will be no time for sorrow."

Where John McJannet presented the ill-disciplined, lily-livered Iraqi troops as a negligible threat, Shipman and Oliver quote an authoritative and well-informed source hiding nothing from his men about the dangers they were about to face. The idea that our brave boys might be reduced to tears is something that the *Sun* and the *Star* would never even contemplate, although those who have witnessed or experienced CSR (combat stress reaction) know that weeping is the least of its symptoms. The collocation *brutally honest* is often misused but it is entirely appropriate for the description of how the bodies of fallen comrades would be unceremoniously disposed of.

Lt Col Collins was also quoted telling his men that they had been sent to Iraq as liberators rather than conquerors, so the UK flag would not be flown and British soldiers were expected to show respect for the people and their customs. Furthermore, he reminded his troops that Iraqi soldiers who surrendered were entitled to be treated in accordance with international law, and he warned them that unnecessary killing would not be tolerated. In stark contrast, the *Star*'s excessive use of the adjective *British* and faintly ridiculous reports of the expertise and heroism of Britain's military personnel seemed calculated to conjure up an image of triumphant British troops covering Iraq with Union Jacks as they recorded one easy victory after another, while no mention was made of the danger that in the stress of mortal combat some UK soldiers might be tempted to behave less than correctly.

In the case of the Falklands War, we have seen that the *Sun*'s gung-ho jingoism and contempt for the Argies was not shared by the *Daily Express*, which instead reported on the conflict in far more measured tones and expressed concern for the number of casualties among Argentinian soldiers, sailors and pilots. Twenty-one years later, the *Daily Star*'s approach to the Iraq War was barely distinguishable from that of the *Sun*, and again the *Daily Express* demonstrated that a right-wing tabloid could support a decision to go to war without demonising the enemy or brushing over the horrors of armed conflict.

The Labour prime minister who was praised by the *Daily Express* found his fiercest critic in the paper that normally supported his party: the *Daily Mirror*. Alone among the tabloids, the *Mirror* under Piers Morgan's editorship vigorously opposed the war from the beginning and used strong words and even stronger images to attack the two avowed Christians determined to lead their respective nations into armed conflict.

Almost a year before the war began, the investigative journalist John Pilger (2002) wrote in the *Mirror*, and also published on his website, an article alleging that George W. Bush's desire to oust Saddam Hussein had nothing to do with liberating the Iraqi people from a tyrannical regime: 'The Bush administration is determined to attack Iraq and take over a country that is the world's second largest source of oil. The aim is to get rid of America's and Britain's old friend, Saddam Hussein, whom they no longer control, and to install another compliant thug in Baghdad'. To Pilger '(t)he fiction of Blair as a steadying hand on his Texas buddy' was demonstrated by the prime minister's determination to commit British troops in defiance of the advice of his own military advisers, while the case for overthrowing the Iraqi regime was based on three lies: (i) that Saddam had weapons of mass destruction just eleven years after 93% of his arsenal had been destroyed during the Gulf War; (ii) that Iraq had in some way been involved in the 9/11 attacks; and (iii) that it was Saddam, and not the USA and Britain, who was preventing desperately needed humanitarian aid from reaching the Iraqi people.

In addition to Pilger, the *Mirror*'s defence correspondent at the time, Tom Newton Dunn (who later moved on to the *Sun*), and the columnist, Ros Wynne-Jones, also wrote hard-hitting articles about the scale of civilian casualties and the dubious reasons for going to war. However, the *Mirror*'s anti-war stance was most evident in a series of front-page splashes featuring a single striking image and few but judiciously selected words. It is probably true to say that we have all seen unflattering photographs of ourselves that we would like to eliminate without trace, but for a public figure who is caught on camera many times each day it is practically impossible to get an unfortunate image removed from a paper's archives. The *Mirror*'s front page of 14 March 2003 was dominated by a decidedly disquieting photo of Tony Blair with a creepy smile and a demonic look in his eye (Daily Mirror Headline 2003a). The punning headline 'PRIME MONSTER?' appeared to refer to Mr Blair's untypically ghoulish appearance in that particular photo, but the subhead shifted the focus to how posterity will view the prime minister: 'Drag us into this war without the U.N. Tony and that is how history will judge you. For God's sake man, DON'T DO IT'. After the two-word headline aimed at the readers, there is a switch in person deixis as the 24-word subhead speaks directly to the prime minister, addresses him by his first name and then by the informal *man*, signals exasperation with the idiomatic 'For God's sake', and concludes with an emphatic imperative in upper case. A Labour-supporting newspaper addresses a Labour prime minister with the tone of someone imploring a friend not to do something that will have disastrous consequences not just for the rest of his life, but also for his reputation long after his death.

The following day three million people took to the streets of London to support the Stop the War demonstration. The *Daily Mirror* had urged its readers to take part and on the day provided a huge number of placards. The paper also teamed up with the War Child charity to produce the 18-track compilation album *Hope*, which featured artists of the calibre of Paul McCartney and David Bowie, and raised £150,000 for child victims of the Iraq War.

Despite the size of the Stop the War demonstration and the urgency of the *Mirror*'s plea to Tony Blair to think about how history would judge him, Britain entered the war to overthrow Saddam Hussein on 20 March 2003. Two days later, the 'Shocking and Awful' headline of the chapter title appeared above a full-page photo of Baghdad in flames (Daily Mirror Headline 2003b).

The *Daily Mirror*'s opposition to the war was not appreciated by the government of the day. Thirteen years later, when the Chilcot Inquiry published its report of Britain's role in the Iraq War, Ros Wynne-Jones (2016) recalled the political climate in the spring of 2003: '13 years ago, our opposition cost us readers, and it brought acrimonious divisions between the Mirror and the Labour government. Angry phone calls came in nightly from Number 10 to editor Piers Morgan's office'.

Morgan was sacked in May 2004 after his paper had been the victim of a hoax. On the first of the month, the *Mirror* had published photographs of an Iraqi prisoner apparently being abused by soldiers of the Queen's Lancashire Regiment, photos that were subsequently shown to be fake. Although the paper's publisher, Trinity Mirror, apologised unreservedly to the regiment concerned and to the Army in general, Morgan's insistence that he had acted in good faith and his reluctance to issue a personal apology resulted in his instant dismissal. Milmo and Carter (2004), however, revealed that although the fake photos did not discredit the US military, there was an American hand in the removal of Britain's most committed anti-war editor:

> It became clear that Mr Morgan's fate lay in the hands of a small band of US shareholders. Five of the 10 biggest investors in Trinity Mirror – who

speak for nearly a third of its shares – are American, and it is believed that yesterday at least one was ready to make representations to the board about Mr Morgan's decision to use the pictures.

Although the *Daily Mail* and its sister paper, the *Mail on Sunday*, were initially in favour of military intervention in Iraq, there was always a certain ambivalence in their position in that they also hosted authoritative dissenting voices, including the military historian Max Hastings and the former foreign correspondent in Moscow and Washington, Peter Hitchens. When the bombing was over, it quickly became evident that the Bush administration had gone into Iraq without having a coherent strategy for handling the post-Saddam confusion, and that was when the *Mail*'s editorial line changed radically. Indeed, the *Times* journalist and later to be minister in the Cameron, May and Johnson Conservative governments, Michael Gove (2004), wrote a piece in *The Spectator* entitled 'The deadly Mail'. For Gove, the once reliably right-wing, pro-Washington *Mail* had become 'a full-throated, anti-war, anti-US, anti-Bush propaganda sheet' and there had been 'a remarkable consensus from almost all its columnists on the folly of the Iraq war and the culpability of those crassly simplistic zealots across the pond'.

Gove must have had his own reasons for singling out just one newspaper since in reality, when the US Army's search for Saddam's supposed weapons of mass destruction failed to come up with anything significant, the *Mail* merely led the way as all the papers that had believed Bush and Blair realised that they had been duped into supporting a war based on a mendacious pretext. *Mail* columnists were undeniably quick off the mark, however. Thirty-three days after the start of the war, on 22 April, Stephen Glover (2003) mocked the British government's insistence that evidence of a secret cache of deadly weapons would eventually be found and concluded that if nothing was discovered 'the destruction of Iraq was built on a lie'; on 1 May, Keith Waterhouse (2003) wrote '[…] it will slowly come to be recognised that the second Gulf War was an immense con-trick, an act of political legerdemain on a breathtaking scale, as seedy a piece of work as the three-card trick as performed in an Oxford Street closing down sale shop doorway'; on 18 May, Peter Hitchens (2003) condemned the Bush administration for their ignorance of the country they had invaded and total absence of a post-war plan: 'Many Iraqis are haggard with worry and lack of sleep. And yet in their guarded compounds, where the power always works and air conditioning cools the 95-degree heat, the American rulers of the city continue to show the clueless complacency that has marked their occupation since it began'. By 2009, it was not a columnist but an unsigned editorial (Daily Mail Comment) that declared: 'The truth is that, with the connivance of a shamefully supine Opposition, Britain was deceived into entering an illegal and tragically costly war – and Iraq reduced to anarchy – on the basis of lies and distortions, cooked up by a cabal'.

It was in 2009 that Blair's successor, Gordon Brown, announced that there would be an inquiry into the circumstances of the Iraq War chaired by Sir John Chilcot. Many people feared that the investigation would be a cover-up, and suspicions increased as the years passed. However, when the 2.6 million-word report was finally published on 6 July 2016, it was found to be anything but a whitewash. The chief findings were: (i) there had not been a sufficient case for war because a weakened Saddam did not represent a major threat and claims that he possessed weapons of mass destruction had been based on suspect intelligence; (ii) there had not been a satisfactory legal basis for war; (iii) the UK, and Tony Blair in particular, had not been able to exert significant influence on Washington's handling of the war; (iv) preparation and planning for the war and the past-war reconstruction had been inadequate; and (v) the military intervention did not achieve its declared goal.

The next day the tabloids tore into Tony Blair. Beneath the headline 'MONSTER OF DELUSION', Slack et al. (2016) in the *Daily Mail* wrote that the report of the Chilcot Inquiry 'savaged the former prime minister for his conduct at every stage of the process that dragged Britain into the catastrophic war'. The front page of the *Daily Express* bore the headline 'SHAMED BLAIR: I'M SORRY BUT I'D DO IT AGAIN' and Alison Little's article (2016) reported on the families of dead or disabled troops calling for the former prime minister to be tried for war crimes. The *Daily Star* (2016) also focused on the families of military victims with the headline 'BLAIR IS WORLD'S WORST TERRORIST', a slight misquotation of words uttered by Sarah O'Connor, whose brother, Bob, was killed in Iraq in 2005. The *Sun*, which twelve years earlier had described a prominent critic of the war as 'a spineless reptile that spits venom', featured a full-page photo of Tony Blair and the headline 'WEAPON OF MASS DECEPTION' above the opening paragraphs of an article by none other than Tom Newton Dunn, who in 2003 had been working for the *Mirror* and had had a leading role in that paper's daily attacks on the Bush/Blair strategy. The *Daily Mirror* itself announced Jason Beattie's article (2016) with a full-page photo of Bush and Blair together and the headline 'I'll be with you whatever…', which was a quote from a memo the British PM had sent the president eight months before the start of the war. To Beattie, that memo (cited in the Chilcot report) vindicated the *Mirror* for having presented Blair's uncritical and unquestioning support of George W. Bush as behaviour more becoming of a poodle than a head of government.

In 2003, four of the five tabloids considered in this chapter were in favour of the war, and as such, they were out of touch with public opinion. When the hostilities officially ceased, the evident lack of a coherent strategy to stabilise the country, the failure to find a secret arsenal of terrifying weapons and the continued loss of life due to acts of terrorism combined to oblige the pro-war papers to question their earlier enthusiasm for invading Iraq, quickly so in the case of the *Mail*, more incrementally for the *Express*, the *Star* and the *Sun*. When the Chilcot report was published in 2016, there was unanimity and all five tabloids could be said to reflect public opinion.

The language used to savage Tony Blair in 2016 was eerily reminiscent of that used to demonise Saddam Hussein in 2003: he was the world's worst terrorist, a murderer, a war criminal, a monster. Before 2016, Blair's political career had already been fatally damaged by the continued chaos of Iraq, but the publication of the Chilcot report was the stake through the heart to ensure that there would be no unlikely resurrection. It remains to be seen whether history will evaluate him primarily for his vital contribution to the Good Friday Agreement of 1998 that committed Northern Ireland's two communities to the search for political rather than military solutions, or whether the *Mirror* was right in predicting that he would be remembered as the 'Prime Monster'.

## References

Ashton, Emily. 2014. Stick it up your Juncker. *Sun*, June 2.
Assinder, Nick. 2004. Charles welcomes tabloid attacks. *BBC News Online*, September 21. http://news.bbc.co.uk/2/hi/uk_news/politics/3676200.stm. Accessed 22 July 2019.
Beattie, Jason. 2016. I'll be with you whatever… *Daily Mirror*, July 7.
Boyce, D.George. 2005. *The Falklands War*. Basingstoke and New York: Palgrave Macmillan.
Chippindale, Peter, and Chris Horrie. 2013[2]. *Stick It Up Your Punter!: The Uncut Story of the "Sun" Newspaper*. New York: Pocket Books. Kindle edition.
Daily Express Editorial. 1984. Democracy will prevail. *Daily Express*, October 13, pp. 8, 9.
Daily Express Editorial. 2003. In this war against terror we are all in the front line. *Daily Express*, March 20, p. 12.
Daily Express Headline. 1984. Unbowed! *Daily Express*, October 13.
Daily Mail Comment. 2009. So the Iraq War, which began in spin and lies, will end the same way. What an insult to democracy. *MailOnline*, June 16. https://www.dailymail.co.uk/debate/article-1193289/DAILY-MAIL-COMMENT-So-Iraq-War-began-spin-lies-end-way-What-insult-democracy.html. Accessed 30 July 2019.
Daily Mail Headline. 1984. They missed her by two minutes. *Daily Mail*, October 13.
Daily Mirror Headline. 2003a. Prime Monster. *Daily Mirror*, March 14.
Daily Mirror Headline. 2003b. Shocking and Awful. *Daily Mirror*, March 22.
Daily Star. 2003a. The tour de France. *Daily Star*, March 20, p. 8.
Daily Star. 2003b. Your txts. *Daily Star*, March 20, p. 9.
Daily Star Headline. 1984. Miracle. *Daily Star*, October 13.
Daily Star Headline. 2016. Blair is world's worst terrorist. *Daily Star*, July 7.
Dudley Edward, Ruth. 2017. Behind the smile, Martin McGuinness was a mass murderer with menace in his eyes—Who only turned to peace when he was beaten. *MailOnline*, March 21. http://www.ruthdudleyedwards.co.uk/journalism17/DMail17_01.html. Accessed 24 May 2019.
Evans, Michael, and John Warden. 1982. Fear for 700 on Argentine warship SUNK! *Daily Express*, May 4.
Glover, Stephen. 2003. Where are the weapons that justify this war? *Daily Mail*, April 22.

Gove, Michael. 2004. The deadly Mail. *The Spectator*, April 17.
Greenslade, Roy. 2002. A new Britain, a new kind of newspaper. *Guardian Online*, February 25. https://www.theguardian.com/media/2002/feb/25/pressandpublishing.falklands. Accessed 1 May 2019.
Greenslade, Roy. 2003. They've lost the battle, will they support the war? *Guardian Online*, March 17. https://www.theguardian.com/media/2003/mar/17/mondaymediasection.Iraqandthemedia. Accessed 2 July 2019.
Hattersley, Roy. 1997. *Fifty Years On: A Prejudiced History of Britain Since the War*. London: Abacus.
Hitchens, Peter. 2003. Iraq's Year Zero. *Mail on Sunday*, May 18.
Horrie, Chris. 2002. Gotcha! How the Sun reaped spoils of war. *Guardian Online*, April 7. https://www.theguardian.com/business/2002/apr/07/pressandpublishing.media. Accessed 21 May 2020.
Johnson, Jason. 2017. It's not how you begin… It's how you end. *Irish Sun*, March 22.
Joseph, Anthony. 2015. Outrage over 'shameful' plot to allow killers from the Northern Ireland Troubles to get away with murder if they confess—Without telling victims' relatives. *MailOnline*, September 11. https://www.dailymail.co.uk/news/article-3230483/Plot-allow-Northern-Ireland-Troubles-killers-away-murder.html. Accessed 21 May 2019.
Kearns, David. 2017. Last farewell. Thousands of mourners line the streets for Martin McGuinness' funeral—With Bill Clinton, the President and the Taoiseach among those paying their respects. *Irish Sun*, March 23. https://www.thesun.ie/news/757053/thousands-of-mourners-line-the-streets-for-martin-mcguinness-funeral-with-bill-clinton-the-president-and-the-taoiseach-among-those-paying-their-respects/. Accessed 25 May 2019.
Leonard, Tony. 2003. Chemical blast alert. *Daily Star*, March 20.
Little, Alison. 2016. Shamed Blair: I'm sorry but I'd do it again. *Daily Express*, July 7.
McJannet, John. 2003a. First Blood. *Daily Star*, March 20.
McJannet, John. 2003b. Time to chuck evil Saddam out of the Last Chance Saloon. *Daily Star*, March 20.
McJannet, John. 2003c. We'll try the tyrant for mass murder. *Daily Star*, March 20.
Milmo, Dan, and Helen Carter. 2004. Mirror editor sacked over hoax. *Guardian Online*, May 15. https://www.theguardian.com/media/2004/may/15/mirror.politicsandthemedia. Accessed 26 July 2019.

Newton Dunn, Tom. 2016a. We've gotcha backs. *Sun Online*, April 5. https://www.thesun.co.uk/archives/politics/205906/weve-gotcha-backs/. Accessed 5 May 2019.

Newton Dunn, Tom. 2016b. Weapon of Mass Deception. *Sun*, July 7.

Oliver, Jonathan. 2003. Britons reject Blair support for war with Iraq. *MailOnline*. https://www.dailymail.co.uk/news/article-131558/Britons-reject-Blair-support-war-Iraq.html?login. Accessed 1 July 2019.

Pilger, John. 2002. How dare George Bush preach peace to Israel when he's meeting Blair to plan war on Iraq? *Daily Mirror* and johnpilger.com. April 5. http://johnpilger.com/articles/how-dare-george-bush-preach-peace-to-israel-when-hes-meeting-blair-to-plan-war-on-iraq. Accessed 25 July 2019.

Plaice, Ellis. 1982. Attacked cruiser 'Sunk'—says Argentina. *Daily Mirror*, May 4.

Sandbrook, Dominic. 2007. *White Heat: A History of Britain in the Swinging Sixties*. London: Abacus.

Sandbrook, Dominic. 2017. To the liberal elite and its media Martin McGuinness was a great man. To ordinary Britons he was a murdering, torturing thug. No wonder so many despise the ruling classes. *MailOnline*. March 26. https://www.dailymail.co.uk/news/article-4347894/To-ordinary-Britons-Martin-McGuinness-murdering-thug.html. Accessed 24 May 2019.

Shipman, Tim. 2003. In for the Kill. *Daily Express*, March 20.

Shipman, Tim, and Sarah Oliver. 2003. We won't all come back. *Daily Express*, March 20, pp. 2, 3.

Slack, James, Jason Groves, and Ian Drury. 2016. Monster of Delusion. *Daily Mail*, July 7.

Snow, Tony. 1982. Gotcha. *Sun*, May 4.

Sommerlad, Nick, and Jilly Beattie. 2015. Terrorists and soldiers accused of horrific murders in Northern Ireland's Troubles can confess and walk free. *Mirror Online*, September 10/11. https://www.mirror.co.uk/news/uk-news/terrorists-soldiers-accused-horrific-murders-6421140. Accessed 21 May 2019.

Sun Reporter. 2017. The Sun Says: Why should evil legacy of Martin McGuinness be forgotten while the Troubles' veterans are hounded for trying to keep peace? *Sun Online*, March 22. https://www.thesun.co.uk/news/3145980/why-should-evil-legacy-of-martin-mcguinness-be-forgotten-while-the-troubles-veterans-are-hounded-for-trying-to-keep-peace/. Accessed 25 May 2019.

Terry, Walter, and Christopher Potter. 1982. Stick it up your Junta. *Sun*, April 20.

Travis, Alan. 2014. Thatcher was to call Labour and miners 'enemy within' in abandoned speech. *Guardian Online*, October 3. https://www.theguardian.com/politics/2014/oct/03/thatcher-labour-miners-enemy-within-brighton-bomb. Accessed 19 May 2019.

Walters, Guy. 2011. Britain was right to sink the Belgrano: Newly released intelligence proves the Argentine ship had been ordered to attack our Task Force. *MailOnline*, December 30. https://www.dailymail.co.uk/news/article-2080490/Belgrano-Britain-WAS-right-sink-ship-attacked-Task-Force.html. Accessed 18 May 2019.

Waterhouse, Keith. 2003. Damned elusive, that Tony Blair. *Daily Mail*, May 1.

Willetts, David. 2017. Unforgiven. *Sun*, March 22.

Wynne-Jones, Ros. 2016. Chilcot Report is just the start in a quest to find truths about the Iraq War. *Mirror Online*, July 6. https://www.mirror.co.uk/news/uk-news/chilcot-report-just-start-quest-8360430. Accessed 26 July 2019.

# 4

# From 'Rivers of Blood' to 'Migrants Are Like Cockroaches': The Tabloids and Race

On 22 January 1934, an article appeared in the *Daily Mail* under the headline 'Hurrah for the Blackshirts'. It was written by the newspaper's owner, Harold Harmsworth, better known by the title Viscount Rothermere, and it strongly urged readers to vote for Sir Oswald Mosley's British Union of Fascists, popularly known as the Blackshirts. Harmsworth declared:

> At this next vital election Britain's survival as a Great Power will depend on the existence of a well-organised Party of the Right, ready to take over responsibility for national affairs with the same directness of purpose and energy of method as Mussolini and Hitler have displayed.
> Such a movement, making "Action" its motto instead of "Drift", will draw a surprising measure of support from former Socialists, who have discovered that the leaders of that party also value words above deeds.
> That is why I say Hurrah for the Blackshirts! They are a sign that something is stirring among the youth of Britain. They are the symbol of that new realism in public life which alone can rouse it from its torpor.

While the *Daily Mail* was expressing approval of Hitler, Mussolini and Mosley—and also serialising the anti-Semitic hoax *The Protocols of the*

*Elders of Zion* a decade after the *Times* had revealed it to be a forgery—the *Daily Mirror* was showing that the Nazis' racial theories were based on dodgy science and misused terminology. On 19 August 1938, an unsigned editorial comment entitled 'PURE NONSENSE' asserted:

> The ideal of pure race is, of course, totalitarian hysteria.
> A learned professor clarifies this Nordic-Aryan-Jewish business. Aryan applies to speech. Nordic to breed. Jewish to cult or creed. German Jews are Alpines and the Yiddish language is Aryan in basis.
> The pure race idea is about as vague and unrealisable, and we might add unnecessary, as the prehistoric myth.

The modern tabloid did not yet exist when the *Mail* and the *Mirror* expressed such divergent views of the Fascist movements and anti-Semitic ideology of the 1930s. After the War, few dared express anti-Semitic sentiments while witnesses to and survivors of the Shoah were numerous and their testimonies unchallenged, and when the subject of race appeared on the front pages once again, the protagonists were not Jews but immigrants from the Caribbean or the Indian subcontinent. A precise date can be identified for the re-opening of the debate: 20 April 1968.

The reference to 'rivers of blood' in the chapter title is the usual misquotation of a sentence uttered by Enoch Powell in a speech to a Conservative Association meeting in Birmingham in April 1968 (the full text of which was published on the *Daily Telegraph*'s website in 2007). What the shadow minister and classical scholar actually said, quoting Virgil's *Aeneid*, was: 'As I look ahead, I am filled with foreboding; like the Roman, I seem to see "the River Tiber foaming with much blood"'. The cause of Powell's foreboding was his conviction that if immigration from the Caribbean and the Indian subcontinent were not halted, rising resentment and fear among the native population was likely to lead to violent clashes with the newcomers. He also quoted less acclaimed sources than Virgil: white residents of his Wolverhampton constituency. One cited the case of how, eight years earlier, 'in a respectable street in Wolverhampton a house was sold to a Negro', which led to a domino effect so that by 1968 only one white person was left in the street, a widow who had turned her home into boarding house but, because of her refusal to accept black tenants, found herself with unoccupied rooms and, consequently, serious financial difficulties. In April 1968, the word *Negro* was still widely used and boarding houses could still put signs in their windows reading: 'No Blacks, No Dogs, No Irish' (although that was shortly to change). The woman said to be the last white person in a street full of West Indians was not an invention but her hostility towards the new residents was: her name was Drucilla Cotterill, she got on fine with her neighbours, 'sometimes baby sat their children, and they sent flowers to her funeral' (Mount 2019).

The timing of Powell's speech was significant for two reasons: (i) in the spring of 1968 the Race Relations Bill was making its way through Parliament and was vigorously opposed by those who felt that freedom of speech was being sacrificed in order to outlaw discrimination; (ii) after many years in which anyone who really wanted a job could find one, unemployment had started to rise quite rapidly, which created tension between working-class whites and immigrants in the labour market to add to the competition that already existed for rented accommodation. Indeed, it is largely forgotten today that Powell insisted that he was addressing the concerns of working-class people, and that his subsequent sacking from the shadow cabinet led to manifestations of support for him from the trade unions. London dockers marched on the House of Commons to demonstrate their moral support for a conservative politician, while the *Daily Mirror* reported on a five-hour strike by members of the Constructional Engineering Union employed by John Thompson Water Tube Boilers Ltd of Wolverhampton (Knight 1968): 'A spokesman for the men explained: "We do not necessarily agree with everything Mr Powell said in his speech. But we support his right to express them. A token strike seemed the best way of showing this"'. Today, of course, a 'token strike', organised not over an industrial dispute but to defend the principle of freedom of speech, would be as unthinkable as calling a person of colour a 'Negro'.

It was the question of free speech that made many people feel uneasy about the Race Relations Bill presented by Harold Wilson's Labour government. To some commentators, in a liberal democracy no opinion, however odious it might be, should be suppressed. Indeed, two days after Powell's speech George Gale (1968), writing in the *Daily Mirror*, expressed the view that the Bill was bound to worsen race relations in Britain:

> It looks very much as if the Race Relations Bill has already become the country's single biggest incitement to racial hatred.
> Later, if it be enacted and rigorously enforced, then I suspect that those who are punished or otherwise penalised under it will have their racial prejudices hugely reinforced, and millions of sympathisers besides.

Despite the misgivings of Gale and others, the Race Relations Act came into being later in the year, and in Great Britain (but not Northern Ireland) it became an offence to refuse housing, employment or public services to people on the grounds of their colour, race or ethnicity.

Today it is difficult to read an article about contemporary politics that does not include the words *populism* and *populist* with tedious regularity, but in 1968 those terms were neither overused nor misused. However, in his perceptive analysis of Powell's timing, Wilfrid Sendall (1968), writing in the *Daily Express*, used a third p-word to account for the actions of a shadow minister who had gone off to Birmingham 'deliberately to pull the lid off the cauldron and even to stoke up the furnace' after he had previously been working with colleagues to formulate the Conservative Party's policy regarding the Labour government's Bill:

> That this was by design there can be no question, for Mr. Powell made his own arrangements for publicity, avoiding the normal Central Office machinery.
> The deduction is inevitable that Mr. Powell, realising that the official party line to which he had subscribed fell far short of expressing the public feelings on the issue, went out to grab the popularity for himself.

Powell's speech left the party leader, Edward Heath, with little choice but to fire him from the shadow cabinet, and he never again held an important political office, eventually leaving the Conservatives to join the Ulster Unionist Party. However, he became a maverick figure who was to remain a thorn in the side of the Conservative Party for the rest of his days. His speech, which half a century on can be seen to have been corrosive and hysterical, shifted the topic of race and immigration to the top of the sociopolitical agenda and it has remained a hot issue in the tabloid press ever since.

During the 1970s, '80s and early '90s immigration continued, although the *Sun, Star, Mail* and *Express* systematically exaggerated the extent of the influx with their water metaphors of natural disaster: *flood, deluge, tidal wave,* etc. It was never a mere trickle but neither was it a tsunami. Similarly, military terms and words denoting great numbers of dangerous people (*invasion, hordes, mobs*) were hardly appropriate given that immigrants were far more likely to be the victims of violence than the perpetrators (today, thankfully, the expression *Paki-bashing* is rarely heard but in the 1970s and '80s both the term and the action were not uncommon). Tensions undoubtedly existed, sometimes boiled over into violence, but the far-right parties that sought to disseminate racial hatred—first the National Front, then the British National Party—had little success in local elections and none at all at national level. The populations of Britain's major cities became blacker and browner, millions of immigrants and their children assimilated into UK society, lamb vindaloo began to rival fish and chips as our favourite take-away, and the nation's state schools did not receive the credit they deserved for their role in helping ethnic-minority children integrate.

The British Government's own statistics give a much-needed sense of perspective to the alleged tidal wave of immigrants prior to the mid-1990s:

> The number of people migrating to the UK has been greater than the number emigrating since 1994. For much of the twentieth century, the numbers migrating to and from the UK were roughly in balance, and from the 1960s to the early 1990s the number of emigrants was often greater than the number of immigrants. Over the last twenty-five years, both immigration and emigration have increased to historically high levels, with immigration exceeding emigration by more than 100,000 in every year since 1998. (Sturge 2019: 3)

One reason for higher immigration was a sharp increase in asylum applications from the mid-1990s to the peak year of 2002 (Blinder 2019). A second was the enlargement of the European Union in 2004 and the subsequent arrival of economic migrants from the new EU member states, with the number of Poles resident in the UK reaching 905,000 by 2018 (Sturge 2019: 24). For the first time, immigration was responsible for a significant population increase in certain parts of the country, and the strain on schools and other public services was exacerbated by the austerity measures and cuts in public spending favoured by the Cameron-Clegg, Cameron and May governments from 2010. Unsurprisingly, the activities of ISIS/Daesh were seized upon by the less reflective sections of society to justify explicit Islamophobia. These three factors—a real rather than imagined increase in immigration, a prolonged period of austerity and acts of terrorism committed in the name of Islam—combined to create a toxic brew, and those who drank of it were emboldened to challenge the conventional wisdom that multiculturalism enriches society. Their view was seldom based on empirical data and rational argumentation, but relied on the emotive language of ill-informed racism and visceral Islamophobia. When statistical evidence was referred to, numbers tended to be used selectively and misleadingly, as we see in the first two headlines considered below. The right-wing tabloids played their part in scapegoating immigrants, while the anti-racist *Daily Mirror* discovered that readers of its online edition did not always share its journalists' tolerance.

The *Daily Mail* did use credible data, a report published by the Office of National Statistics, in a lengthy article highlighting the sheer numbers of immigrants entering the country, but the report's findings were summarised in the headline and subhead in a highly selective manner (Slack et al. 2015):

> **Just how many more can we take? PM pledges to get a grip as migrants add a city the size of Coventry to population in only a year**
>
> - **Net migration hit 318,000 in 2014—the second highest total ever recorded**
> - **Leaves PM further than ever from meeting his 'tens of thousands' pledge**
> - **David Cameron blamed former Lib Dem Coalition partners for the failure**

The *Daily Mail*'s position is immediately made clear from the rhetorical question in the headline, while equating a population figure with a city is an old trick to make the number seem unmanageable (no mention is made of the fact that the UK only has 242,500 km$^2$ in which to squeeze a second Coventry, which means fitting in another 1.3 people per km$^2$). The expression 'to get a grip' implies that the situation has got out of hand and firm action is now required. The subhead draws attention to David Cameron's failure to reach his own target for reducing immigration, and his pinning the blame on his Liberal Democrat coalition partners in the previous government is explained in the article in a specific accusation directed at Vince Cable, the former Business Secretary (unsurprisingly, businesses were happy to have cheap labour supplied by Romanian and Bulgarian migrants).

The article was written when Cameron was negotiating with Brussels to secure improvements in the terms of Britain's membership of the EU, which he hoped would convince voters in the referendum planned for the following year that it was no longer necessary or desirable for the UK to leave the European Union. Consequently, the article focuses on EU migrants, the squalid rented accommodation in which many of them live (surely the fault of the landlord rather than the tenant) and, curiously, the huge number of National Insurance numbers issued to foreigners, which is a necessary prerequisite to enable them to pay income tax and contribute to the economy. The article ends with Cameron's proposals to change conditions for migrant workers, at least two of which are clearly in conflict with the EU's policy of freedom of movement for workers: to discriminate against EU nationals by denying them the right to tax credits and in-work benefits that low-paid British workers have; to oblige EU nationals to have a job offer before travelling to the UK.

Two years earlier the *Daily Express* also made quite innocuous numbers appear to be catastrophic (Russell 2013):

**EU flooded with 1,000 asylum seeker applications EVERY day**

The EU was flooded with nearly 350,000 applications from asylum seekers over the past 12 months – a rate of almost 1000 a day.

A round figure of 1000 sounds like a lot until we note that it refers to applications processed by all the EU member states. We cannot simply divide by 28 and conclude that each country handles 36 applications for asylum each day because it is unlikely that many refugees wish to settle in Hungary or Poland. However, the 'nearly 350,000 applications' are shared by those member states that have traditionally taken in refugees, and no single country can be said to be 'flooded'. Indeed, when we read the article with the aid of a calculator, we discover that Germany and France handle 42% of the applications and that the UK's share of 29,950 per year works out at 82 per day, which as floods go is barely newsworthy.

The headline is also deceptive in that the inattentive reader might take it that 1000 asylum seeker applications mean 1000 extra refugees every day. In reality, of course, applications can be, and frequently are, rejected. Indeed, the article goes on to specify that France rejects 84% of applications, Belgium 71%, Germany 65%, Britain 60% and Italy 23%. The author of the article, Benjamin Russell, makes the simplistic observation that some countries adopt a tougher stance than others. To understand the different rejection rates, it is necessary to consider where asylum seekers come from: because of its proximity to Libya, Italy rescues people in the Mediterranean who are bona fide asylum seekers fleeing war zones, while France is targeted by a great many people who turn out to be economic migrants.

Much of the most unpleasant tabloid reporting concerned the so-called *Calais Jungle*. This was essentially a shanty town close to the port of Calais populated by mostly African migrants hoping to get an opportunity to reach Britain via the Channel Tunnel. A high percentage were from Syria, Somalia, Eritrea or Iraq, so the humanitarian case for allowing them to stay in Europe was strong, but many did not want to apply for asylum in France. Some succeeded in clambering aboard lorries going to Britain, but others were seriously injured or even killed when endeavouring to get through the Tunnel. The camp eventually grew to about 10,000 people before the French Government demolished it in October 2016. In the months leading up to the Brexit referendum of June 2016, the pro-Leave *Sun*, *Mail* and *Express* (as usual, the *Mirror* was the exception) made much of the threat to the UK's security of so many mostly male, mostly Muslim migrants ready to risk life and limb to get to England.

On 31 July 2015, striking ferry workers in Calais set up roadblocks of burning tyres, which left the overstretched police unable to stop an estimated 4000 migrants from attempting to storm the Eurotunnel. For several hours, the port was in a state of chaos, and long tailbacks of vehicles built up on both sides of the Channel. Leo McKinstry (2015), writing in the *Daily Express*, saw the crisis as a consequence of the EU's failure to police its frontiers and portrayed the migrants as mere scroungers eager to live comfortably on the UK's welfare state. A substantial part of his article is given below:

**Calais crisis is becoming a symbol of the flawed EU, blasts LEO MCKINSTRY**

As marauding gangs of immigrants continue to disrupt the Channel Tunnel, Calais is fast becoming a lawless zone of conflict and intimidation. But the consequences of this collapse in order are not confined to the French port.
[*Omissis*]
Effectively one of the world's busiest transport routes is being held to ransom by a horde of aggressive foreigners who have no right even to be in Europe.
Predictably, the British and French politicians have been woefully ineffectual in this crisis.
They have failed to take any robust steps, such as clearing the squalid immigrants' camps on the edge of Calais, or deporting the criminal gangs or sending in the army to beef up security.
Such feebleness is outrageous. But they are so in thrall to the doctrine of multiculturalism, so wedded to their belief in ethnic minority victimhood, that they are terrified of vigorous action.
[*Omissis*]
The fact is that the current mawkish portrayal of the Calais migrants has to be challenged. We are constantly told in sobbing tones by the media that they are "desperate", not least because they are supposedly forced to endure such filthy conditions at their makeshift camp. But this is a so-called "humanitarian crisis" entirely of their own making.
They are not fleeing persecution or living in fear.

In fact, they have temporarily settled in one of the most advanced, free countries in the world.

Far from being vulnerable, they are arrogant young men, brimming with a sense of entitlement to live wherever they want.

[*Omissis*]

Yes, they are desperate, but only to exploit Britain's welfare system. They are benefit seekers, not asylum seekers.

"In England, once I go, it will be very easy for me. They will give me a house," one squatter told an interviewer last November. "Everything in England is comfortable," said another.

We have absolutely no obligation to these people. Most of them have neither any connection with our country nor any understanding of our heritage, language or culture beyond the recognition that we are a pathetically soft touch.

In their capacity to inflict international chaos, they have turned the Calais disruption into a grim symbol of how our once well-ordered, cohesive society is now threatened by a lethal cocktail of mass immigration, multi-culturalism and European integration.

The eagerness of the Calais migrant squatters to tear down security fences is a vivid metaphor for the wholesale destruction of our borders in recent years.

Incredibly, the annual number of arrivals to Britain has now reached 624,000, fuelling a social revolution where British people are often left to feel like aliens in their own land.

We now live in a society where Mohammed is the most popular boy's name and where white Britons are now in a minority in entire conurbations like Luton, London and Leicester.

The failure of the authorities to act at Calais has its parallel in the reluctance of Britain's civic institutions to deal with social problems among ethnic minorities, such as female genital mutilation against women of African origin, the rise of Islamic extremism, or the eagerness of Muslim sex gangs in towns like Rotherham to prey on vulnerable white girls.

For the lure of the welfare honeypot for the Calais migrants is mirrored by millions of other foreigners who have come to Britain. Not all of them want to work.

As a report from the think tank Migrant Watch concluded, people from migrant communities are much more likely than the indigenous population to rely on benefits, live in social housing and be economically inactive.

> The Calais crisis is also a monument to the disastrously flawed ideology of the EU, whose drive for federal unity has prevented the member states from upholding their own national interests of protecting their own peoples.
> In the name of harmonisation and free movement, we have been left defenceless. Without the EU's removal of borders across Europe, the migrants would never have reached Calais in the first place. Calais should be the place where European civilisation makes a stand against its own destruction.
> If our rulers continue to wring their hands over immigration, we are doomed.

While Enoch Powell saw a river foaming with much blood, 47 years later Leo McKinstry feared we might be doomed, and for both men the cause of the impending catastrophe was the submergence of British identity beneath a deluge of immigrants.

McKinstry repeatedly emphasises the violent or intimidatory behaviour of the Calais migrants. They are 'marauding gangs', 'aggressive foreigners', 'arrogant young men' and 'brimming with a sense of entitlement'. He also refers to them as 'squatters', which is technically correct since the migrants were camping on land near the port without authorisation, although today the word is normally used for people who have committed the criminal act of breaking into unoccupied properties. To grant such dangerous individuals, the right of residence in the UK would be unwise given the precedents of immigrants who have brought practices like female genital mutilation into the country or have preyed on 'vulnerable white girls'. The stereotype of the criminal and sexually predatory black man is not supported by hard data. Although black people in Britain are more likely to be arrested than whites, arrests do not always result in successful prosecutions: the report *Prosecutions and convictions* (HM Government 2018) reveals that in 2017 the percentage of defendants actually convicted was 78.7% for blacks, 79% for people of mixed race, 80.3% for Asians and 85.3% for whites.

Like Slack et al. and Russell, McKinistry cites figures selectively. He claims that the number of immigrants entering Britain annually is 624,000 without citing the source of the statistic, or explaining how such a figure is reached given that immigration rates fluctuate from year to year, and without acknowledging that there is also emigration from the UK. Some of his assertions are not substantiated, such as his claim that the migrants are 'benefit seekers, not asylum seekers' without demonstrating that the British welfare system is more generous than that of France, while his reference to 'criminal gangs' at the Calais camp gives no details of the identities or activities of these supposed delinquents. A recent report (Ritschel 2019) supports his claim that Muhammed is the most common name given to male babies in Britain, but the next 19 in the Top 20 are non-Muslim and often Biblical (with his own name, Leo, in seventh place). On the one occasion, he cites a source—the think tank Migrant Watch—he chooses an organisation that defines itself as non-political but has been accused of being no more than a right-wing pressure group that employs questionable methodology to produce 'whatever logical contortion is required to turn facts about immigrants into a weapon to beat them with' (Dunt 2016).

Perhaps the most offensive assertion in the article is: 'They are not fleeing persecution or living in fear'. While the French authorities were clearly not persecuting the Calais migrants, it is nevertheless an extraordinarily insensitive statement to make about people who had fled war and terrorism in their own countries and had covered much of the distance from a refugee camp in Turkey to Calais on foot. It was not even true that all of the migrants were living without fear in France since among their number there were unaccompanied women and minors.

To support his conviction that the migrants are only interested in living off Britain's welfare state, McKinstry quotes two 'squatters' briefly explaining how things will be 'easy' and 'comfortable' for them once they reach England. He does not name them, or give any information about their background, or reveal to whom they expressed their opinions. They are just people who 'have neither any connection with our country nor any understanding of our heritage, language or culture'. In the same paper on the same day, another article clarifies in its headline and subhead that the most obviously criminal act was committed not by migrants, but by French ferry workers (Reynolds et al. 2015):

Calais goes UP IN FLAMES: Migrants fight to get into UK as ferry workers block harbour
FLAMES filled the air in Calais after striking French ferry workers blocked roads with burning tyres leaving the port now resembling a WARZONE

In a rather more balanced report, Reynolds et al. cite a spokesperson for the Freight Transport Association expressing concern for the safety of lorry drivers given the tenacity with which some migrants endeavour to hitch a lift through the Channel Tunnel. However, they also spoke to a couple of asylum seekers, one of whom was Mohammad Al-Mohammad, a 26-year-old Syrian who did not quite fit McKinstry's profile of the migrant who has no knowledge of the heritage, language or culture of the UK. He spoke good English, had a degree in English literature from the University of Aleppo, said he had a brother already living in England, and hoped to study for a master's degree in the UK.

Returning to McKinstry's article, his most withering remarks are reserved for politicians and administrators who, he believes, have allowed sentiment to overrule sense where immigration is concerned. They are 'in thrall to the doctrine of multiculturalism' and 'wedded to their belief in ethnic minority victimhood', while their 'mawkish portrayal' of the Calais migrants is expressed in 'sobbing tones'. Wodak (2015: 188) notes that for the political right of the twenty-first-century solidarity with the weakest and most vulnerable has not only ceased to be a virtue but has become something worthy only of contempt: 'Proponents of solidarity are frequently labelled as do-gooders, naive and over-zealous [...] solidarity is viewed as an anachronistic concept not suitable for an individualistic, neo-liberal and globalized world'. Add the 'fallacy of sameness' (ibid.: 54), the notion of a culturally homogenous native population, and solidarity can be depicted as something imposed upon the community either at supranational level (by the EU, for example) or by a national government out of touch with ordinary people allegedly characterised by uniformity of values. Leo McKinstry accuses Brussels of preventing member states from protecting their national interests and Westminster of leaving Britons feeling 'like aliens in their own land', allegations he was to elaborate upon some months later during the build-up to the Brexit referendum.

McKinstry's article demonstrates that freedom of speech has not really been curtailed by race relations legislation. He expresses views that some people would consider offensive but nothing in this piece is actionable.

As the 'Calais Jungle' continued to grow, the British Government eventually bowed to pressure to allow minors to enter the UK. Most did not have documents indicating their date of birth, and the headline to Sam Tonkin's article for the *MailOnline* (2016) cast doubt upon whether they really were under 18: 'Another all-male coachload of "child" migrants arrives in Britain – but officials WON'T say how many there are and WON'T do dental checks to prove they're really children'. The online article features a series of photos of the latest arrivals, some of which depict strapping young lads with stubbly chins. The Home Office had ruled out the use of dental checks on the grounds that the practice would be unethical, and, in any case, such examinations did not verify age with sufficient accuracy. As regards the numbers of the new arrivals, Tonkin uses the almost obligatory word 'wave', then immediately and probably unwittingly, demonstrates that it is an entirely inappropriate term given the arithmetic of the situation: 'A third wave of "child" migrants arrived in Britain from the Calais Jungle today – but the Home Office refused to carry out dental checks to prove their real age. Around 12 migrants – all burly lads aged anywhere between 15 and 21 – were escorted off a coach and taken inside a Home Office building, before being released'. The first of many photos reveals that the 'coach' transporting the wave of twelve was actually a minibus.

The headline states that all the young migrants are male and it is this aspect that some readers focused on in their feedback. For Chelsea10, the peculiar sexual threat posed by dark-skinned men informed his/her observation: 'Coming to a school near you. Lock up your daughters!!!' M69- had no doubt that the females would arrive later: 'Someone asked "where are the girls?" I'll tell you where they are, they are back home and when these "boys" get citizenship they will want their wives and daughters to join them as it is their human rite (*sic*) to a family life'.

In October 2016, the French Government began an operation of clearing the camp and transporting the migrants to official immigration centres. Among the last 3000 there were some who were determined not to be moved, and on the morning of 26 October a group of Afghans began torching their shacks and tents in protest against the demolition of the camp. Fire was always a great danger since most of the remaining refugees had gas canisters for cooking, and French and volunteer British firefighters spent hours putting out the flames. Martin Fricker (2016), writing for the *Mirror Online*, quoted an aid worker saying that the very dangerous form of protest was 'a sign that people feel they have nothing to lose again'. Fricker's article is straight reporting devoid of comment, but opinion was supplied by readers' feedback. The tone and content of some of those comments were not what one might have expected from readers of a left-leaning newspaper whose editorial line was that Europe had a duty to help people fleeing from war or persecution. Of course, the readership of online editions is politically heterogeneous. A reader nicknamed paultbay, evidently not a man to be intimidated by the Taliban, wrote: 'they seem to be prepared to fight to get to Britain, pity they hadn't of stayed in their countries and fought like men instead of running and leaving their families behind to make it to the Britain with the streets paved with gold for those who want to sponge'. The sexual threat of bearded foreigners worried macdaddypastyman: 'And they had the cheek to complain about the time it took the French fire service to put out the fires THEY started!!! These are NOT the kind of people I want living anywhere near myself or my daughter!!!'

The Independent Press Standards Organisation (Ipso) states on its website that its mission is 'to support those who feel wronged by the press, to uphold the highest professional standards in the UK press, to determine whether standards have been breached and provide redress if so'. Ipso is not without its critics, most notably the press campaign group *Hacked Off*. Since it is funded by its member publications, that is, by the very newspapers it is supposed to regulate, it is sometimes accused of being a watchdog on a leash. Indeed, the redress for having used inaccurate or offensive content rarely goes beyond the requirement to publish a correction or an adjudication, while many instances of radically tabloided truth do not attract the attention of Ipso at all.

However, the *Sun*'s main article on 23 November 2015—'1 in 5 Brit Muslims' sympathy for jihadis'—was investigated by Ipso and was found to have breached the Accuracy Clause of its Editors' Code. On 13 November 2015, a series of terrorist attacks took place in Paris that caused a total of 130 deaths, and afterwards the *Sun* commissioned the market research agency Survation to conduct a telephone poll of British Muslims. The report of the findings in the print and online editions was illustrated with a photograph of Mohammed Emwazi, popularly known as 'Jihadi John', a British Muslim who went to Syria to fight for Islamic State and was eventually killed in a drone strike. The organisation Muslim Engagement and Development (MEND) reported the article to Ipso, who in February 2016 ruled that the *Sun* 'had failed to take appropriate care in its presentation of the poll results, and as a result the coverage was significantly misleading' (Ipso ruling 09324-15 2016). Essentially, *sympathy* and *support* had been treated as synonyms, while it was not clarified that some respondents had interpreted *sympathy* as meaning *regret* or *sorrow*. The remedial action required of the *Sun* was the publication of Ipso's adjudication 'on page 4 or 5, or further forward', a sanction that almost certainly did not cause the newspaper's owner and editor much distress.

The *Daily Star* did its bit to present Muslims in a poor light by finding a way to link Islam with one of Britain's most notorious serial killers. Between 1975 and 1980, Peter Sutcliffe, otherwise known as the Yorkshire Ripper, brutally murdered thirteen women and mutilated their bodies. After his conviction, he was diagnosed with paranoid schizophrenia and spent more than three decades in the Broadmoor high-security psychiatric hospital, but in August 2016 he was declared mentally fit enough to be transferred to a normal prison and he was sent to HM Prison Frankland in Durham. In an unsigned article (Daily Star 2016) headlined 'Yorkshire Ripper turns to Islam: Muslim inmates to protect Sutcliffe behind bars' it was reported that Sutcliffe had received death threats since being moved. A 'source' is quoted as saying, 'HMP Frankland is ruled by gangs and you are either in a white gang, black gang or Asian gang. If you are a child killer, rapist or mass murderer, the only gang who are going to let you in are the Muslims but you have to convert to Islam'.

The real scandal of this story ought to be the claim that in one of Her Majesty's prisons it is not the guards but gangs of inmates who run the place (although when an article written by 'Exclusive' relies on the testimony of 'a source', it is legitimate to harbour some slight doubt about the veracity of the report). For the *Daily Star*, the scandal is that Muslims are willing to protect a serial killer and even welcome him into their religion, and there is not a word of censure for the prison authorities who have ceded control of their institution. It is explicitly stated that moving Sutcliffe from Broadmoor to Frankland saves about £250,000 a year of taxpayers' money; it is tempting to infer that the anonymous author believes that still greater savings could be made if only the interfering Muslims would mind their own business and allow the other prisoners to murder the Yorkshire Ripper.

In October 2016, the European Commission against Racism and Intolerance (ECRI) published a 41-page, 149-paragraph report on the UK. In a section on hate speech, Paragraph 40 states: 'ECRI notes that certain tabloid newspapers, which are the most widely-read national dailies, are responsible for most of the offensive, discriminatory and provocative terminology' (ECRI 2016: 18). The *Sun* is singled out, specifically the piece written by a columnist who likened migrants to cockroaches (the text is treated in more detail below). In paragraph 41 (ibid.), the '1 in 5 Brit Muslims' sympathy for jihadis' article is cited, along with the case of a trans schoolteacher who committed suicide after being outed by the *Daily Mail*.

Paragraph 54 criticises Ipso (ibid.: 22), noting the less than draconian sanctions it imposes on errant newspapers: 'IPSO makes provision for investigations but the procedure is cumbersome with many opportunities for the target newspaper to obstruct and delay. As a result, while fines are possible (up to £1 million), none has so far been imposed'.

In June 2017, *Vice* magazine sought to find out why the UK tabloids continued to get away with Islamophobic front pages by interviewing their own media lawyer, Jade Allen, and Diall Duffy of Ipso (Ewens 2017). It emerged that: (i) inciting hatred is difficult to prove in court; (ii) it is more difficult to prosecute for inciting religious hatred than racial hatred; (iii) newspapers risk serious consequences if they defame an individual but making a more generalised attack on a broad group of people is a much less hazardous enterprise; and (iv) it is in the nature of the tabloids to push boundaries.

One person who certainly pushes boundaries, smashes taboos and steamrollers other people's sensitivities is the controversial TV personality and newspaper columnist Katie Hopkins. She was a contestant on the TV programme *The Apprentice* in 2007 and her abrasive, opinionated and downright rude behaviour quickly established her as a highly controversial figure, loathed by many but a person guaranteed to boost viewing figures. Appearances on other television shows followed, including *I'm a Celebrity… Get Me Out of Here!* and *Celebrity Big Brother*, then she demonstrated that she could be as provocative in writing as she was on screen when she started writing for the *Sun* and the *MailOnline*. The right-wing views expressed most forthrightly in her tabloid columns are considered thoroughly obnoxious by many commentators but she appears to relish the opprobrium she attracts.

The reference to 'cockroaches' in the chapter title alludes to Katie Hopkins' column on page 11 of the *Sun* on 17 April 2015. Four days after more than 400 migrants drowned in the Mediterranean while trying to reach Italy from Libya, her headline was 'Rescue boats? I'd use gunships to stop migrants'. The piece was removed from the *Sun*'s online archive in December 2016, which was a case of too little and too late since the most offensive comments had already been re-posted all over the web. She shed no tears for men, women and children who had fled from war and/or hunger in their own countries, had endured rape and torture in Libya, only to drown on the last stage of their journey to a better life: 'No, I don't care. Show me pictures of coffins, show me bodies floating in water, play violins and show me skinny people looking sad. I still don't care'. But, of course, asylum seekers are nowhere near as vulnerable as they would have us believe: 'Make no mistake, these migrants are like cockroaches. They might look a bit like "Bob Geldof's Ethiopia circa 1984", but they are built to survive a nuclear war'. And those that manage to reach the UK are ruining the country: 'Some of our towns are festering sores, plagued by swarms of migrants and asylum seekers, shelling out benefits like Monopoly money' (Hopkins 2015).

Cockroaches are not the most lovable of God's creatures. There are two reasons why they struggle to win a place in our hearts: firstly, they are considered vermin, and as such they are associated with filth and are therefore a threat to the health of human beings; secondly, they are insects, creepy-crawlies that most people, vegans included, swat or stamp upon without compunction. In her choice of simile, Hopkins presents migrants as the equivalent of potentially noxious creatures whose lives have no value. She then moves from simile to metaphor in her description of British towns as 'festering sores, plagued by swarms of migrants and asylum seekers'. In quick succession, we have a noun phrase denoting a repulsive but at least localised medical problem, a past participle associated with death on a mass scale and a collective noun normally used for insects. In short, migrants are dehumanised and presented as a serious health risk.

Ipso received more than 400 complaints about Hopkins' column (Ponsford 2015), the majority of which concerned Clause 12 (Discrimination) of the Editors' Code. In addition, there were further complaints regarding Clause 2 (Opportunity for right of reply), Clause 4 (Harassment), Clause 5 (Intrusion into grief or shock) and Clause 6 (Reporting of children). All were rejected with Ipso's ruling clarifying that the Editors' Code does not cover matters of taste and offence. There were also complaints concerning Clause 1 (Accuracy) and for these Ipso's ruling was announced some weeks later, and once again the ruling was that there had been no breach of the Editors' Code. The Complaints Committee concluded that the column clearly represented Hopkins' opinions and would not be mistaken by readers as a factual report. Further clarification was also given of the earlier rejection of complaints regarding Clause 12 (Discrimination):

> The Committee acknowledged the strength of feeling the column had aroused. It took this opportunity to note publicly that the terms of Clause 12 specifically prohibit prejudicial or pejorative reference to individuals; they do not restrict publications' commentary on groups or categories of people. In this instance, the references under complaint were not to any identifiable individuals. As such, Clause 12 was not engaged. The Committee made clear that it does not have jurisdiction to deal with potential breaches of the law, but understood that the police were currently investigating the matter. (Ipso ruling 02741-15 2015)

The Metropolitan Police did indeed conduct investigations to see whether Katie Hopkins had been guilty of incitement to racial hatred but concluded that she would not face charges. Duell (2015) reported the news with the observation 'Cops get attack of common sense at last'. Scotland Yard was probably not amused to see published on *MailOnline* the letter from Detective Inspector Howard Holt informing Hopkins that she would not be charged. The columnist herself told readers that while being questioned under caution she had 'delivered a long Hopkins rant about the importance of free speech', which might have made Inspector Holt wonder whether the Crown Prosecution Service had been a little hasty in deciding not to proceed with criminal charges. Duell's evident contentment that Hopkins was not to be investigated further may have been related to the fact that a few weeks earlier the controversial columnist had decided to leave the *Sun* in order to reach far more monthly users at *MailOnline*; the former had only recently abandoned its ill-judged experiment with a paywall while the latter's freely accessible website was attracting more than 13 million daily visitors.

We have seen that Enoch Powell's so-called rivers of blood speech was delivered when the Race Relations Bill was being discussed in Parliament, and some commentators felt that the proposed legislation represented an unacceptable threat to freedom of expression. If the story of Katie Hopkins' 'cockroaches' column tells us anything, it is that the misgivings many people had in 1968 were misplaced. Half a century on it is still possible to say or write hateful things about an entire population and acquire fame and fortune while doing so. Which is not to say that Katie Hopkins has not paid a price for her spiteful, ill-informed excesses. Her extreme right-wing views and extraordinary lack of empathy made her thoroughly detested by millions of people, and in the end the same media that had exploited her ability to raise audience and circulation figures decided that she had become too toxic. Her contract with *MailOnline* was terminated in 2017 and at the time of writing she is broke, rarely seen on TV and limited to social media to express her opinions.

To counter accusations of racism, the right-wing tabloids sometimes give extensive coverage to a racially-motivated crime committed by whites. The best-known case concerns the black teenager Stephen Lawrence, who was knifed to death by a gang of white youths on 22 April 1993 as he waited at a bus stop in south-east London. Suspects were quickly identified but twelve days after the murder Stephen's parents called a press conference to complain that the Metropolitan Police were not pursuing the case with much urgency. Five men were eventually arrested and two were charged, but the Crown Prosecution Service concluded that the evidence was insufficient. The Lawrences then brought a private prosecution against three of the five men but that too failed in 1996 for lack of evidence. It was widely felt that negligence and/or incompetence on the part of the police meant that opportunities to gather sufficient evidence had been missed, and it began to look as if Stephen Lawrence's racist killers had got away with murder. There were calls for an enquiry into the handling of the case, which the *Daily Mail* energetically supported.

It was not the sort of case that the *Mail* would normally turn into a *cause célèbre* but the editor, Paul Dacre, had a personal reason for pursuing this particular hate crime: Stephen's father, Neville Lawrence, had once done some plastering work at Dacre's house and the editor had met Stephen and his brother Stuart. He sprang into action in February 1997 after the jury at the inquest into Stephen Lawrence's death quickly reached the conclusion that he had been unlawfully killed by five white men in an unprovoked racist attack. But the gang of five had already been acquitted in court of Stephen's murder and under the double jeopardy rules of the time could not be tried again. Dacre, however, was determined to see justice done. Fifteen years later Stephen Wright (2012) outlined the long and ultimately successful campaign by the *Daily Mail* to secure a retrial and a conviction. It began on 14 February 1997 with a front-page splash consisting of photos of the five men below the following headline and subhead:

## MURDERERS

The Mail accuses these men of killing. If we are wrong, let them sue us

The five were named: Gary Dobson, Neil Acourt, Jamie Acourt, Luke Knight and David Norris. In approving this front page, Paul Dacre was running a double risk. In the UK, the media cannot comment upon an active case; to do so often leads to prosecution for contempt of court, which can result in a jail sentence. It all depended on whether the case of Stephen Lawrence's stabbing was deemed to be still active. The second risk was that one of the five men was the son of a certain Clifford Norris, who was reputed to be a gangster and the sort of man who was not above eliminating people who upset him. As it happened, after a week Dacre learnt that he was not going to be charged with contempt of court and public reaction was mostly highly positive, which might have gone some way to deterring Clifford Norris from doing anything rash. As Addison (2017: position 4543) puts it: 'The story has, to many, come to define his editorship, and it was the only front page that hung for years in a frame in his office'.

Wright (2012), often citing his own articles, then goes on to recall the successive stages in the *Mail*'s campaign: pressure for an inquiry into how the police investigated the murder, the MacPherson Inquiry's revelation of institutional racism in the Metropolitan Police, calls to end the double jeopardy rule in an age of rapid advances in forensic science and the subsequent change in the law, demands for police officers who did not do their duty to be prosecuted, a compensation payment to Stephen's parents from the Metropolitan Police, a retrial after new developments in forensic investigation and the convictions for murder of two of the gang of five.

The *Daily Mail*'s tenacity in pursuing the Stephen Lawrence case was commendable. It was a one-off, however, a token investigation that could never adequately compensate for the harm done by an enormous number of articles about Black or Asian Britons and foreign immigrants that are not just unpleasant but also factually inaccurate (in February 2017 Wikipedia defined the *Mail* as an unreliable source). Migrants from Syria or Afghanistan do not have the advantage of having done plastering work for Paul Dacre or his successor, Geordie Greig.

The other UK tabloid named by the European Commission against Racism and Intolerance in its 2016 report, the *Sun*, periodically attacks public figures who make racist remarks. In 2009, it was Nick Griffin, then leader of the British National Party, who was described as a 'fascist bigot' and his contribution to a televised discussion programme dismissed as 'vile TV outpourings' (Wooding et al. 2009). More recently the veteran comedian John Cleese sparked controversy when he tweeted that in his opinion 'London was not really an English city any more'. The journalist and author Mick Hume (2019) wrote a short piece for the *Sun* describing the once very funny Cleese as 'a very grumpy old git' who has become 'all bile, bitterness, hate and humbug'. He then goes on to extol the advantages of multiculturalism and diversity, which he contrasts with Cleese's 'fantasy of what Ye Olde England was like'. Many of us would argue that Cleese's criticisms of twenty-first-century London appear to be motivated more by nostalgia than racism or hate, and that Hume's definition of the comedian's comments as a 'rant' is an exaggeration. However, his affirmation that it is London's very diversity that makes the city 'strong' and 'vibrant' allows the *Sun* to deny that it is relentlessly hostile towards immigrants and Muslims. As with the *Mail*'s campaign to get Stephen Lawrence's killers brought back to court, we have to consider the relative numbers: for every *Sun* column criticising an individual's racist sentiments, there are many more front-page splashes denigrating entire communities in British cities or in a refugee camp in Calais.

So are the right-wing tabloids racist? The simple answer is yes, but their content is rarely actionable since trained journalists know that if they direct their insinuations, smears or explicit accusations at groups rather than individuals they are not at great risk of prosecution. Furthermore, the industry's independent regulator, Ipso, tends to slap wrists rather than impose fines that might give newspaper owners pause for thought. However, there is an important contrast with 1934 when Viscount Rothermere expressed his admiration for Oswald Mosley's British Union of Fascists: none of the UK tabloids wants anything to do with the extreme right-wing, xenophobic parties—from the National Front to the British National Party to the English Defence League—that over the decades have tried and failed to make a real impact on British politics. When Nigel Farage was leader of the UK Independence Party, he did not hesitate to expel members who made racist comments, and his Ukip was favourably presented in the pro-Brexit tabloids, but when the party lurched towards the far right under subsequent leaders it was largely ignored by the popular press. It is not entirely clear whether the tabloids eschew Fascist organisations as a matter of principle or simply because history shows that such parties never manage to gain a foothold in the UK.

# References

Addison, Adrian. 2017. *Mail Men: The unauthorized story of the* Daily Mail, Kindle edition. London: Atlantic Books.

Blinder, Scott. 2019. Migration to the UK: Asylum and refugees. *The Migration Observatory at the University of Oxford*, January 4. https://migrationobservatory.ox.ac.uk/resources/briefings/migration-to-the-uk-asylum/. Accessed 11 August 2019.

Daily Mirror Editorial. 1938. Pure Nonsense. *Daily Mirror*, August 19.

Daily Star. 2016. Yorkshire Ripper turns to Islam: Muslim inmates to protect Sutcliffe behind bars. *Daily Star Online*, September 4, updated July 20, 2019. https://www.dailystar.co.uk/news/latest-news/yorkshire-ripper-islam-muslim-inmates-17114476. Accessed 20 August 2019.

Daily Telegraph Comment. 2007. Enoch Powell's 'Rivers of Blood' speech. *Telegraph.co.uk*, November 6. https://www.telegraph.co.uk/comment/3643823/Enoch-Powells-Rivers-of-Blood-speech.html. Accessed 9 August 2019.

Duell, Mark. 2015. Cops get attack of common sense at last: Katie Hopkins will not face charges over allegations that she incited racial hatred in migrant article. *MailOnline*, November 3. https://www.dailymail.co.uk/news/article-3301963/Katie-Hopkins-not-face-charges-allegations-incited-racial-hatred-article-comparing-migrants-cockroaches.html#comments. Accessed 23 August 2019.

Dunt, Ian. 2016. Buried in a Migration Watch report: The truth about immigration. *Politics.co.uk*, June 13. https://www.politics.co.uk/blogs/2016/06/13/buried-in-a-migration-watch-report-the-truth-about-immigrati. Accessed 16 August 2019.

ECRI Report on the United Kingdom, October 4, 2016. Strasbourg: Council of Europe. https://rm.coe.int/fifth-report-on-the-united-kingdom/16808b5758. Accessed 21 August 2019.

Ewens, Hannah. 2017. How Tabloids Get Away with Islamophobic Front Pages. *Vice.com*, June 20. https://www.vice.com/en_uk/article/bj8am5/how-tabloids-get-away-with-islamophobic-front-pages. Accessed 21 August 2019.

Fricker, Martin. 2016. Apocalyptic scenes as Calais Jungle migrants burn tents with aid workers desperately battling to remove gas canisters. *Mirror Online*, October 26, 2019. https://www.mirror.co.uk/news/world-news/apocalyptic-scenes-calais-jungle-migrants-9127901. Accessed 18 August 2019.

Gale, George. 1968. The law should take no account of race. *Daily Mirror*, April 22.

Harmsworth, Harold (Lord Rothermere). 1934. Hurrah for the Blackshirts. *Daily Mail*, January 22.

HM Government. 2018. Prosecutions and convictions. *UK Government*, October 10. https://www.ethnicity-facts-figures.service.gov.uk/crime-justice-and-the-law/courts-sentencing-and-tribunals/prosecutions-and-convictions/latest. Accessed 16 August 2019.

Hopkins, Katy. 2015. Rescue boats? I'd use gunships to stop migrants. *Sun*, April 17, p. 11.

Hume, Mick. 2019. John Cleese's racist tweet row about London proves he has ceased to be funny. *Sun*, May 31. https://www.thesun.co.uk/news/9189672/john-cleese-racist-tweet-row-opinion/. Accessed 25 August 2019.

Ipso ruling 02741-15. 2015. Greer v The Sun, July 20. https://www.ipso.co.uk/rulings-and-resolution-statements/ruling/?id=02741-15. Accessed 23 August 2019.

Ipso ruling 09324-15. 2016. Muslim Engagement and Development (MEND) v The Sun, February 17. https://www.ipso.co.uk/rulings-and-resolution-statements/ruling/?id=09324-15. Accessed 20 August 2019.

Knight, Victor. 1968. Heath slaps down Powell 'inuendo'. *Daily Mirror*, April 23.

McKinstry, Leo. 2015. Calais crisis is becoming a symbol of the fatally flawed EU. *Daily Express*, July 31. https://www.express.co.uk/comment/columnists/leo-mckinstry/595124/Calais-is-becoming-a-symbol-of-the-fatally-flawed-EU. Accessed 14 August 2019.

Mount, Ferdinand. 2019. Wedded to the absolute. *London Review of Books* 41 (18): 5–8.

Ponsford, Dominic. 2015. IPSO rejects Katie Hopkins migrant 'cockroaches' complaints: Editors' Code does not cover 'taste and offence'. *Pressgazette.co.uk*, May 6. https://www.pressgazette.co.uk/conde-nast-first-digital-only-launch-website-alpha-geeks-ars-technica/. Accessed 23 August 2019.

Reynolds, Mark, Rob Virtue, Scott Campbell, and Alison Little. 2015. Calais goes up in flames: Migrants fight to get into UK as ferry workers block harbour. *Daily Express*, July 31. https://www.express.co.uk/news/world/594851/Eurotunnel-Calais-migrants-Britain-Channel-Theresa-May-government-security-immigration. Accessed 17 August 2019.

Ritschel, Chelsea. 2019. Most popular baby names of 2019 so far in the UK revealed. *Independent*, June 26. https://www.independent.co.uk/life-style/baby-names-popular-uk-babycentre-2019-olivia-muhammed-a8974461.html. Accessed 16 August 2019.

Russell, Benjamin. 2013. EU flooded with 1,000 asylum seeker applications every day. *Express Online*, August 9, 2013. https://www.express.co.uk/news/uk/420865/EU-flooded-with-1-000-asylum-seeker-applications-EVERY-day. Accessed 12 August 2019.

Sendall, Wilfrid. 1968. The Tories must read the lesson right. *Daily Express*, April 23, p. 8.

Slack, James, Steve Doughty, and Tamara Cohen. 2015. Just how many more can we take? PM pledges to get a grip as migrants add a city the size of Coventry to population in only a year. *MailOnline*, May 22. https://www.dailymail.co.uk/news/article-3091929/Just-PM-pledges-grip-migrants-add-city-size-Coventry-population-year.html. Accessed 12 August 2019.

Sturge, Georgina. 2019. *Migration Statistics*. London: House of Commons Library. https://brexit.hypotheses.org/files/2018/02/SN06077.pdf. Accessed 11 August 2019.

Tonkin, Sam. 2016. Another all-male coachload of 'child' migrants arrives in Britain—But officials won't say how many there are and won't do dental checks to prove they're really children. *MailOnline*, October 19. Accessed 3 January 2020.

Wodak, Ruth. 2015. *The Politics of Fear*. Los Angeles, London, New Delhi, Singapore, and Washington, DC: Sage.

Wooding, David, Nick Parker, and Ryan Sabey. 2009. Backlash hits BNP chief. *Sun*, October 24.

Wright, Stephen. 2012. The Mail's victory: How Stephen Lawrene's killers were finally brought to justice years after our front page sensationally branded the evil pair murderers. *Daily Mail*, January 3, 2016. https://www.dailymail.co.uk/news/article-2080159/Stephen-Lawrence-case-How-killers-finally-brought-justice.html. Accessed 24 August 2019.

# 5

# Totties, Time Warps and Traitors to the Sisterhood: The Tabloids and Sex

The lexeme *tottie* (or *totty*) has an interesting history. In the nineteenth century, it denoted a prostitute and possibly evolved from the diminutive form of the name Dorothy (Thorne 2014: 445), but in the twentieth century its use came to be largely restricted to the all-male environment of the armed services, particularly the Royal Navy, and referred to a sexually attractive woman but not necessarily one motivated by mercenary considerations. It had practically disappeared from everyday English until the tabloids, particularly the *Sun* and the *Daily Star*, revived it in the 1990s. Today it denotes a sexually enticing young woman and lends itself to alliterative headlines featuring words like *top*, *titty* and *telly*. The nearest male equivalent would probably be *hunk*, but there is a fundamental difference between the two terms: describing a man as a *hunk* does not imply that he has no positive attributes other than his physique, while the connotations attached to the female term make *intelligent tottie* sound like an oxymoron.

The tabloids have adopted other expressions to refer to parts of the body or sexual activity that are rarely, if ever, used by the general public in everyday speech. Although they take great interest in celebrities' coital preferences, they eschew the word *fuck*, whether written in full or with asterisks to replace letters other than the initial *f* (although the imperative *f\*\*\* off* with asterisks is used in inverted commas to quote someone's verbal intemperance). The vulgar verb is typically replaced by *bonk* (often involving a pun with *bonkers*) or *romp* (which suggests sex of a boisterous kind), both words that belong more firmly to the lexicon of the tabloids than to that of the general public. Other euphemistic substitutions are *have a fling, have a tumble* and *have nookie*, all expressions that focus on the playfulness of sex and convey little or nothing in the way of moral censure. Similarly, for newspapers that feature so many photos of generous breasts, there is a surprising reluctance to use the word *tits*. The usual substitutions—*boobs* and *knockers*—are polysemous lexemes that lend themselves to the creation of puns, while *knock* collocates with a series of adverb particles to form phrasal verbs.

Buttocks may be referred to by the informal British words *bum, bot* (abbreviation of *bottom*) and *backside* but it is becoming increasingly common to see the American slang words *butt* and *booty*. The *Sun* employed this last expression in the punning headline 'Booty contest' (Price 2016) to announce an extraordinarily well-documented investigation to identify the owner of 'Britain's best bum'. The two contestants for this title are the British media personality Carol Vorderman and the American actor and model Kim Kardashian, and the article provides precise statistics concerning the height, width and total surface area of each woman's posterior (details of how such figures were obtained and who conducted the research are not revealed). Alliteration and rhyme feature in the 'battle of the bots' to discover who has the 'Rear of the Year', although the journalist evidently failed to think of a word to collocate with 'derrière'. Finally, a clairvoyant is consulted to inform readers as to what the two women's bottoms reveal about their personalities (she is dubbed a 'rumpologist'). Many people would consider this detailed comparison to be offensive to women and more in tune with the social climate of the 1970s than with that of 2016, although the author of the piece, Lee Price, would doubtless argue that it is just harmless fun and that the two women concerned can hardly complain given that they owe much of their success to their attractive bodies. The claim that the tabloids sometimes appear to be stuck in a time warp is investigated below.

A recent slang coinage is *wedgie*, which is the situation in which a person's underwear gets stuck thong-like between his/her buttocks, and a variation is *front wedgie* when a woman's tight-fitting panties or bikini bottoms end up between the labia majora of her vagina. The tabloids generally consider the colloquial substitutes for the word vagina to be too vulgar to use, or at least, not sufficiently jocular, although once again asterisks may be employed to quote someone's deliberately offensive language, as in 'he called me a stupid c***'. To refer to female genitalia, it is nearly always *vagina*; indeed, *vagina(s)* appears no fewer than eighteen times in an illustrated article in the *Sun* in which 'a former bikini waxer' draws upon her professional experience to describe the five main types she has identified (Pemberton 2018). No informal or slang alternatives are used.

There is a lexical gap here that must be of concern to tabloid editors given their habitual preference for colloquial language, but in September 2019 the *Daily Star* found the word it needed in African American slang. When the online retailer Fashion Nova posted photos of a new bodysuit on Instagram, online shoppers felt that it was likely to give them a front wedgie and was therefore a garment that they would be reluctant to wear in public (Roberts 2019). One responder went further in noting that apart from the danger of exposing a little too much of herself, a PVC bodysuit with such a crotch design might well cause the wearer some physical discomfort: 'My coochie hurts just looking at this'. The origin of the slang expression can be traced to the title of Willie Dixon's blues song *Hoochie Coochie Man* in which the first word refers to bootlegged liquor and the second to the female genitalia, which are more likely to be exposed when a woman is drunk. The woman's observation was incorporated into the article's headline (in inverted commas), and it now remains to be seen whether *coochie* will become established as the acceptably risqué word, with all its potential for puns, that will liberate the tabloids from the need to use a formal term that offers few opportunities for plays on words.

The online article described above includes images of beautiful young women wearing the highly revealing bodysuit, most of whom are models paid by Fashion Nova but there are also photos re-posted from the accounts of independent 'Instagram Stars'. Social media have given women who wish to use their aesthetically pleasing bodies to attract followers and advertisers the opportunity to be autonomous, and it could be argued that the demise of the *Sun*'s page-3 girls and of the *Daily Star*'s topless models had more to do with the digital revolution than with decades of protests against the demeaning of women. What is certain is that photos of sexy young women remain, but now their breasts are covered. On April Fools' Day 2019, nearly half a century after the *Sun*'s first topless page-3 girl, a young lady named Ellie became the *Star*'s very last glamour girl to pose without a bikini top. Her photo reappeared nine days later on *MailOnline* with an article reporting on female politicians' welcoming of the *Star*'s topless ban, but in true tabloid style also noted the angry reaction of glamour models who feared that they would lose work and, in a quote attributed to nobody, dismissed anti-page-3 campaigners as 'no bra-wearing man-haters' (Dyer 2019).

So Ellie's photo in the *Daily Star* marked the end of an era. The *Sun* had eliminated topless page-3 girls from its print edition in 2015, although bare breasts continued to be posted on its website until 2017, including a New Year's Eve 2016 collection of 'titillating photographs' from 1976 to 2016 and a female journalist's description of 'jaw-droppingly beautiful shots through the years' (Barns 2016). The *Daily Mirror* and the *Sunday People* had stopped publishing photos of topless models in the 1980s, while the *Mail* and the *Express* never had their equivalents of page-3 girls in the first place, although both, particularly the former, adopted the alternative strategy of publishing amply illustrated stories about good-looking female celebrities. Over the years the *Sun*, the *Star* and the now-defunct *News of the World* vigorously, and sometimes nastily, attacked critics who accused them of exploiting and degrading women. Those who did not view the photographs of naked women as just a bit of innocent fun were labelled humourless prudes, wet blankets and sanctimonious killjoys. The worst treatment was reserved for female critics, who were depicted as sour old women motivated by envy because they were not, and never had been, remotely similar in appearance to the slim, beautiful and very sexy women on page 3. The main target was the Labour MP Clare Short, whose attempt to push through legislation banning topless page-3 girls so incensed Kelvin

MacKenzie that the *Sun* described her as 'too ugly to rape' (Rhodes 2017).

After the turn of the century, the *Sun* endeavoured to counter accusations of shamelessly exploiting the female body by complementing photos of sexy young women with a smaller number but equally unclothed images of hunky young men. Until fairly recently something often seen on the wall in all-male working environments was the sexy calendar featuring twelve buxom models, one for each month. In November 2008, the *Sun* urged female readers to purchase a 2009 calendar depicting twelve male models posing as building labourers, each with his jeans slung low to reveal a significant percentage of his backside (Battle 2008):

> **Brit builders: some like it bot**
> **By BELLA BATTLE**
> A new calendar called Builders Bottoms 2009 shows 12 of the sexiest men we've ever seen on a building site - and they've all got their bums out.
> Nab yourself a copy now at urbanphotography.co.uk and ogle six more fellas in our slideshow above.

The alliterative headline alludes to Billy Wilder's film *Some Like It Hot*, a comedy that shook up the morally and sexually conservative Hollywood of 1959; Britain in 2008 and was more than ready for the role reversal of good-looking young men exposing their bodies to amuse or excite women. The verb *ogle* normally follows a male subject, but the imperative here is clearly aimed primarily at female readers. To critics of the tabloids' page-3 culture, however, an occasional pretence of evening things up in this way was never going to be deemed an appropriate counterweight to their habitual exploitation of female flesh.

The same tabloids that publish photos of beautiful young women in provocative poses are ferocious in their attacks on sex offenders. An article on the *Sun*'s website attributed to Alain Tolhurst (2018) is actually just a summary of an investigation conducted by ITV's *Good Morning Britain* programme about convicted sex offenders, more than half of whom had committed offences against children, whose original sentences had stated that after serving their prison sentences they would remain on the sex offenders' register for the rest of their lives (which involves strict limitations on their freedom to travel). Following a change in the law in 2012, those who were juveniles themselves at the time the offences were committed were allowed to appeal to be taken off the register, and *Good Morning Britain* revealed that 1230 had successfully done so. Tolhurst's piece, as well as an unsigned editorial, use the language of moral outrage in condemning a legal reform that allows rapists and child abusers to change address and travel where they want without having to inform the police. This concern about the risk to potential victims of sex crimes loses a little credibility, however, given that on the same web page there are photos not designed to appeal to a man's higher instincts and links to stories that are not of an edifying nature.

When the *Sun* introduced the page-3 girl in 1970, Larry Lamb and his team could justify their decision on the grounds that they were merely reflecting the norms and mores of their time, stating that 'the Permissive Society is a fact, not an opinion' (Bingham 2009: 222). Similarly, the *Star*'s decision to cover the glamour girls' breasts represented a belated acceptance that five decades on attitudes had changed. However, the impression that certain tabloids are stuck in a time warp is actually strongest when nudity is not an issue. In March 2017, the Prime Minister, Theresa May, and Nicola Sturgeon, Scotland's First Minister, went head-to-head in a televised debate on, among other things, the question of Brexit and Scottish independence. The next day the *Mail*'s front page featured a photograph of the two women seated side-by-side, both smartly dressed and, since they were in a sitting position, with the hems of their skirts above their knees. The headline was 'Never mind Brexit, who won Legs-it!' and the related article on pages 6 and 7, written by the regular *Mail* columnist Sarah Vine (2017a), noted that 'the most powerful women in British politics were wearing remarkably similar outfits' before proceeding to describe in great detail their clothes (including brands and prices), shoes, make-up and hairstyles. In her determination to observe every sartorial particular, Vine evidently failed to register what the two politicians actually said during the TV programme. Naturally, the article, but most of all the headline, were roundly condemned as an affront not only to the two tough, intelligent individuals directly concerned, but also to career women in general, and within 24 hours Ipso received some 300 complaints.

Unusually for *MailOnline*, this article can no longer be accessed, but a not dissimilar piece (though with a very different headline) written by the same columnist (Vine 2017b) and posted on the same day is available. This second article again describes the two women's outfits but also focuses on their body language and general demeanour, speculating upon the subliminal influence upon TV viewers. The final two sentences actually touch upon politics as Vine opines that Scottish viewers would have noted 'the reliable, measured, considerate and cautious politics of Mrs May and the safety of a Union that has endured for 300 years'. This conclusion is based on style rather than content and just happens to be perfectly in sync with the editorial line of a paper that campaigned aggressively for Brexit in 2016 but is also fiercely opposed to Scottish independence.

Another area in which the right-wing tabloids are sometimes out of step with the majority of the population is that of attitudes towards homosexuality. In the 1970s words like *poofter*, *queer*, *lezzie*, *pansy* and *bumboy* were freely used, while the emergence of AIDS in the 1980s was initially seen as a disease limited to male homosexuals, and therefore not such a bad thing. When Hugh Whittow (1985) of the *Sun* wrote 'A vicar yesterday branded the gay plague AIDS as the wrath of God' many readers doubtless agreed that the pervs were getting what they deserved. As the century drew to a close, however, public attitudes changed radically and the tabloids failed to move with their readers. In November 1998, the Minister of Agriculture in Tony Blair's government, Nick Brown, went public about having had a two-year relationship with a male lover, a confession that was forced upon him when he discovered that Rupert Murdoch's Sunday tabloid, *The News of the World*, was going to out him. *The News of the World* went ahead with the story anyway even though it was no longer a scoop, then the *Sun* followed up with a front-page editorial under a headline addressing Prime Minister Tony Blair: 'Tell Us the Truth, Tony – Are We Being Run by a Gay Mafia?' The editorial was written by the *Sun*'s political editor, Trevor Kavanagh (1998), who wondered whether Britain was in the hands of 'a gay Mafia of politicians, lawyers, palace courtiers and TV bigwigs', and declared that the public had a right to know how many homosexuals were in positions of power.

Readers did not react as Kavanagh had expected. Some days later the *Guardian*'s Martin Walker (1998) chose the *Los Angeles Times* for an article whose headline neatly summed up the state of play: 'As Public Grows Tolerant, Chattering Class Doesn't'. He cited the results of an opinion poll commissioned by his own paper which found that 52% of Britons found homosexuality to be 'morally acceptable' and exactly the same percentage believed that being gay was perfectly compatible with serving as a Cabinet minister. Only 33% thought homosexuals should not be in the government. Walker saw parallels between the *Sun*'s failure to detect the public's growing acceptance of homosexuality and the fact that while opinion formers in America had got themselves into a lather about Bill Clinton's behaviour, notably his relationship with one Monica Lewinsky, American voters had endorsed the President's leadership in midterm elections: 'Just as much of America's chattering classes in Washington and the media found themselves behind the curve of rising public tolerance of sexual vulnerabilities, so much of the British press has misjudged the changing public mood'.

The change in public mood went into overdrive in the first decade of the twenty-first century. In 2010, the *Sun* commissioned a YouGov survey that asked the question: Should gay people be cabinet ministers? Just twelve years after the *Guardian*'s poll cited above, the consensus was that the question should not be asked at all: 'But by asking, the tabloid has exposed something else, something important, something its editor and that of all right-wing newspapers should take note of. There is now a yawning chasm between the press and the public in their attitudes towards homosexuality' (Strudwick 2010).

By the second decade of the century, presenting gay people in a negative light had become a risky business for the tabloids. Same-sex marriage became legal in the UK (but not Northern Ireland) in 2014. In 2017, the medal-winning Olympic and Commonwealth Games diver, Tom Daley, married his male partner and the current report of the ceremony on the *Daily Express*'s website is not controversial (Giles 2017). In this version, the headline reads: 'Tom Daley, 22, and Dustin Lance Black, 42, marry in romantic Romeo and Juliet ceremony'. In the original version, the word *marry* was placed between inverted commas, which many people found offensive because it seemed to insinuate that heterosexual couples marry properly but for gay couples it is not the same thing.

There may also be economic consequences for a newspaper that does not grant absolute parity between gay and straight couples. Less than a year after their marriage Tom Daley and Dustin Lance Black announced that they were going to be parents and were photographed with an ultrasound scan of the baby in the womb of the unnamed surrogate mother. A *Daily Mail* columnist commented in an article under the headline 'Please don't pretend two dads is the new normal: RICHARD LITTLEJOHN says children benefit most from being raised by a man and a woman' (Littlejohn 2018). Anticipating accusations of homophobia, he made his position very clear: 'I supported civil partnerships long before it was fashionable and I'd rather children were fostered by loving gay couples than condemned to rot in state-run institutions, where they face a better-than-average chance of being abused'. He goes on to state that homosexual couples can be excellent parents but he finds the exhibitionism of the prospective fathers distasteful and feels that the practice of surrogate motherhood is a 'trend towards treating women as mere breeding machines'. The article is wittily written and poses some important questions, and in tone and content is anything but a homophobic rant, yet it provoked considerable hostility. The campaign group Stop Funding Hate immediately declared that the column was homophobic and contacted the company Center Parcs, whose advertisement had appeared next to Littlejohn's piece in the print edition. Center Parcs duly announced that it would no longer advertise in the *Daily Mail*, and shortly afterwards the Southbank Centre made the same decision (Barns 2018).

Less than half of the average Briton's lifespan earlier, a newspaper ran no risk at all if its headlines screamed about the gay plague and the wrath of God. It is difficult to think of any other aspect of social life in which attitudes have changed so radically in such a relatively short period of time, and it is only now that the tabloids face losing advertising revenue that they are catching up with their readers.

We have already seen that an article about two female political leaders that focused almost exclusively on their appearance and clothes was written by a woman. Similarly, a piece on the *Sun*'s website celebrating forty years of page-3 girls was written by a woman. The editor of the *Daily Star* from December 2003 to February 2018 was Dawn Neesom (and she is still a columnist for that paper), who had previously worked for *Woman's Own* magazine and had been woman's editor at the *Sun*. Throughout her fifteen-year editorship, she did nothing to reform the *Star*'s blokeish culture, the decision to bring back bikini tops coming after her male successor, Jon Clark, had taken over. Another traitor to the sisterhood, Rebekah Brooks (née Wade), was editor of the *News of the World* for three years before assuming the same role at the *Sun* from 2003 to 2009, and like Dawn Neesom she made no attempt to encourage different attitudes towards women's bodies. Indeed, it is surely not coincidental that on Rebekah Wade's first day in charge at the *Sun*, the page-3 girl was also called Rebekah.

The *Daily Mail* has a long record of publishing articles by female columnists whose views on gender issues are far from feminist in nature, which is ironic since it is the only national daily newspaper in the UK with more female than male readers. The very first edition of the paper on 4 May 1896 featured a women's page, and today that single page has grown into the *Femail* supplement, several extravagantly illustrated pages covering clothes and cosmetics, health tips, food and recipes, diets, advice for parents and mother-to-be, celebrity gossip, photos of cute pets and, of course, the Princesses Kate and Meghan with their offspring. Articles about equal pay are unlikely to feature, and the opinions of certain female columnists suggest that while there has been a radical change in attitudes towards homosexuality, there has not been a similar revolution in notions of the role of women in society. The title of one of Jan Moir's columns (2014) is unequivocal: 'So much for feminism! All today's girls want is to be brides'. She goes on to mock Harriet Harman, a Labour MP and campaigner for gender equality, and ridicules attempts to combat gender stereotypes:

> It's almost laughable. All that painstaking work Harriet Harman did on equality, all those efforts to ban gender-specific toys for children, all those fine brains devoted to encouraging women to think of themselves as 'the boss' rather than someone who was 'bossy' – and still a generation of girls dream of nothing more than being a special bride for a lovely day.

Statistics from reliable sources indicate that more and more young couples do not bother to get married, which casts doubt upon the claim that there is a generation of girls whose sole aim in life is to be the beautiful protagonist of a romantic wedding ceremony. Jan Moir bases her arguments on 'research by Interflora', thus equating a flower delivery network with a recognised public opinion and data analytics company.

It has become a commonplace to say that millennial women want to have it all—a successful career, a satisfying relationship and the joy of motherhood—and it is not difficult to point to examples of women in positions of power and responsibility who appear to have achieved that aim. However, the title of another piece written by a female columnist in the *Mail* refutes in strong terms the idea that such a balancing act is really possible: 'Sorry girls, you can't have a career AND a happy relationship' (Platell 2012). With great frankness, Amanda Platell ascribes the failure of her marriage and of three long-term relationships to the fact that she had always put her career first, her priorities having been partly determined by her inability to have children. She believes that the men with whom she had tried to share her life had difficulty accepting her professional success:

> Most men judge themselves by their careers. It makes them feel vulnerable if their wife or partner's career is more successful. That doesn't make for happy relationships. Women, on the other hand, will usually accommodate a more successful husband and will often put being a good wife and mother ahead of a career.

Some decades ago such a distinction would have been considered self-evident, even banal, but by the second decade of the twenty-first century it had become for many people an inaccurate and unhelpful stereotype. This column generated 112 responses from readers, some of whom agreed with Platell's views but a clear majority disagreed, sometimes in strong terms, and many cited their own successful combining of career, marriage and motherhood. Some challenged the stereotype of men resenting their female partner's success, again with reference to personal experience, a few thought Platell's description of her very long working day indicated an inability to organise her time, and one person objected to the word 'girls' in a headline aimed at grown women. Just as the online edition of a specific tabloid is read by people who do not agree with that paper's political stance, so the website of the only tabloid with a majority of female readers is visited by people who do not concur with the way women are depicted by its journalists.

The prize for the most provocative headline used by a female columnist in the *Mail* surely goes to Angela Epstein (2008): 'I'm a FEMALE male chauvinist – and proud of it'. The article begins with her recollection of her profound unease during a flight when the captain addressed the passengers and she realised that the plane was being flown by a woman. She acknowledges that '[t]he sisterhood may blanch at my reaction' but states that while she admires women who achieve success, 'when it comes to *real* power, I feel so much happier if a man holds the reins' (Epstein's italics). On the question of whether she is being 'treacherously disloyal' to her sex, she insists that before 'the braburners[1] start hurling the embers of their lingerie' at her, they should be aware that she is hardly alone in holding such views. To make her point, she refers to two elections in which a female candidate was defeated by a male adversary—Hillary Clinton against Barack Obama in the Democratic primaries of 2008 and Ségolène Royal against Nicolas Sarkozy in the French presidential elections the previous year—and implies that in both cases it was women's votes that ensured the victories of the male candidates. To demonstrate that she practises what she preaches in wanting men to be in charge of serious matters, she informs her readers that she had chosen a male obstetrician to oversee each of her four pregnancies. In twenty-first-century Britain, few men would talk of the biological unsuitability of women for certain roles or professions unless they were in a safe, all-male and probably rather boozy environment. In 2008, Angela Epstein did not hesitate to describe 'testosterone-fuelled power' (Sarkozy) and a woman who succumbed to 'the hormonal urge to blub when faced with a setback' (Hillary Clinton) in an article that by now has been read by millions.

If Angela Epstein has a 1950ish conception of gender roles, her views on the institution of marriage also appear to be expressed by a woman constrained in a girdle and wearing backseam stockings: 'The secret to wedded bliss? Your friends divorcing! The unhappier they are, the more smug you'll feel says ANGELA EPSTEIN' (Epstein 2014). This headline clearly sets the tone for the article that follows, which gives instances of the author deriving pleasure from witnessing the pathetic spectacle of divorced female friends pretending to enjoy their regained independence, and comparing their wretchedness with her own happily married complacency. She makes no mention of the plight of divorced male friends; evidently divorce is disproportionately traumatic for women:

> I like to be around freshly minted divorcees and actively encourage them to come for dinner or pop in for coffee. And my reasons are unapologetically pragmatic. Watching an ex-wife navigate a party teeming with couples is a frank reminder that her fabled grass isn't any greener – all fresh starts and new opportunities – it's just more grass. And it looks markedly less lush than my carefully tended lawn.

Epstein is critical of couples who, in her view, get divorced for trivial reasons—her message being divorce in haste, repent at leisure—and cites another friend who left her husband merely because she was fed up (it would be interesting to know how many friends she has left since the publication of this column). She dedicates a single sentence to cases in which there are reasons that make it impossible for a wife to persevere with her marriage; one of those reasons is 'serial affairs', which implies that a single affair does not constitute a motive for divorce.

271 readers posted comments on this article and most were highly critical of Epstein, further evidence that the tabloids' online editions are visited by people who do not agree at all with much of what they read. The most common accusation was that only a cynical, self-serving and thoroughly unpleasant individual would appear to listen sympathetically as friends spoke of their problems, only to ridicule them in her column for the *Mail*. It is quite possible, however, that in reality Angela Epstein does not think that divorced women are pathetic and does not believe females are incapable of flying a passenger jet. Controversy is grist to her mill, and the language used in the two articles cited here is so perfectly calculated to outrage what Epstein herself calls the sisterhood that it all begins to look somewhat contrived. Having created a media niche for herself as the woman feminists love to hate, it may now be difficult for her to change direction.

## Note

1. In 1968, a group of feminists protested against a beauty pageant in New Jersey by throwing in a trash can and burning symbols of the objectification of the female body—cosmetics, high-heeled shoes and, in a handful of cases, bras—and since then male critics of feminism have used the expression *bra-burners* as a derogatory term to depict feminists as shrill and rather ridiculous. It does not normally form part of a woman's lexicon.

## References

Barns, Sarah. 2016. Nippy New Year! Titillating photographs show Page 3 models ringing in the New Year with champagne and strategically-placed tinsel. *Sun Online*. 31 December 2016. https://www.thesun.co.uk/living/2509050/titillating-photographs-show-page-3-models-ringing-in-the-new-year-with-champagne-and-strategically-placed-tinsel/. Accessed 7 September 2019.

Barns, Tom. 2018. Center Parcs pulls advertising from Daily Mail over 'homophobic' column on Tom Daley and Dustin Lance Black's baby announcement. *MailOnline*. 17 February 2018. https://www.independent.co.uk/news/uk/home-news/center-parcs-stops-daily-mail-advertising-tom-daley-baby-column-stop-funding-hate-companies-support-a8215191.html. Accessed 9 September 2019.

Battle, Bella. 2008. Brit builders: Some like it bot. *Sun*. 15 November 2008. https://rashmanly.com/2008/11/16/24582/. Accessed 4 January 2020.

Bingham, Adrian. 2009. *Family Newspapers? Sex, Private Life and the British Popular Press 1918–1978*. Oxford: Oxford University Press.

Dyer, Chris. 2019. After nearly 50 years, the last topless Page 3 girl vanishes from Fleet Street: Daily Star covers up models four years after The Sun lead (*sic*) the way citing 'changing times and tastes'. *MailOnline*. 11 April 2019. https://www.dailymail.co.uk/news/article-6909041/Daily-Star-covers-Page-3-models-citing-changing-times-tastes.html. Accessed 7 September 2019.

Epstein, Angela. 2008. I'm a female male chauvinist—And proud of it. *MailOnline*. 10 January 2008. https://www.dailymail.co.uk/femail/article-507148/Im-FEMALE-male-chauvinist–proud-it.html. Accessed 13 September 2019.

Epstein, Angela. 2014. The secret to wedded bliss? Your friends divorcing! The unhappier they are, the more smug you'll feel says Angela Epstein. *MailOnline*. 23 June 2014. https://www.dailymail.co.uk/femail/article-2665395/The-secret-wedded-bliss-Your-friends-divorcing-The-unhappier-smug-youll-feel-says-ANGELA-EPSTEIN.html#comments. Accessed 14 September 2019.

Giles, Kayleigh. 2017. Tom Daley, 22, and Dustin Lance Black, 42, marry in romantic Romeo and Juliet ceremony. *Express Online*. 7 May 2017. https://www.express.co.uk/celebrity-news/801386/Tom-Daley-Dustin-Lance-Black-marry. Accessed 9 September 2019.

Kavanagh, Trevor. 1998. Tell Us the Truth, Tony—Are We Being Run by a Gay Mafia? *Sun*. 9 November 1998.

Littlejohn, Richard. 2018. 'Please don't pretend two dads is the new normal': Richard Littlejohn says children benefit most from being raised by a man and a woman. *MailOnline*. 17 February 2018. https://www.dailymail.co.uk/debate/article-5397713/Please-dont-pretend-two-dads-new-normal.html. Accessed 9 September 2019.

Moir, Jan. 2014. So much for feminism! All today's girls want is to be brides. *MailOnline*. 14 March 2014. https://www.dailymail.co.uk/debate/article-2580623/Jan-Moir-So-feminism-All-todays-girls-want-brides.html. Accessed 12 September 2019.

Pemberton, Becky. 2018. No need to ovary act. There are apparently five different types of vagina… so are you a Ms Barbie or a Ms Puffs? *Sun Online*. 28 March 2018. https://www.thesun.co.uk/fabulous/3308350/different-vagina-type-ms-barbie-puffs/. Accessed 6 September 2019.

Platell, Amanda. 2012. Sorry girls, you can't have a career AND a happy relationship. *MailOnline*. 27 September 2012. https://www.dailymail.co.uk/femail/article-2209170/AMANDA-PLATELL-Sorry-girls-career-AND-happy-relationship.html. Accessed 13 September 2019.

Price, Lee. 2016. Booty contest. *Sun Online*. 5 April 2016. https://www.thesun.co.uk/archives/news/626670/booty-contest/. Accessed 6 September 2019.

Rhodes, Mandy. 2017. Clare Short on a new dawn in British politics: A 'time of idiots'. *Holyrood*. 23 May 2017. https://www.holyrood.com/articles/inside-politics/clare-short-new-dawn-british-politics-time-idiots. Accessed 7 September 2019.

Roberts, Sophie. 2019. 'Front wedgie' bodysuit mocked by shoppers: 'My coochie hurts looking at this'. *Daily Star Online*. 4 September 2019. https://www.dailystar.co.uk/fashion-beauty/front-wedgie-bodysuit-mocked-shoppers-19427781. Accessed 6 September 2019.

Strudwick, Patrick. 2010. Press are more homophobic than the public. *Guardian Online*. 1 June 2010. https://www.theguardian.com/commentisfree/2010/jun/01/sun-poll-gay-cabinet-homophobic. Accessed 9 September 2019.

Thorne, Tony. 2014. *Dictionary of Contemporary Slang*. London: Bloomsbury.

Tolhurst, Alain. 2018. 'Should be on for life': Shocking investigation reveals 1.200 sex offenders have got themselves removed from the register—Despite being put on for life. *Sun Online*. 26 July 2018. https://www.thesun.co.uk/news/6859192/shocking-investigation-reveals-1230-sex-offenders-have-got-themselves-removed-from-the-register-despite-being-placed-on-there-for-life/. Accessed 14 September 2019.

Vine, Sarah. 2017a. Never mind Brexit, who won Legs-it! *Daily Mail*. 28 March 2017. https://www.pressreader.com/uk/daily-mail/20170328/281479276248035. Accessed 8 September 2019.

Vine, Sarah. 2017b. One was relaxed, every inch a stateswoman while her opposite number was tense and uncomfortable: Sarah Vine says May v Sturgeon was a knockout victory for the PM. *MailOnline*. 28 March 2017. https://www.dailymail.co.uk/debate/article-4354996/SARAH-VINE-says-v-Sturgeon-victory-PM.html. Accessed 8 September 2019.

Walker, Martin. 1998. As Public Grows Tolerant, Chattering Class Doesn't. *Los Angeles Times*. 15 November 1998. https://www.latimes.com/archives/la-xpm-1998-nov-15-op-42961-story.html. Accessed 9 September 2019.

Whittow, Hugh. 1985. AIDS is the wrath of God, says vicar. *Sun*. 7 February 1985.

# 6

# 'Ve vill Occupy ze Sunbeds Here at Precisely 5 a.m....!': National Stereotypes and Britain's Relationship with Europe

No tabloid editor would dream of letting their journalists refer to UK citizens of Afro-Caribbean or Asian origin as N*****s and P***s, yet it continues to be common practice to call our European neighbours Frogs, Krauts, Dagos and Wops. Tired old national stereotypes are recycled, as are references to Britain's glorious past and, inevitably, 'our finest hour' during the Second World War.

A chapter title chosen by Katy Greenland (2000: 15), a psychologist who specialises in social identities and intergroup contact, makes it clear that it is futile to try to eliminate generalised representations of specific populations: 'Can't live with them, can't live without them: stereotypes in international relations'. Similarly, Moyle (2004: 112) sees stereotypes as inevitable: 'Most people agree that stereotyping is part of the human condition and is, therefore, an unavoidable part of life'. They are not wholly negative; on the contrary '[…] categorization and stereotyping is a fundamental adaptive tool that we use in perceiving the social world' (Greenland 2000: 19). Positive and negative national stereotypes tend to be two sides of the same coin. I have lived in Italy for more than thirty years and on countless occasions people have told me that the national genius is the capacity for creative improvisation that permits Italians to come up with last-minute solutions. Flipping the coin gives us the negative stereotype of the Italians' habitual lack of foresight and planning that leads to the very problems that necessitate such eleventh-hour improvisation. In contrast, the Germans are admired for their organisation, discipline and ability to work together, but when those qualities are taken to excess a negative stereotype is triggered of a population characterised by inflexibility, boorishness and belligerence.

The title of this chapter is the caption to a cartoon by Bernard Cookson, whose work appeared in a number of publications, most notably the *Daily Express* and the satirical magazine *Punch*. The cartoon depicts five paunchy German men on a Mediterranean beach, each of whom has supplemented his standard swimwear with garments rarely seen in such a setting: two wear military caps, another a helmet and all five have swastika armbands. As their leader outlines their strategy to occupy all the sunbeds at dawn the next morning, he uses a stick to draw in the sand as we have seen commanding officers do in films set in wartime. It was published in the *Sun* on 7 April 1987 along with a full-page article entitled 'Vot makes Krauts holiday louts?'. Husemann (2000: 59) reveals that the cartoon and the article complaining of German tourists grabbing the best sunbeds, piling their plates high at the breakfast buffet and jumping queues were actually inspired by a report in the German tabloid *Bild* the previous month about the aggressive behaviour of German holidaymakers in Tenerife. The *Daily Mail* latched onto the *Bild* article the very next day, the *Sun* developed the theme further, and thus was born the caricature of the German sunbather putting his towel on the sunbed early in the morning when, to use another negative stereotype, British tourists are still in bed nursing their hangovers. It is a stereotype that has stood the test of time: thirty-one years later Neal Baker (2018), writing for the *Sunonline*, reported on holidaymakers in Cornwall discovering a sizeable area of Porthmeor Beach cordoned off by tents and windbreaks. Although there was no hard evidence to attribute the land grab to German tourists—the headline refers to 'German beach-towel *tactics*' (italics added)—the fact that the area of beach was sectioned off early in the morning led holidaymakers to use social media to blame nationals traditionally associated with such behaviour (although a minority accused Londoners with second homes in Cornwall). Although the article was updated the following day, the new version neither confirmed nor denied that this German tactic was indeed adopted by German people.

Whenever there is a football match between England and Germany, the tabloids' knee-jerk response is to dust off the language of two world wars in punning or rhyming headlines often featuring offensive epithets to refer to the historic adversaries. England hosted the UEFA European Football Championship in 1996, and when it was known that the home team's opponents in the semi-final would be Germany, the *Daily Mirror*'s attempt to lampoon the militaristic tone of its red-top rivals backfired disastrously. On 24 June, the *Mirror*'s front-page splash featured a photomontage of the players Stuart Pierce and Paul Gascoigne wearing First World War-style tin helmets with the word 'ACHTUNG!' above the image and 'SURRENDER' below it. The subhead made fun of many Germans' inability to pronounce the two *th-* English consonants as it recalled the formula German troops used when they captured British servicemen during the Second World War: 'For you Fritz, ze Euro 96 Championship is over'. In a narrow right-hand column, a spoof editorial entitled 'Mirror declares football war on Germany' was a parody of the real declaration of war announced in 1939. It began:

> I am writing to you from the Editor's Office at Canary Wharf, London. Last night the Daily Mirror's ambassador in Berlin handed the German Government a final note stating that, unless we heard from them by 11 o'clock that they were prepared at once to withdraw their football team from Wembley, a state of soccer war would exist between us.

Satire always runs the risk of overstepping the limits of acceptable taste, and the *Mirror*'s intended send-up was seen by many as xenophobic and gratuitously disrespectful to Germans. When Piers Morgan, the same editor who would later rigorously oppose Britain's participation in the Iraq War, was asked if his paper would resort to racial stereotypes in an article about the West Indies cricket team, he is reported as having replied, 'No, we wouldn't, that would be deeply offensive – these are Germans' (Garland and Rowe 2001: 158). So insulting Afro-Caribbeans merely because they were Afro-Caribbeans was out, while Germans were fair game.

They still were fourteen years to the day later. 24 June 2010 was the day after England's 1-0 win over Slovenia in the World Cup tournament hosted by South Africa. That victory meant that England were through to the quarter-final stage where their opponents would be Germany, and the *Daily Star*'s headline was 'JOB DONE NOW FOR THE HUN' (Savage 2010). Tom Savage's report focused on the relief of English fans who had been unimpressed by the team's performances in the group stage and had feared that they would be flying home early, so the headline was a gratuitous insult that bore no relation at all to the content of the article. During the First World War, the press often referred to Germans as the Hun(s) and the word appears in W.E. Johns' *Biggles* books for boys about the heroics of Captain James Bigglesworth flying his Sopwith Camel aeroplane (texts that have not been used in state schools for decades owing to their imperialistic tone). Today the word is practically never used with its original denotation outside the pages of the tabloids. Indeed, young people may not take it to refer to a fifth-century barbarian at all since in the twenty-first-century *hun* is either an abbreviation of *honey* as a term of endearment or a slang term for multi-level marketeers whose honeyed tones aim to convince people to invest in pyramid schemes.

But these are Germans. As Smith and Higgins note (2013: 109): 'In many forums, including popular journalism, the historical relationship with Germany in particular has become part of Britain's national sense of itself'. The two nations have a complicated history of rivalry tempered by mutual respect, although something more is required to convince the popular press of one of those countries that ninety-two years after the end of the First World War it is all right to revive a term of abuse from that conflict to insult an entire population (while *Bild Zeitung* feels no corresponding urge to reciprocate in kind). From the two reports of England v Germany matches considered here, it seems that that something else might simply be a failure to understand that for most people xenophobia is xenophobia, and is not mitigated by a few witty puns. The tabloids will argue that their treatment of other Europeans is mock xenophobia rather than the real thing, just a bit of fun (comparable with their photos of topless totties) that no one with a functioning sense of humour should find genuinely offensive. In so doing, they underestimate the impact their supposedly harmless banter has on their targets: 'The British act as though their xenophobia was a private joke. But it isn't. Our insulting comments are relayed back to the people at whom they are directed by means of their own correspondents in London. And, as any British diplomat working in Europe will tell you, they have an effect' (Hooper 2001).

Over the last forty years, the tabloids' portrayal of our continental neighbours has grown nastier as their editorial lines (with the usual exception of the *Daily Mirror*) have become increasingly hostile towards the EEC and its successors the EC and the EU. With hindsight, we can see that the Brexiteers who won the referendum of 2016 began pressing for Britain's withdrawal in 1990, and that their campaign was launched in an interview published not in a tabloid, but in the magazine *The Spectator*. On 14 July 1990, the Secretary of State for Industry, Nicholas Ridley, gave an interview that ended his political career but had a lasting and growing influence, so much so that *The Spectator* republished the full text twenty-one years later (Jones 2011). In July 1990, German reunification was in process and the president of the Bundesbank, Klaus-Otto Pohl, was due to visit the UK to discuss the benefits of a joint European monetary policy and a fully fledged currency to replace the electronic European Currency Unit (ECU). Ridley had little doubt about what monetary union would mean: 'This is all a German racket designed to take over the whole of Europe. It has to be thwarted. This rushed take-over by the Germans on the worst possible basis, with the French behaving like poodles to the Germans, is absolutely intolerable'. His thesis was that Germany was already dominating the EEC, monetary union would definitively establish German hegemony, and that the UK should never cede sovereignty to unelected commissioners in thrall to the German giant (perfectly represented by the physically intimidating Chancellor Helmut Kohl): 'You might just as well give it to Adolf Hitler, frankly'. The interviewer, Dominic Lawson, played the Devil's advocate insisting upon Germany's good intentions, but he could not resist using the metaphor of the beach towel with reference to the way German business leaders were winning contracts in Eastern Europe.

Ridley's words caused uproar and Mrs. Thatcher immediately demanded his resignation. The allusions to Hitler and the Second World

War were seen as particularly distasteful and also somewhat hysterical. The headline to Lawson's report of the interview was 'Saying the unsayable about the Germans', but in the years that followed Ridley's views became progressively more sayable. When the text was republished in 2011, the headline was: 'From the archives: Ridley was right'. Three years later Dominic Lawson (2014) recalled the interview and wondered, 'But was he right all along?' He thought that Ridley must have felt vindicated when German inflexibility was instrumental in Britain's humiliating exit from the European Exchange Rate Mechanism (ERM) on Black Wednesday (16 September 1992). He also noted that the sovereign debt crisis in Greece sparked off by the general financial crisis of 2007–2008 saw the German government depicted as Nazis in the Greek media, while Chancellor Merkel's insistence upon German *Uberwachung* (oversight) of the public sector in Greece led to comparisons with the Nazi occupation of the country during the war. What was once the unsayable about the Germans could now be trumpeted, as indeed it was once the Brexit referendum campaigns got going.

The other historical relationship that has become part of Britain's national sense of itself is the one with France, and it is no coincidence that only the 'Frogs' are insulted as regularly as the 'Krauts' in the tabloids. A few months after the Ridley interview the Brexit cause was transferred from a Tory Old Etonian to Kelvin MacKenzie's *Currant Bun*. The target was the President of the European Commission, Jacques Delors, whose sin of being Margaret Thatcher's ideological enemy was compounded by the fact that he was also French. As we noted with 'Gotcha!', when a front-page splash earns particular notoriety, the *Sun* tends to recycle it, and the deeply offensive attack on Delors and his homeland was celebrated on the 25th anniversary of its original publication on 1 November 1990 (Parsons 2016).

## Up Yours Delors

> At midday tomorrow Sun readers are urged to tell the French fool where to stuff his ECU.
> The Sun today calls on its patriotic family of readers to tell the feelthy French to FROG OFF!

In the headline, subhead and first sentence cited above, an astonishing concentration of offensiveness is achieved in just thirty-eight words. The tendency of French people to lengthen English vowels is ridiculed in 'feelthy French', while it is perfectly legitimate to produce a headline in which the rhyme depends on mispronunciation of Delors's name. The words *frog* and *froggie* are traditional insults for French people but here the noun is converted to a verb to create an imperative normally expressed using a different four-letter word beginning with *f*. It is taken for granted that the 'patriotic family of readers' concurs with the insults directed at Delors and his compatriots.

It was to get worse over a quarter of a century as a series of treaties establishing greater European unity coincided with developments in British politics that saw hostility towards Europe grow ever stronger in the right-wing tabloids. The first was Margaret Thatcher's fall from power in November 1990, not as the result of an election defeat, but because senior colleagues decided that they had had enough of a prime minister who delighted in bashing the EEC with her handbag. Although the *Sun* had lost its warrior-queen, it nevertheless campaigned for her decidedly less charismatic successor, John Major, in the 1992 general election, and when the sitting prime minister gained an unexpected victory the UK's best-selling newspaper claimed credit for having turned things around for the Tories with a typically immodest headline—'It Was the Sun Wot Won It'—variations of which have been widely used after practically every subsequent election.

Major led a party that was divided over the question of further European integration with a considerable number of Thatcher loyalists implacably opposed to anything that smacked of federalism. On the 1st of November 1993, the Maastrict Treaty went into force, and on that day the European Economic Community became the European Community. Even to people who had read nothing about Maastricht, that name change was sufficient to understand that the European project was now about far more than free trade. The process that would eventually lead to the creation of the European Union with a single currency had begun, and in both the country and the Parliamentary Conservative Party there were profound misgivings to which the *Mail, Express* and *Sun* gave shrill voice. Although Major had negotiated opt-out clauses for the UK (notably on the single currency), he had difficulty getting the Maastricht Treaty ratified by Parliament, partly because he had a small majority but mostly because of internal dissent. Indeed, the Treaty was initially rejected because of the votes of Conservative MPs who became known as the Maastricht Rebels, and ratification was only achieved when Major made the second attempt a vote of confidence. Later the prime minister referred to the Maastricht Rebels as 'bastards' at the end of a television interview when he thought the microphones were switched off. That comment was never aired, but a tape was leaked to the *Daily Mirror*, who ensured that the deep split in the governing party was known to all.

Tony Blair won the general election of 1997 and his rebranded New Labour did not make the right-wing tabloids fear that a Marxist one-party state was just around the corner (indeed, the *Sun* went on to switch its allegiances to the new government). Although the Labour Party had its Eurosceptic faction, the great majority of its MPs were pro-EC, so at government level tensions over Europe were eased. The tabloids, however, did not tone down their hostility towards greater integration and, most of all, monetary union. Then in 1999 the European Commission handed the Eurosceptics a huge propaganda victory. Acting on the denunciation of a whistle-blower, the European Parliament investigated the affairs of the Commission and uncovered incidences of mismanagement, fraud and favouritism, which led to the resignation of the President, Jacques Santer, and all the commissioners, including those who were not personally guilty of any wrong-doing. It was a gift for the tabloids: Santer was a francophone Luxembourger and the most ridiculous case of favouritism concerned the former prime minister of France, Edith Cresson, who was found to have awarded contracts to her dentist for work for which he was manifestly unqualified. In contrast, the two British commissioners, Neil Kinnock and Leon Brittan, had conducted themselves correctly.

The discovery of corruption was seized upon by the tabloids, but Brussels' long-term political aims remained the chief preoccupation. Press coverage of Europe during the 1990s was summed up by Anderson and Weymouth (1999: 23) as follows:

> [...] a significant proportion of British press reporting concerning the EU has portrayed the latter as primarily a foreign-dominated forum for fish wars and sausage spats, and as a launching platform for those who wish to 'drag sovereignty away from the mother of parliaments' and to subject Britain to a 'mercilessly centralising' bombardment of rule by Euro-money and Euro-directive [...]

As the twenty-first century began, the process of European integration took another step forward with the Treaty of Nice of 2001, although a rare setback was the rejection of a European Constitution in referenda in France and the Netherlands. The Treaty of Lisbon was signed in 2007, and when it became effective on the 1st of December 2009 the European Union as we now know it came into being. Eurosceptics in the UK were particularly concerned about two aspects of the Lisbon Treaty: it introduced qualified majority voting for many policy areas, which meant that Britain could no longer simply veto anything it didn't like; the EU's Charter of Fundamental Rights became legally binding, which some saw as an unacceptable loss of sovereignty.

Two more Presidents of the European Commission, Romano Prodi (1999–2004) and Manuel Barroso (2004–2014), were criticised by the *Sun-Mail-Express* triumvirate but they were never subject to the viciousness that had been directed at Jacques Delors, and attacks on their views and policies were never extended to their nations and populations. Delors was a 'Frog' but the *Sun* did not call Prodi a 'Wop' or Barroso a 'Pork'n'cheeser'. After David Cameron announced that he planned to hold a referendum on continued EU membership, the *Daily Mail* quoted Barroso's reaction to the notion of the UK going it alone: 'Today even the largest, proudest European nation cannot hope to shape globalisation – or even retain marginal influence – by itself. [...] What would be the influence of the prime minister of Britain if he was not part of the EU? It would be zero' (Chapman 2014). It is not difficult to imagine how the *Daily Mail* would have reacted if a French President of the European Commission had had the temerity to assert that Britain on its own would count for nothing in the world, but Barroso's observations, though not uncontested, did not spark off a vitriolic, xenophobic counter-attack on the ludicrous Lusitanian and his port-swigging country-men and -women. The then chairman of the Conservative Party, Grant Shapps, was quoted disagreeing with Barroso, but the article contained no personal attacks or offensive national stereotyping.

Being French was the cardinal sin, although Frog-speaking Belgians and Luxembourgers were not to be trusted either. More than three months before the *Mail*'s low-key treatment of the outgoing President of the European Commission, the same paper adopted an altogether more hostile approach towards his designated successor, Jean-Claude Juncker (Jones 2014). He is described as a 'louche little man' who 'slurps cognac with his breakfast' and during his eighteen years as prime minister of Luxembourg had wasted vast sums of public money on grandiose schemes that turned out to be white elephants. Juncker always had funds available for his madcap projects owing to his penchant for 'giving succour to secretive finance houses, tax-dodging tycoons and corrupt Third World dictators'. We are informed that early on in his political career Juncker had befriended Jacques Santer, the President of the European Commission who had had to resign following the worst scandal in the Commission's history, a link that some readers might take as evidence that senior politicians from Luxembourg are not known for their rectitude. Finally, we learn that Juncker's father-in-law had been one of Hitler's propaganda commissars and had had a role in enforcing the Nuremburg Laws. While it is acknowledged that Juncker should not be held to account for someone else's sins, there is implicit criticism in the fact that he had never spoken of this matter and that the news was only broken thanks to the German media.

A Portuguese who said that Britain outside the EU would be totally irrelevant was not insulted but a Luxembourger who had yet to take office took a pounding, including an attack that anyone who has an embarrassing in-law would consider decidedly below the belt. It would appear that to the Brexit-supporting tabloids, Belgium and Luxembourg are considered pillars of the EU Establishment given that they were founding members of the EEC and several institutions of the European Union are based in their respective capital cities. Worse still, for linguistic reasons both countries can be depicted as nearly France. More recent and more peripheral members of the EU are not seen as fully signed-up participants in the dastardly European plot to snatch more and more power from democratically elected sovereign states; indeed, awkward new arrivals, such as Poland and Hungary, are treated almost as allies (that Hungary was the only member-state to join David Cameron in opposing Juncker's appointment was noted with approval).

Once the date for the Brexit referendum was fixed, the Leave and Remain campaigns swung into action. Four of the national tabloids—the *Sun*, the *Daily Mail*, the *Daily Star* and the *Daily Express* (combined monthly browsers in 2016: 300 million)—were unequivocally for getting out of the EU. The *Daily Mirror* and the London paper the *Evening Standard* (combined monthly browsers: 87 million) supported Remain, while the position of the freely distributed *Metro* was not clear (Melson 2016). I have dealt with the nature of the pre-referendum campaigns elsewhere (Buckledee 2018) and the way in which the Brexiteers employed passionate and colourful language with powerful metaphors while the Remainers plugged away at a Project Fear agenda consisting of dire predictions of economic disaster. The two campaigns grew increasingly unpleasant as the voting day (23 June 2016) approached, and after that date the reciprocal hostility did not diminish in the slightest. On the contrary, the country was more divided than ever as the Remainers accused the Brexiteers of having misled the public into believing that leaving the EU would be straightforward, and the Leavers accused the 'Remoaners' or 'Remaniacs' of not respecting the result of the biggest democratic vote in British history. Each side accused the other of having lost their hold on reality, even of mental incapacity, with *delusional* a recurrent lexical choice. Another much-used lexeme was *elite*, which sometimes referred to ill-defined manipulators in the worlds of finance, politics and the media who were plotting to prevent Britain from ever leaving the EU, and sometimes identified high profile Old Etonians in the Brexit camp.

Tony Parsons (2019) for the *Sun* does not use the word *delusional* but describes how the elite (defined as Parliament, the Civil Service and the BBC) 'have fought with the passion of true, eye-swivelling believers to keep us shackled to Brussels'. His thesis is that in a country that has traditionally had no truck with 'loony fringe extremism', the risk is that 'the democracy deniers of the British establishment are creating the perfect conditions for the rise of the nutters'.

Two short pieces published on the same day in the pro-EU *Daily Mirror* attacked the other elite, defined as wealthy male Conservative MPs who had attended Britain's most expensive independent school, Eton College (where a boy's education will cost his parents £240,000), followed by either Oxford or Cambridge. It was March 2019 and Theresa May's proposed Brexit deal had just been rejected by the House of Commons for the third time, leaving the (still, just about) governing party still committed to Britain's withdrawal from the EU but without a clue as to how to realise that objective. On the 29th of that month, both Reade (2019) and Maguire (2019) placed the blame for what was almost universally seen as an utter shambles on the heads of a group of Old Etonians, most notably the man whose reckless gamble of holding a referendum had created the mess, David Cameron, and two other products of Eton and Oxford, Boris Johnson and Jacob Rees Mogg. Maguire describes a 'shameless Brexit elite' consisting of 'slippery chancers', including 'serial liar Boris Johnson' and a Jacob Rees Mogg who is 'all three-piece suit and no spine'. He concludes that 'Britain's poisoned and ripped apart for the egos of conceited Tories thinking they were born to rule'. Reade writes of an 'Eton mafia', men who belong to 'the most elite of elites' and have such a strong sense of entitlement that they 'can't even see how they abuse their privilege'. He also provides statistics on how the products of Britain's top independent schools (6.7% of the total school population) occupy an extraordinarily high percentage of positions among military officers, judges, surgeons, MPs and even actors. In pre-Internet days, regular readers of the *Daily Mirror* would have approved of Reade and Maguire's focus on the perniciousness of social class and privilege; in 2019 nearly half of the readers' who posted online feedback disagreed with the two articles, and a few insulted the respective authors in vulgar terms.

For the pro-Brexit tabloids, unrepentant Remainers were out-of-touch with the British people and perhaps with reality. The same Dominic Lawson who in 1990 had been taken aback by Nicholas Ridley's conviction that the EEC was a German racket to take over the continent, then in 2014 wondered whether Ridley was right all along, by 2018 had completed his journey and could announce in the *Daily Mail* that 'Brexit's enemies are such a deluded, comical rabble' (Lawson 2018). He then proceeds to name five prominent campaigners seeking to prevent Britain's withdrawal from the EU—three former members of the Commons and two members of the Lords—and notes that the attempt to overturn the result of a referendum in which 33,577,342 people voted was 'led entirely by men who either have tired of the need to win support at the ballot box, or never bothered in the first place' (Lawson 2018).

Where Lawson directs his irony at the questionable democratic credentials of those hoping to block Brexit, Nick Ferrari in the *Daily Express* (2019) ridicules Brexit opponents' insistence on referring to a possible second vote on the issue as a 'People's Referendum'—'remember, it was obviously only robots, cocker spaniels and Martians who voted last time'—and accuses the 'duplicitous, out-of-touch elitists' of showing contempt for the 17,410,742 citizens who voted to leave the EU: 'They see any Leave voter as a knuckle-dragging Neanderthal who is at best stupid, at worst a rabid racist'.

In early July 2019, three EU presidents elect due to take office towards the end of the year were announced: Ursula von der Leyen, a German, would replace Jean-Claude Juncker and become the first female President of the European Commission; another woman, Christine Lagarde from France, would take over from the Italian Mario Draghi as President of the European Central Bank; Donald Tusk's successor as President of the European Council would be a Belgian, Charles Michel. The *Express* (Weston 2019) quoted Nigel Farage describing the passing of the reins as 'a Franco-German stitch-up' in which '[T]he French and Germans have got the big jobs, and another Belgian has got a huge job unbelievably' while the countries of southern and eastern Europe had been treated like second-class member states. On the same day, Stephen Glover (2019) for the *Mail* also used the expression 'Franco-German stitch-up' (as did the pro-EU *Guardian*) and was scathing about the far-from-transparent procedure for deciding upon the new appointments: 'Cutting grubby deals in private, as European leaders have been doing, is not merely undemocratic. It leads to outcomes that are likely to be injurious to the citizens of the EU'.

The *Sun* finally found a European hate-figure to bear comparison with Jacques Delors when Guy Verhofstadt became the European Parliament's Brexit Coordinator. As a Belgian, and therefore nearly French, who has a federalist vision of Europe that he can express in clear English, he ticks all the boxes to qualify for an unsigned editorial (*Sun* 2019) that opines that: 'No more repugnant figure struts the corridors of Brussels than the curtain-haired slimeball Guy Verhofstadt. Try as they might, even the drunk Juncker or the peacock Barnier cannot match the Belgian's detestable blabbermouthed arrogance'. So in just thirty-four words the *Sun* managed to insult a Belgian, a Luxembourger and a Frenchman. A dig at the Germans comes a little later with a reference to the Nazi occupation of much of the continent, with the insinuation that Europeans like Verhofstadt would do well to remember their historic debt to Britain. This editorial generated 73 readers' comments, some of which insulted Verhofstadt and other prominent EU figures in even more offensive terms, but a fair percentage criticised the boorish nature of the piece.

That the Germans and French (plus nearly French) have always been the prime targets of the tabloids' negative national stereotyping is undeniable, and from the Delors-Thatcher clash to the fallout from the Brexit referendum, the EEC-EC-EU process has provided the perfect vehicle for both reasoned arguments and hysterical allegations about a Franco-German alliance, or stitch-up, to realise a vision of Europe that some countries see as a potential threat to their sovereignty and independence. Hostility to the EU is not, of course, the same thing as hostility to European people, and the *Sun*'s deplorable language in attacking Verhofstadt, Juncker and Barnier does not represent the views of the majority of Britons. There is some consolation in reading feedback from a reader who writes: 'As so often in the past you get it completely wrong. The EU has by and large been rather gracious in dealing with this UK-homemade utter disaster. It will go into history as Britain's Waterloo, but this time Britain being on the receiving end'.

# References

Anderson, Peter J., and Tony Weymouth. 1999. *Insulting the Public? The British Press and the European Union.* London: Routledge.

Baker, Neal. 2018. Pitched Battle: Furious locals slam German beach-towel tactics of tourists who marked off massive stretch of Cornish beach with tents. *Sun Online*, August 3. https://www.thesun.co.uk/news/6933096/porthmeor-beach-st-ives-towel-tents-hogging-space/. Accessed 20 September 2019.

Buckledee, Steve. 2018. *The Language of Brexit*. London and New York: Bloomsbury Academic.

Chapman, James. 2014. Britain would be irrelevant without us, claims EU chief… and he says plan to cap migration is illegal, too. *MailOnline*, October 20. https://www.dailymail.co.uk/news/article-2799517/britain-irrelevant-without-claims-eu-chief-says-plan-cap-migration-illegal-too.html. Accessed 4 October 2019.

Daily Mirror Editorial. 1996. Mirror declares football war on Germany. *Daily Mirror*, June 24.

Ferrari, Nick. 2019. MPs sink to a new low, at our expense. *Express Online*, March 3. https://www.express.co.uk/comment/columnists/nick-ferrari/1094970/brexit-news-mps-expenses-cheats-parliament-theresa-may-jeremy-corbyn. Accessed 7 October 2019.

Garland, Jon, and Michael Rowe. 2001. *Racism and Anti-Racism in Football*. Basingstoke: Palgrave Macmillan.

Glover, Stephen. 2019. Appointing their leaders with a grubby backdoor stitch-up like this, thank God we're leaving the EU. *MailOnline*, July 3. https://www.dailymail.co.uk/debate/article-7211109/STEPHEN-GLOVER-Thank-God-leaving-EU.html. Accessed 7 October 2019.

Greenland, Katy. 2000. 'Can't live with them, can't live without them': Stereotypes in international relations. In *Stereotypes in Contemporary Anglo-German Relations*, ed. Rainer Emig, 15–30. Basingstoke: Macmillan Press Ltd.

Hooper, John. 2001. Blind prejudice. *Guardian Online*, September 2. https://www.theguardian.com/media/2001/sep/02/raceintheuk.comment. Accessed 21 September 2019.

Husemann, Harrald. 2000. We will fight them on the beaches. In *Stereotypes in Contemporary Anglo-German Relations*, ed. Rainer Emig, 58–78. Basingstoke: Macmillan Press Ltd.

Jones, David. 2014. Cognac for breakfast? Dave's EU nemesis has far worse skeletons in his closet, including his nasty habit of blowing taxpayers' millions on white elephants. *MailOnline*, July 5. https://www.dailymail.co.uk/news/article-2681298/Cognac-breakfast-Daves-EU-nemesis-FAR-worse-skeletons-closet-including-Nazi-father-law-rumours-love-child.html. Accessed 4 October 2019.

Jones, Jonathan. 2011. From the archives: Ridley was right. *Spectator Online*, September 22. https://blogs.spectator.co.uk/2011/09/from-the-archives-ridley-was-right/. Accessed 22 September 2019.

Lawson, Dominic. 2014. Is the EU just a German racket to take over Europe? Nearly 25 years ago, a Tory minister told dominic Lawson it was—And lost his job in the firestorm that followed: But was he right all along? *MailOnline*, July 4. https://www.dailymail.co.uk/news/article-2680183/Is-EU-just-German-racket-Europe-Nearly-25-years-ago-Tory-minister-told-DOMINIC-LAWSON-lost-job-firestorm-followed-right-along.html. Accessed 22 September 2019.

Lawson, Dominic. 2018. How blessed we are that Brexit's enemies are such a deluded, comical rabble. *MailOnline*, March 15. https://www.dailymail.co.uk/debate/article-5225401/Brexits-enemies-deluded-comical-rabble.html. Accessed 7 October 2019.

Maguire, Kevin. 2019. Shameless Tory elite have poisoned and ripped apart UK over Brexit. *Mirror Online*, March 23. https://www.mirror.co.uk/news/politics/kevin-maguire-shameless-tory-elite-14204966#comments-section. Accessed 7 October 2019.

Melson, Craig. 2016. Brexit: Where do the papers stand? *Political Intelligence*, May 27. https://www.political-intelligence.com/brexit-where-do-the-papers-stand/. Accessed 5 October 2019.

Moyle, Lachlan R. 2004. An imagological survey of Britain and the British and Germany and the Germans in German and British cartoons and caricatures, 1945–2000. Doctoral thesis posted online. https://repositorium.ub.uni-osnabrueck.de/bitstream/urn:nbn:de:gbv:700-2005020415/2/E-Diss389_thesis.pdf. Accessed 19 September 2019.

Parsons, Tony. 2016. Europe's dream? It crumbled and died… *Sun Online*, April 6. https://www.thesun.co.uk/archives/politics/116590/europes-dream-it-crumbled-and-died/. Accessed 23 September 2019.

Parsons, Tony. 2019. If the elite stop us from leaving the EU, those on the fringes of society will feel enabled. *Sun*, January 13. https://www.thesun.co.uk/news/opinion/8181469/elite-stopping-britain-leaving-the-eu/. Accessed 5 October 2019.

Reade, Brian. 2019. Elite guard of Eton rifles are shooting Britain in the foot over Brexit. *Mirror Online*, March 23. https://www.mirror.co.uk/news/uk-news/brian-reade-elite-guard-eton-14204599#comments-section. Accessed 7 October 2019.

Savage, Tom. 2010. Job done Now for the Hun. *Daily Star*, June 24. https://www.dailystar.co.uk/news/latest-news/job-done-now-hun-18235087. Accessed 21 September 2019.

Smith, Angela, and Michael Higgins. 2013. *The Language of Journalism*. London and New York: Bloomsbury Academic.

Sun editorial. 2019. The Sun says curtain-haired slimeball Guy Verhofstadt proves he's the most repugnant figure in Brussels. *Sun Online*, May 8. https://www.thesun.co.uk/news/9024871/guy-verhofstadt-theresa-may-eu-documentary/. Accessed 7 October 2019.

Weston, Katie. 2019. Nigel Farage lashes out at 'Franco-German stitch-up' in fiery rant—'Never heard of him'. *Express Online*, July 3. https://www.express.co.uk/news/world/1148781/eu-news-latest-nigel-farage-show-today-live-david-maria-sassoli-parliament-president-uk. Accessed 7 October 2019.

# 7

# 'Drug Trial Moment of Horror' to 'European Health Tourist Scam': Investigative Journalism and Other Merits of the Tabloids

The British tabloids are xenophobic, sometimes downright racist. They commoditise the female body and pour scorn upon feminists. They callously exploit grief and suffering, pry into sides of people's lives that ought to remain private, and destroy reputations with allegations that are little more than malicious gossip. Not content with tabloiding the truth, they sometimes resort to unequivocal lying. They are unprincipled, ruthless and vulgar. Many would agree with the contributor to the *Antidotes for Chimps* website (Anonymous 2018) who wrote: 'With those kinds of ethics, it's clear that the only good use for a tabloid is keeping a copy in the bathroom, for wiping your arse with when the toilet paper has run dry'.

This chapter will look at the more meritorious aspects of the popular press over the last sixty years, for they exist even though some people would sooner consent to having molten lead poured into their ears than admit that the tabloids might have done some good on occasion. We might begin with the fact that unlike the anonymous author of the opinion cited above, tabloid journalists and/or editors take responsibility for what they write. More to the point, the popular newspapers have on many occasions exposed cases of corruption, dishonesty and plain incompetence and have provided a platform for investigative journalists of the calibre of John Pilger (*Daily Mirror*) and David Rose (*Mail on Sunday*). Furthermore, it can be argued that over the years the tabloids have done rather more than the quality papers have to launch campaigns on behalf of the weaker members of society or to raise funds to help individuals in desperate circumstances.

The first quotation in the chapter title is a front-page headline in the *Daily Mirror* on 7 November 1962. The *Mirror* had taken the unusual step of sending a correspondent to Belgium to follow the trial of a woman who admitted to having killed her one-week-old child but based her defence on the fact that she had taken the drug thalidomide during pregnancy, which resulted in her baby being born with grotesque deformities. The headline describes the shocked silence in the court when a photograph of the unfortunate child was exhibited. Five days later, after Suzy Vandeput and her co-defendants—her husband, her mother, her sister and a doctor—had been acquitted of murdering the baby girl, the *Mirror* dedicated its centre pages to an interview with Mrs. Vandeput in which she explained why she had felt that she could not allow her child to live: 'My baby would never forgive me when she was older for having let her grow up – let's face it – a freak' (Stephens 1962). The *Daily Mirror* avoided passing judgement on what Vandeput had done, although the paper's popular agony aunt, Marjorie Proops (1962), drew on her considerable experience of listening to people's misfortunes to point out that there are also mothers who let their disabled children grow up and do not regret the decision.

Thalidomide was created by the Grünenthal Group in Germany in 1953 and was prescribed as a treatment for pregnant women's morning sickness, but it was withdrawn in 1961 after an article in the *Lancet* medical journal linked it with serious birth defects. Over half a century victims' families battled to obtain appropriate compensation, and the tabloids played their part in keeping the issue alive until the British government finally offered belated apologies and a £20million support package in 2010 (two more years were to pass before the Grünenthal Group also apologised). As recently as 2018, the *Daily Mirror* returned to the subject when the German government reneged on a promise that 'the health needs of British thalidomide survivors would be covered at the same level as German nationals' (Parry 2018).

The second quotation in the chapter title is part of a headline in the *Sun* on 1 September 2018 about fake European Health Insurance Cards (EHIC) that people in EU member states were using to get health treatment in their own countries charged to the NHS. The first sentence of the article reminds readers that a *Sun* exposé eight months earlier had alerted the Government to this scam, but notes that nothing had yet been done to tighten up application procedures for EHIC cards (Dathan 2018). There is a photograph of a fake card bearing the name of someone called Theresa May. It is estimated that since 2006 the NHS had paid £200 million to European hospitals for the treatment of patients in possession of fake EHIC cards, a figure that the *Sun* helpfully informs us is the equivalent of 8600 extra nurses. Prime culprits are identified, but with a passive reporting clause that leaves the journalist with the option of letting unnamed sources carry the can if the accusation proves to be untrue: 'Many Polish families are said to get the cards for relatives, who use them to reduce health costs at home'.

Health scandals sell newspapers, especially when there is the suspicion that health professionals and/or politicians have attempted to withhold information from the public. A case in point would be the so-called mad cow disease, the popular name for bovine spongiform encephalopathy (BSE), a neurodegenerative disease of cattle, and variant Creutzfeldt-Jakob disease (vCJD), a fatal degenerative brain disorder of humans that appears to be linked to the consumption of beef from cows infected with BSE. In the 1980s, cattle on a number of farms in the south-west of England developed a strange neurological disease and at first the Ministry of Agriculture, Forestry and Fisheries (MAFF) did nothing. In 1987, the disease was identified as BSE, by which time it was spreading to other parts of the country. The following year the slaughter of infected cattle began but the official line was that British beef was perfectly safe to eat because the disease could not be transmitted to humans (although in 1989 specified offals, such as brains, were banned). May 1990 saw the Minister of Agriculture, John Gummer, invite TV cameras to an outdoor event in his constituency so that he and his four-year-old daughter, Cordelia, could be filmed munching away on British beef burgers. Much to the amusement of the assembled media folk, Cordelia declined the proffered burger, but the publicity stunt went ahead as her father chomped on British minced beef with some relish. The symptoms of classic CJD are similar to those of dementia and victims of this rare disease usually fall ill in their sixties, but the illness is practically unknown among young people. Even as John Gummer was reassuring the public, however, the scientific community was investigating the risk that BSE could jump species as vCJD. The hypothesis acquired greater credibility as big cats in zoos died of a neurological disease that looked very much like BSE, then in 1994 a teenage girl died of CJD. The following year a nineteen-year-old man was diagnosed as having a degenerative brain disorder, and his death was later attributed to vCJD, the variant form. But in 1995 the Government was not yet ready to admit that there was a link between BSE and CJD.

Enter the *Daily Express*. In 1990, this Conservative-supporting paper accepted the Government's assessment of the absolute safety of British beef. In the same month as John Gummer's performance with the reluctant Cordelia, a front-page headline read 'Mad Cow Madness' and an article by the paper's consumer editor, Paul Crosbie (1990), quoted the view of the Food Minister, David Maclean, that those local education authorities that had removed beef from school meals had overreacted 'without a shred of scientific advice'. Five years later, another article by Crosbie (1995) reported that one in four Britons had decided to exclude beef from their diet and cited two television programmes that had investigated the issue: *Watchdog*, the BBC's consumer programme, and Granada's *World in Action*, the second of which had uncovered evidence that beef from cattle infected with BSE was still reaching butcher's shops despite safeguards introduced to prevent this from happening. The following month the *Express* returned to the subject of school meals and reported that many more local authorities had taken beef off the menu following protests by parents who 'fear there may be a direct link between contaminated beef and Creutzfeldt-Jakob Disease, the human version of BSE' (Smith et al. 1995). An unsigned editorial the next day referred to 'an impressive application of parent power' (Daily Express Opinion 1995).

By late 1995, a significant percentage of the population had become sceptical of official reassurances about British beef as it was beginning to look as if the Government had been rather complacent, and instead of adopting a precautionary approach had chosen to prioritise the economic interests of British farmers. The *Daily Express* will always back a Conservative government but over the mad cow story was not prepared to set itself against millions of people who suspected (rightly as it later transpired) that their health had not been protected as it should have been. When a scientific study was published suggesting that BSE could not be transmitted to people as CJD, the story was not splashed on the front page as proof that John Major's Government had got it right and the left-wing scaremongers had been discredited. Instead, the paper's medical correspondent, Paul Fuller (1995), reported on the findings in measured tones: 'Researchers who carried out tests on mice believe they have proved that the chances of BSE jumping the species barrier from cattle to humans to cause Creutzfeldt-Jakob Disease are extremely remote'. A keyword is 'believe'; the researchers express what they see as a likelihood but do not claim to have definitively demonstrated that there is no link between BSE and CJD. Similarly, the scientifically trained Fuller exercises caution in evaluating the development and even notes that a former health adviser to the Government is among the millions who have given up beef. He was right to be circumspect: just two years later the causal link between BSE and vCJD was no longer in doubt. By 2014, there had been 177 deaths in Britain and 52 in the rest of the world. Among the UK victims was the 23-year-old daughter of one of John Gummer's friends. A handful of the cases were attributable to blood transfusions or unsterilised surgical instruments but the overwhelming majority of deaths were the result of eating British beef. In my own small way, I too have been slightly affected: in my country of residence my attempts to donate blood have been politely declined due to the fact that I made visits to the UK in the late 1980s and early '90s.

No one in the MAFF had been guilty of criminal negligence but there had been serious misjudgements that meant that when action was finally taken it proved to be too little too late. When, a few years later, concerns were raised that the measles, mumps and rubella (MMR) vaccine could trigger autism in children, recent memories of the mad cow debacle had left the public predisposed to distrust official reassurances. The scare was sparked off by a 1998 article in the *Lancet* by Dr. Andrew

Wakefield, but since other researchers were unable to reproduce his findings health authorities continued to advise parents to make sure their children had the MMR jab. On this occasion, some of the tabloids' coverage did more harm than good. When Marsh and Orr (2002) for the *Daily Mail* reported on a cluster of cases of measles in part of London, they correctly noted that in the area concerned only 65% of children had had the MMR vaccine, which is under the official threshold below which the risk of an epidemic becomes serious. However, they dedicated approximately a third of their article to the anecdotal evidence of parents who were so convinced of the MMR-autism link that they had elected not to have their children vaccinated, but did not give a doctor an opportunity to explain the properly documented risks of permitting the return of three diseases that had been practically eradicated.

The fake news that the MMR jab causes autism has been remarkably resilient despite the fact that Andrew Wakefield is now an ex-doctor, struck off the UK medical register in 2010 after having been exposed as a fraud who falsified his research findings. The persistence of this scare story is primarily down to misinformation online rather than the British tabloids, as is evidenced by the spread of anti-vax mumbo-jumbo in countries other than the UK.

The issues of poverty and the welfare state see the ideological positions of the various tabloids become evident. In 2014, the charity Shelter, which campaigns for the homeless, marked its 50th anniversary with an exhibition of photographs taken by Nick Hedges between 1968 and 1972. They show the appalling living conditions endured by the poor in privately rented slums in a number of English cities. Two years later, the *Mirror Online* posted nine of those photos of squalid, cramped and damp rooms with peeling wallpaper and broken floor tiles, and the inhabitants struggling to maintain dignity despite the conditions (Panther and Hedges 2016). A tenth photograph, however, was recent; it showed Sandrine in a ridiculously cluttered room that appeared to serve as kitchen, bedroom and dining room. We are told that she shared a bathroom with neighbours in the block of flats in Enfield, North London, and in the absence of a bed, slept across two plastic garden chairs. Until she could no longer afford the rent even for accommodation of this nature and was evicted, and to be safe and warm after dark was reduced to sleeping on night buses. In the article, Nick Hedges recalls his emotions when taking the original photographs while Lewis Panther focuses on the new housing crisis as a chronic shortage of affordable public housing has led to soaring rents in the private sector for accommodation that is sometimes unfit for human habitation. Several of the readers who posted comments pointed the finger at Mrs. Thatcher, whose policy of letting local authorities sell council houses to sitting tenants at discounted prices was a vote-winner, but was also the start of the process that led to the crisis of today. Some also noted that building council houses was not a policy of Tony Blair's New Labour government.

When the *Sun*, the *Express*, the *Star* or the *Mail* write about the poor the aim is often to show that they are not really poor at all, but are just a bunch of idle scroungers living off benefits paid for by hard-working readers of the *Sun*, the *Express*, the *Star* or the *Mail*. To take just one example, an article posted on the *Daily Star Online* in 2016 and updated three years later (Jolly 2019) bears the headline 'REVEALED: How UK's most notorious benefits scroungers spend OUR cash' and gives instances of claimants who spend their benefits on such things as online gambling, luxury goods and cosmetic breast surgery. It rather stretches credibility when the individuals concerned speak frankly to the *Daily Star*, supply their full names and even consent to having their photographs published, and apparently do not object to being described as an 'unemployed teen layabout', an 'octomum' (i.e. the mother of a 'brood' of eight children), a 'serial convict' and a 'mum-of-12' who sees a thirteenth child as a way to get the increased benefits she requires to pay for 'a boob job'. When people freely admit to sponging off the state and seem not to care if inspectors from the Department of Work & Pensions happen to read Bradley Jolly's article, it is legitimate to suspect that we are dealing with an extreme case of tabloiding the truth.

Precisely one month after the updating of the article described above, a report co-written by the same Bradley Jolly was published on the *Mirror Online* (Mohammed and Jolly 2019). It gives an entirely different picture of the unemployed as it describes the daily routine of a young man who found himself homeless and, having no family to fall back on, ended up living under a bridge. He spends his days reading books, avoiding drug pushers and advertising his employability as a graphic designer with no problems with drugs or alcohol. The *Star* and the *Mirror* do not see the unemployed in quite the same way, and Jolly clearly knows how to keep different editors happy.

The right-wing tabloids have little sympathy with the unemployed, who are habitually presented as not so much out of work as workshy. With pensioners, it is an entirely different matter, perhaps because the elderly represent a sizeable chunk of readers of paper editions. Any government that does not ensure that pensions at least keep pace with inflation can expect to be taken to task. Even the BBC's hardly draconian decision to scrap free TV licences for the over-75s sparked outrage, with *MailOnline* (Tingle 2019) employing emotive language in reporting on individual pensioners who were variously 'devastated', 'fighting back tears' and likely to 'vegetate' without the non-means tested perk of free television (the poorest OAPs receiving Pension Credit would continue to be exempt from the licence fee).

The Welfare Reform Act of 2012 introduced an 'under-occupancy penalty' for public housing tenants considered to have more living space than they really needed. In practice, 'under-occupancy' meant having a bedroom that was not regularly used, and it was hardly surprising that this measure quickly came to be known as the bedroom tax. Tenants poor enough to receive housing benefit had that benefit cut if they had a spare bedroom. The measure hit certain people unfairly: couples whose son or daughter at university or in the armed services came home to mum and dad during the holidays or when on leave; separated parents whose children came to stay with them at the weekend; disabled people whose spare bedroom had become a storeroom for the special equipment they needed. Since successive Conservative governments had deliberately run down the stock of public housing, and the Welfare Reform Act was introduced by David Cameron's first government, unsurprisingly the right-wing tabloids had little to say about the bedroom tax. Not so the *Mirror* and its sister paper the *Sunday People*.

In the print edition of the *People* and on the *Mirror*'s website, Mudie and Nelson (2013) described the last hours of Stephanie Bottrill, who committed suicide because she could no longer afford to live after her two children moved out. The reduction of £80 per month in her housing benefit left her unable to both pay the £320-a-month rent and feed herself. In a farewell note to her son, she wrote: 'Don't blame yourself for me ending my life. The only people to blame are the Government'. Since her son and daughter were having difficulty paying for the funeral, the *Sunday People* made a contribution.

However reluctant the right-wing tabloids might be to criticise the Conservatives' economic policies, individuals belonging to or associated with the party are not protected if they abuse their power, get involved in shady business deals or become embroiled in a really juicy sex scandal. Throughout John Major's tenure as prime minister, and indeed during Margaret Thatcher's final years, so many senior figures in the party were caught either with their fingers in the till or with their pants down that the expression 'Tory sleaze' gained wide circulation. In 1994, Alan Duncan resigned as Parliamentary Private Secretary after it was revealed that he had acquired a council house at a discounted price by exploiting a scheme intended to help the underprivileged become homeowners; in the same year, the Minister for the Environment and Countryside, Tim Yeo, who had earlier expressed concern about the number of unmarried mothers in Britain, was found to have fathered a child during an extramarital affair; in 1995, the Chief Secretary to the Treasury, Jonathan Aitkin, sued the *Guardian* for alleging that he had had improper business relations with two British-Lebanese arms dealers, but the case collapsed and he was jailed for perjury. In these and many other cases, the Conservative-supporting tabloids gave no quarter merely because the misdeeds were committed by Tories. Prurience linked to hypocritical moralism is a vital element in the tabloids' appeal, and no editor will ever miss out on a good sex scandal merely because the naughty boy (or occasionally girl) happens to be on the right side of the political divide.

When a tabloid reports on an adult having consensual sex with another adult who just happens not to be his/her spouse or partner, the language used is, as noted earlier, the playful terminology of bonking and having a romp. When someone has multiple sexual partners, how that behaviour is described involves gender discrimination: a man is a *Lothario* or a *Casanova* and is admired for his numerous *conquests* while a woman who is similarly successful is unlikely to acquire a literary epithet and the language employed begins to assume a condemnatory quality. Take away the consensual aspect and we are in the realm of sexual assault or rape, and today the terminology usually reflects the gravity of the offence (although insinuations that the rape victim brought the attack upon herself have not yet been entirely eradicated). Then, when one of the participants is not an adult, no one disputes that the abuser has committed a heinous crime and merits such appellations as *monster* or *brute* that the press assigns to him.

The treatment of paedophilia has seen the tabloids at their investigative best and at their irresponsible worst. In July 2000, eight-year-old Sarah Payne was abducted and murdered, and when her killer, Roy Whiting, was apprehended it emerged that he had a previous conviction for abducting and indecently assaulting a girl of nine. Shortly afterwards the now-defunct *News of the World* started campaigning for a 'Sarah's Law' that would allow the public to know if someone convicted of a sex crime was living near them. The Sex Offenders Register was set up in September 1997 but when Sarah Payne was murdered access to it was limited (in any case, Whiting's earlier crime was committed before the Registry came into being). When the editor of the *News of the World*, Rebekah Wade, decided to publish the names of 49 convicted 'paedos', she effectively gave the green light to self-appointed guardians of our vulnerable children to carry out vigilante attacks on those named and shamed and/or their property. The move was condemned by the senior police officers who had to deal with the acts of violence committed by what were practically lynch mobs, but Wade was unrepentant even when it became clear that many of the would-be paedo-bashers were not concerned parents at all, but young, childless men who saw the hysteria following Sarah Payne's death as an excuse to engage in public disorder. Worse still, because of cases of mistaken identity, individuals who had no criminal record of any kind were also targeted. The most grotesque episode involved a person or persons unknown and semantically challenged who daubed 'paedo' on the front door of the house rented by Dr. Yvette Cloete, a paediatrician.

What links the towns of Telford, Rochdale, Huddersfield, Rotherham and Aylesbury, plus the cities of Oxford, Newcastle and Bradford is the fact that in the second decade of the twenty-first century it came to light that in all eight locations gangs of men had for far too many years got away with grooming under-age girls, some as young as eleven, for sexual abuse, including gang rape. The girls' compliance was obtained by giving them alcohol and drugs, and any signs of rebellion were quashed by threats of public exposure or physical violence. Nearly all of the men were of Asian ethnicity and most of their victims were white, a fact that was seized upon by certain tabloids. *MailOnline*'s report of the Newcastle case (Duell 2018) let images do the talking with photographs of the eighteen gang members found guilty of child sexual exploitation (CSE): seventeen brown-skinned men and one white woman. The *Sun* quoted a study conducted by the Quilliam Foundation—a think tank staffed mostly by Muslims that defines itself as 'the world's first counter-extremism organisation'—which found that 84% of the people convicted of child sex grooming offences since 2005 were of Asian origin (Lockett 2017). The *Daily Star* reported on the Telford gang, the worst case to come to light both because of the number of girls involved (up to 1000) and the length of time the rapists were allowed to operate before the police and town council intervened (Blair 2018). Drawing on earlier investigations conducted by the *Daily Mirror*, it was noted that '[…] authorities failed to keep details of child abusers from Asian backgrounds for fear of being accused of "racism"' (original inverted commas). The *Express* reported the testimony of a female detective constable who resigned from the Greater Manchester Police in 2012 because she believed not enough was being done to protect girls in Rochdale (Fielding 2017). She had been given the task of trying to win the confidence of victims who were reluctant to talk to the police, but when she reported to senior officers that the girls were beginning to identify Asian gang members they seemed to lose enthusiasm for pursuing the case.

The right-wing tabloids were relatively restrained regarding the ethnicity of most of the men involved in the grooming gangs (though readers who posted comments were rather less so), and their ire was directed at a society depicted as soft on crime with a justice system that seemed more concerned with the human rights of criminals than with those of their victims. Calls for the castration—and not the chemical kind—of Pakistanis were and are to be found on social media but professional journalists had more sense than to condemn an entire community. Indeed, after the trials and convictions of the Rotherham gang, *MailOnline* gave a Briton of Pakistani heritage, Mohammed Shafiq (2016), the opportunity to express his personal sense of shame (three of the men imprisoned were his relatives) and his anger at the lack of contrition of men who not only saw white women and girls as 'fair game' but also claim that 'it is they who are victims of a racist witch-hunt'. However, Shafiq sees 'a glimmer of hope' in that there is a generational divide among British Pakistanis and '[o]utdated attitudes are slowly being overturned among the young'.

No tabloid journalist has done more to expose grooming gangs and other cases of sexual assaults on minors than Geraldine McKelvie. She and a colleague reported the findings of an 18-month *Sunday Mirror* investigation (Sommerlad and McKelvie 2018) into the Telford grooming gang, which began drugging and sexually abusing girls as far back as the 1980s but although around 200 suspected abusers had been identified, by March 2018 only nine had been imprisoned. The shameful failure to protect vulnerable children is attributed to inexcusable inaction on the part of social workers, town council staff inclined to view the girls as prostitutes rather than victims, police negligence on an extraordinary scale and a general reluctance to risk accusations of racism.

Six months later McKelvie (2018) reported on one young woman's attempts to see justice done, albeit after an unforgivable delay. First raped at the age of twelve, pregnant and forced to have an abortion at thirteen, she had been abused by about seventy men but only one of them had been tried and convicted. Telford is not very big—the population is a little over 150,000—so she had to suffer the indignity of seeing her abusers walking freely around town. However, the local MP (female) and a lawyer (female) were backing her attempts to persuade the Crown Prosecution Service to reconsider an earlier decision not to prosecute key suspects in the case. In addition, she hoped to sue Telford and Wreckin Council, whose social workers had closed her case when the abuse was still taking place.

In 2018, The Holly Project (based in Wellington, near Telford) was set up to provide support services to help the victims of CSE put their lives back together again. Having done so much to report the horrendous abuse suffered by the Telford victims, Geraldine McKelvie (2019) then used crowdfunding to raise more than a thousand pounds for The Holly Project.

The Sunday tabloid *The News of the World* had a reputation for publishing kiss-and-tell sex stories (hence its nickname *The News of the Screws*) but also conducted genuine investigations into unethical or illegal activities. Indeed, in the year before its closure it won the British Press Awards' Scoop of the Year prize for a sting operation in which an Asian journalist posed as an Arab sheikh to expose a corrupt bookmaker and some Pakistani test cricketers involved in a spot-fixing scam. Then the phone-hacking scandal broke as it was revealed that the paper had systematically broken the law by hiring private investigators to gain access to people's mobile phone voicemail accounts. Not just celebrities but anyone who found themselves temporarily in the news ran the risk of having their phones intercepted. Those who recalled Rebekah Wade's campaign for a Sarah's Law to permit people to know if there was a paedo in their neighbourhood used social media to make tongue-in-cheek demands for a Rebekah's Law to give the public the right to know if there was a News International journalist living nearby. More seriously for Rupert Murdoch, a lot of advertising was withdrawn and he closed the paper down in July 2011. The final edition sold 3.8 million copies, which suggested that there were some who were sorry to see it go.

One person who publicly expressed her sorrow was Ros Wynne-Jones (2011), who modestly refers to herself and her colleagues as *hacks* rather than journalists in a spirited defence of the tabloids' record of investigative journalism that has frequently been recognised at the National Press Awards. She notes approvingly that hacks 'possess a naturally deep disdain for authority, establishment and big business', defends the often-maligned tabloid readers who donate generously to charities or good causes, and sees the loss of a well-known title as something no one should be happy about: 'With the demise of the News of the World there is one less public policeman – however bent – on the block'. She concludes with an anecdote from the 1990s concerning a homophobic incident at a pub in Canary Wharf. The next day she saw a colleague with a black eye, and knowing that his views on gay rights were not particularly enlightened, suspected that he might have been the aggressor. Then he told her what had happened: 'There was a couple of poufs getting battered. [...]

I thought, we can't have that going on in this day and age'. Unstated but powerfully implied is the question of how many journalists on the quality papers—tolerant liberals who would never dream of uttering a word like *poufs*—would wade into a fistfight to protect two gay men they didn't even know.

Tabloid readers demonstrate their generosity both in one-off appeals for help and in regular donations at Christmas time. As an example of the former, *Sunday People* readers raised £14,533 for a state-of-the-art robotic arm made by 3D printer for a woman who had all her limbs amputated following a kidney infection that led to sepsis (Willis and Selby 2018). Every December the same paper also organises its Secret Santa Appeal, which in recent years has raised funds for the food bank charity Trussell Trust, the Barnardo's charity for vulnerable children and young people, and The Veterans Charity for ex-servicemen and -women who suffered physical or psychological harm while on active duty. Readers of the right-wing tabloids are no less generous than those of the Labour-supporting *Mirror* and *People*.

Both investigations into cases of corruption or malpractice that damage the collective and the raising of funds to help the needy serve to establish a bond between the tabloids and their readers. The popular newspapers aim to portray themselves as being in tune with the common-sense views of ordinary, decent, hard-working people and explicitly declare their willingness to take on those who represent powerful vested interests. They adapt their language to make it clear whose side they are on: colloquial lexis, grammatically deviant forms and self-consciously working-class language present the tabloids as the voice of the common (wo)man, often in contrast with the linguistic obscurity and evasiveness of experts who are not entirely to be trusted. Today they also quote social media posts to underline their solidarity with ordinary men and women, rather than privileged and overpaid fat cats. On 19 October 2019, the House of Commons sat on a Saturday, the first time it had done so in 37 years, in order to debate Prime Minister Boris Johnson's proposed Brexit deal just twelve days before the official date for Britain's withdrawal from the European Union. At a time when parliamentarians were not highly regarded by the public, Chris Bryant MP suggested that he and his colleague should be paid extra for their sacrifice of turning up to work on a Saturday and having to spend more on weekend childcare. Under a headline that pointed out that MPs earned £80,000 a year, the *Sun* (Christodoulou 2019) sided with, and quoted, shift workers who earned a fraction of Bryant's salary and worked at the weekend rather more frequently than once every 37 years.

> He has been slammed on social media by fuming parents who argue they have to juggle long shifts with looking after their kids.
> One wrote: "Bloody hells bells !!! Are you joking ??? Lots of families work on Weekends, most don't get help with cost of childcare any day of the week ! Most families HAVE to work weekends just to pay the rent !! Absolutely disgusting".

This issue pitted ordinary families struggling after years of austerity against an elite that had not suffered at all, but for the Brexit-supporting *Sun* there was also indignation over the fact that MPs had that day voted for yet another extension to Britain's membership of the EU.

In the autumn of 2019, there was another matter that some tabloids interpreted as self-indulgence by people who simply didn't care about the disruption they caused to the lives of ordinary men and women: it was the series of Extinction Rebellion protests that saw great numbers of people of all ages taking to the streets of London and effectively bringing parts of the capital to a halt. The right-wing tabloids depicted Extinction Rebellion as a white, middle-class phenomenon involving people who were fortunate enough to be able to take time off work or away from their studies to engage in activities of questionable legality. In so doing, they stopped working people from going about their business but did nothing to combat climate change. If actors or other celebrities participated in the protests, they were referred to by the disparaging term *luvvies*, a word that implies a cocooned environment protected from the cares and hassles that the rest of us have to cope with. The *Sun* columnist Rod Liddle (2019) describes them as 'indulged kidults', 'narcissists and bedwetters' and 'the most cosseted and privileged generation we have ever seen'. His use of pronouns establishes a clear dichotomy between *they/them*, the spoilt and self-important protesters, and *we/us*, ordinary people too busy earning a living and paying taxes to have time for such childish and ultimately self-defeating antics. The pronoun *you* also appears, however, as Liddle addresses the protesters directly, switching from low-frequency lexis like *narcissists* and *cosseted* to the sort or terms of abuse that the ordinary bloke in the pub would use: 'How do you think plastic is made, you morons? [...] You want to change the world, you drongos?'

A week later some ordinary men and women, commuters on the London underground, rebelled against the rebels, and Jan Moir (2019) for the *Daily Mail* was delighted. When two Extinction Rebellion protesters tried to block the Jubilee Line by climbing on top of a tube train at Canning Town Station, frustrated commuters elected not to wait for the police, but instead dragged down the would-be eco-warriors. From Moir's description of first the commuters, then the protesters, there is little doubt as to whose side she is on:

> They are the normals, the everyday civilians, the overlooked ordinary Joes just trying to get to work. Or desperate to get home after a draining night shift.
> Hard-working people who never get a favour or a lucky break or the opportunity to smugly tell everyone about how they have just offset their carbon footprint and have solar panels on the swimming pool roof.

In reality, it is unlikely that many of the protesters have swimming pools, while few of London's Tube travellers think of themselves as the downtrodden masses, but Moir, like Rod Liddle, creates an oversimplified dichotomy and places herself, and by extension the newspaper she writes for, firmly on the side of the common (wo)man.

It is easy to be cynical about the tabloids' true motives when they investigate cover-ups and/or incompetence regarding health scandals and sex grooming gangs, or when they expose cases of sleaze among our elected representatives and ridicule MPs whingeing about working on a Saturday, or reveal the extent of slum accommodation in twenty-first-century Britain and the shortage of public housing, or side with Londoners trying to do the environmentally correct thing of travelling by public transport. They are, after all, matters that raise passions, and therefore sell newspapers. The fact remains, however, that the tabloids have on numerous occasions done the public some service by opening cans of worms that certain powerful interests wished to keep firmly and permanently sealed.

## References

Anonymous. 2018. How tabloids are ruining your country. *Antidotes for Chimps.* 14 November 2018. https://antidotesforchimps.com/2018/11/14/how-tabloids-are-ruining-your-country/. Accessed 9 October 2019.

Blair, Anthony. 2018. Britain's 'worst ever' grooming gang: '1,000 girls raped, beaten & even killed by brutes'. *Daily Star Online.* 11 March 2018. https://www.dailystar.co.uk/news/latest-news/telford-child-abuse-grooming-gang-16855479. Accessed 16 October 2018.

Christodoulou, Holly. 2019. 'Disgrace' Brexit vote: Fury as £80 k-a-year MPs claim they should be paid extra for wrecking Brexit on Super Saturday. *Sun Online.* 19 October 2019. https://www.thesun.co.uk/news/brexit/10170302/chris-bryant-childcare-brexit-super-saturday/. Accessed 19 October 2019.

Crosbie, Paul. 1990. Mad Cow Madness. *Daily Express.* 16 May 1990.

Crosbie, Paul. 1995. One in four shuns beef. *Daily Express.* 13 November 1995.

Daily Express Opinion. 1995. A healthy show of parent power. *Daily Express.* 6 December 1995.

Daily Mirror, 1962. Drug Trial Moment of Horror. *Daily Mirror.* 7 November 1962.

Dathan, Matt. 2018. EHIC vow broken. European health tourism scam ripping NHS off by £200million still going eight months after our exposé. *Sun Online.* 1 September 2018. https://www.thesun.co.uk/news/7150270/european-health-tourism-scam-cabinet-vow/. Accessed 10 October 2019.

Duell, Mark. 2018. 'When I woke, I had been raped': Asian grooming gangs' victims tell of horrific ordeals after report reveals 'arrogant' abusers felt 'unlikely to be prosecuted' while preying on 700 girls and woman. *MailOnline.* 23 February 2018. https://www.dailymail.co.uk/news/article-5426395/Report-Asian-grooming-gangs-abusing-700-girls-women.html. Accessed 15 October 2019.

Fielding, James. 2017. Fellow police made my life torture for trying to stop Rochdale sex ring, claims detective. *Express Online.* 19 November 2019. https://www.express.co.uk/news/uk/881325/Police-Asian-grooming-rapists-Rochdale-child-abuse-Maggie-Oliver. Accessed 16 October 2019.

Fuller, Paul. 1995. Tests calm BSE fears. *Daily Express*. 19 December 1995.

Jolly, Bradley. 2019. Revealed: How UK's most notorious benefits scroungers spend our cash. *Daily Express Online*. 10 September 2019. https://www.dailystar.co.uk/news/latest-news/benefits-scrounger-revealed-travis-simpkins-17095165. Accessed 13 October 2019.

Liddle, Rod. 2019. Extinction Rebellion should pack up their plastic tents and virtue-signalling hysterics and get back to work. *Sun Online*. 10 October 2019. https://www.thesun.co.uk/news/10103451/extinction-rebellion-get-back-to-work/. Accessed 20 October 2019.

Lockett, Jon. 2017. 'It's important we talk about it' British-Pakistani researchers say 84 per cent of grooming gang members targeting young girls are Asian. *Sun Online*. 12 December 2017. https://www.thesun.co.uk/news/5109188/grooming-gangs-britain-pakistan-girls-sexual-abuse/. Accessed 16 October 2019.

Marsh, Beezy and James Orr. 2002. Measles cluster adds to fears of an epidemic. *Daily Mail*. 14 February 2002.

McKelvie, Geraldine. 2018. Telford girl abused by up to 70 paedophiles speaks out after fresh hope of justice for town's sex victims. *Mirror Online*. 26 September 2018. https://www.mirror.co.uk/news/uk-news/girl-abused-up-70-paedophiles-13290068. Accessed 18 October 2019.

McKelvie, Geraldine. 2019. We've raised £1,235 to fund The Holly Project, which provides vital support to those affected by child sexual exploitation in Telford. *Just.giving.com*. 21 April 2019. https://www.justgiving.com/crowdfunding/geraldine-mckelvie-1. Accessed 18 October 2019.

Mohammed, Aamir, and Bradley Jolly. 2019. Homeless graphic designer living under a bridge is desperate for work. *Mirror Online*. 10 October 2019. https://www.mirror.co.uk/news/uk-news/homeless-graphic-designer-living-under-20551455. Accessed 13 October 1919.

Moir, Jan. 2019. What joyful revenge on eco zealot Ruperts and the grungsters as Londoners fed up of Extinction Rebellion take matters into their own hands. *MailOnline*. 18 October 2019. https://www.dailymail.co.uk/news/article-7586393/Londoners-fed-XR-matters-hands.html. Accessed 20 October 2019.

Mudie, Keir, and Nigel Nelson. 2013. Bedroom tax victim commits suicide: Grandmother Stefanie Bottrill blames government in tragic vote. *Sunday People*. 14 May 2013. https://www.mirror.co.uk/news/uk-news/suicide-bedroom-tax-victim-stephanie-1883600. Accessed 14 October 2019.

Panther, Lewis, and Nick Hedges. 2016. Slum conditions in 2016 Britain show little has changed since shocking pictures of the 1960s. *Mirror Online*.

13 March 2016. https://www.mirror.co.uk/news/uk-news/slum-conditions-2016-britain-show-7544949. Accessed 12 October 2019.
Parry, Tom. 2018. Germany accused of betraying victims of thalidomide scandal over promise to compensate British victims. *Mirror Online*. 29 April 2018. https://www.mirror.co.uk/news/world-news/germany-accused-betraying-victims-thalidomide-12450929. Accessed 10 October 2019.
Proops, Marjorie. 1962. Think of other women. *Daily Mirror*. 12 November 1962.
Shafiq, Mohammed. 2016. My cousins the Rotherham child abusers and the Asian men who share their twisted view of white girls: A brave and very personal denunciation by a British Pakistani of those in his community who defend grooming gangs. *MailOnline*. 27 February 2017. https://www.dailymail.co.uk/news/article-3466549/My-cousins-Rotherham-child-abusers-Asian-men-share-twisted-view-white-girls-brave-personal-denunciation-British-Pakistani-community-defend-grooming-gangs.html. Accessed 18 October 2019.
Smith, Howard, Alun Rees, and Lisa Reynolds. 1995. Schools in rush to outlaw beef. *Daily Express*. 5 December 1995.
Sommerlad, Nick, and Geraldine McKelvie. 2018. Britain's 'worst ever' child grooming scandal exposed: Hundreds of young girls raped, beaten sold for sex and some even killed. *Mirror Online*. 12 March 2018. https://www.mirror.co.uk/news/uk-news/britains-worst-ever-child-grooming-12165527. Accessed 18.10.2019.
Stephens, Peter. 1962. Why I killed the baby I loved. *Daily Mirror*. 12 November 1962.
Tingle, Rory. 2019. More than 240,000 sign petition opposing BBC's 'shameful' decision to scrap free TV licences for 3.7 m over-75 s—As devastated pensioner says 'TV is a vital lifeline for millions like me'. *MailOnline*. 12 June 2019. https://www.dailymail.co.uk/news/article-7127243/Furious-pensioners-call-licence-fee-payers-boycott-BBC.html. Accessed 14 October 2019.
Willis, Kim, and Alan Selby. 2018. Bionic gran who lost all four limbs 'gets her life back' thanks to 3D printed robotic arm. *Sunday People*. 21 October 2018. https://www.mirror.co.uk/news/uk-news/bionic-gran-who-lost-four-13451126. Accessed 19 October 2019.
Wynne-Jones, Ros. 2011. Red-top redemption: Why tabloid journalism matters. *Independent.co.uk*. 22 July 2011. https://www.independent.co.uk/news/media/press/red-top-redemption-why-tabloid-journalism-matters-2318346.html. Accessed 18 October 2019.

# 8

# From 'Zip Me Up Before You Go Go' to 'Boring Old Gits to Wed': The Tabloids and Celebrities

What the two quotes in the chapter title have in common is that the newspapers concerned subsequently displayed no contrition at all for having used headlines that many people felt were in very bad taste; on the contrary, both later referred to their respective front-page splashes in self-congratulatory tones.

The first headline appeared in the *Sun* in 1998 when the news broke that the pop star George Michael had been arrested in the USA for making a sexual approach to an undercover police officer in a public toilet (his group Wham! had had a big hit with a song entitled *Wake me up before you go go*). The *Sun*'s report of George Michael's humiliation (Graham 1998) exemplifies the tabloids' tendency to elevate public figures to a level not always commensurate with their talent and/or contribution to the general good, only to take great relish in knocking them down as soon as the opportunity presents itself. When a hugely popular singer is arrested, it is news, though whether the story merits front-page coverage to the exclusion of all the other news of the day is questionable. The colloquial language of the subhead—'George Michael nicked for sex act in loo'—ridiculed the pop star, who had not yet come out about being gay. He had little choice but to do so when the *Sun* and other papers quoted the Los Angeles police chief explaining that '[h]e was engaging in a lewd act in front of the undercover officer'.

George Michael died on Christmas Day 2016 at the age of 53, and two days later *Sun Online* published a long tribute to his life and career featuring numerous still photographs and film clips (Parsons 2016). In addition, the tribute quotes extracts from *Bare*, the singer's life story, co-written by Michael with the *Sun* columnist Tony Parsons, and published just two years after the *Zip me up before you go go* headline. Like *Gotcha*, that headline also ended up on a T-shirt, and following the star's death the *Sun*, true to form, did not express the slightest regret for having made fun of a sensitive man at one of the lowest points of his life. That Michael then chose to avail himself of the literary skills of someone on the *Sun*'s payroll is indicative of celebrities' ambivalent relationship with the tabloids.

The second headline in the chapter title comes from an article allegedly written 'By Hugh Cares, Royal Correspondent' that appeared in the *Daily Star* on 11 February 2005 after it was announced that Prince Charles and Camilla Parker-Bowles were to be married. Although the royal family had long ceased to be treated with reverence by the popular media, this headline created quite a stir because many felt that it exhibited an unacceptable and entirely gratuitous level of disrespect. The irreverent tone was maintained in the opening sentence: 'Prince Charles is to marry Camilla Parker Bowles after 34 years of dithering – but last night the nation sighed: "Who gives a damn?"' (Cares 2005). We are informed that the betrothed couple have a combined age of 113 and it is implied that the prince, referred to as 'Chas', may have struggled to get down on one knee to propose.

The next day the *Star* led with the headline 'Disrespectful, treacherous & bloody funny… that's the Daily Star' and the correctly named Gary Nicks (2005) began his self-congratulatory article: 'The Daily Star was the talk of the nation yesterday for horsing around with our brilliant royal wedding coverage'. The American idiom *horse around* is seldom used in Britain and it is legitimate to suspect that Nicks chose the expression not merely to allude to Mrs Parker Bowles' interest in equestrian activities; Thorne (2014: 224) notes that since 2000 *horse* has been used in British slang to mean an unattractive woman, so it is tempting to presume that the aim was also to make an oblique reference to the public's perception of Prince Charles' fiancée as a woman who compared unfavourably with the younger and better looking Princess Diana. To suggest, however indirectly, that the woman destined to marry the heir to the throne was ugly would once have been unthinkable, but the tendency to close the gap between the once untouchable royals and other famous people began in the 1960s, accelerated during Princess Diana's much-televised life and was probably concluded on 11 February 2005. The *Daily Star* had selected its royal targets judiciously given that both were unpopular with the general public; Diana, the sad-eyed people's princess, had fallen victim to the scheming Camilla Parker-Bowles and the two-timing Prince Charles.

Gary Nicks was delighted to point out how his newspaper had distinguished itself from its competitors: 'Rather than filling our pages with sickly reports like our stuffy rivals, we gave the story the tongue-in-cheek treatment it deserved'. The expression *tongue-in-cheek* is typical of the red-tops' practice of claiming that they are only having a bit of fun—be it a report of a royal engagement or a salacious description of a young woman's breasts—and that critics of their language and style are just a bunch of po-faced killjoys.

This chapter examines the symbiotic relationship between celebrities and the tabloid press, and the sometimes fuzzy dividing line between justified investigation and unwarranted snooping. A distinction is made between people who acquire celebrity status as a consequence of their achievements in fields such as show business or sport, and those who have done nothing to earn their fame other than to appear on reality TV or have sex with someone well-known. The former are often in the position that they either no longer need publicity or never sought it in the first place, so they may resent tabloid journalists prying into their lives, perhaps to the extent that they seek to use the law to stop the snooping. The latter can hardly complain that their privacy is not respected since media exposure—whether good or bad—is vital to people who are famous merely because they are famous. Someone who has repeatedly complained about the UK press is Meghan Markle, now the Duchess of Sussex, whose claim that she has received excessively critical treatment is supported by hard data: of 843 articles about her in fourteen print newspapers between mid-May 2018 and mid-January 2019, 43% were negative, only 20% positive and 36% neutral (Duncan and Bindman 2020). At the time of writing, the news has just broken that the Duke and Duchess of Sussex have decided to leave their official roles in the royal family, stop using their Royal Highness titles, become financially self-supporting and spend a considerable part of each year an ocean away from the British tabloids. In the second category a case that has been extensively commented upon concerns the late Jade Goody, who became famous, or infamous, as a result of her TV appearances on *Big Brother* and *Celebrity Big Brother*. Once derided in the tabloids as a mouthy, ignorant chav with a nasty racist streak, her decision to remain in the public eye as she battled with cervical cancer led to almost instant rehabilitation and widespread praise for her contribution to cervical-cancer awareness. She lost her struggle against the disease, and after having lived the last seven years of her short life before television cameras, her funeral was also a major media event.

As noted earlier, tabloiding the truth seldom entails obvious falsehoods but consists in exaggerating or distorting something—a fact, an event or a statement—to produce a version that is no longer truly representative of the original entity. In 2013, the *Daily Mail* misrepresented an article that J.K. Rowling had published on the website of the single parents' charity *Gingerbread*. It was about own experience as a single mother and benefits claimant in Edinburgh before literary success, and the rewards of that success, came her way. In the article, she described a single occasion when a woman attending her church referred to her disparagingly as 'the unmarried mother', but in the report published on *MailOnline* on 28 September 2013 and in the print edition the next day the novelist's recollection of the incident was effectively converted from singular to plural. She stood accused of unfairly claiming that she was subject to repeated abuse by various members of the congregation. Boyle (2014) quotes Rowling's legal team stating that the piece in the *Mail* deliberately gave the impression that she 'had knowingly given a false account of her time as a single mother in Edunburgh in which she falsely and inexcusably accused her fellow churchgoers of behaving in a bigoted, unchristian manner towards her, of stigmatising her and cruelly taunting her for being a single mother'. Seven months later the novelist duly won the libel case and the *Daily Mail* was obliged to print an apology and pay an undisclosed amount in damages, which she donated to charity.

It might seem strange that a national newspaper would take a wholly uncontroversial article on a charity's website, wilfully misrepresent it and thus incur a substantial financial penalty, but there are reasons why J.K. Rowling was targeted. The *Daily Mail* does not approve of single mothers and tends to portray them as women who deliberately get pregnant in order to secure a council flat and state benefits. A single mother who subsequently gets married, adds to her family, becomes a multimillionaire and elects not to move to a tax haven does not quite shake off the stigma of her original sin. Rowling's truly unforgivable misdeed, however, has been to voice her support for an adequate welfare system that helps people through difficult times of the kind she once experienced herself. For the *Daily Mail* welfare benefits merely encourage idleness, put an excessive burden on hard-working taxpayers and reek of socialism. J.K. Rowling's first book after the *Harry Potter* series was *The Casual Vacancy*, which was published a year before the author sued the *Mail*. The *Mail* columnist Jan Moir (2012) wondered whether the novel would live up to the pre-publication hype, then answered her own question: 'On balance, I would have to say no. Not unless you want to have more than 500 pages of relentless socialist manifesto masquerading as literature crammed down your throat'. Rowling's crime is to depict the inhabitants of a run-down council estate as people with multiple difficulties rather than work-shy benefits scroungers with feral children. Specifically, the author portrays sympathetically the character of Krystal, a teenager whose mission in life is to prevent her three-year-old brother from being removed from their heroin-addicted mother and taken into care. For Moir, Krystal is a 'tart with a heart' and Rowling a 'blinkered, Left-leaning demagogue'.

When the BBC made a three-part mini-series of *The Casual Vacancy* and gave it a peak-viewing slot, Moir (2015) returned to the attack: '[T]his contemporary drama depicts the English upper and middle classes as relentlessly awful people – unless they happen to be Asian – while the working class characters are almost all noble savages who have been wronged by society'. Once again she poses a question then answers it herself; this time the issue is why this particular novel was chosen for TV adaptation, and the explanation is that it is an election year and the

BBC—notoriously a bunch of lefties—saw Rowling's portrayal of class war as a vehicle to attack David Cameron and the Conservative Party.

J.K. Rowling was also attacked by the *Sun* columnist Dan Wooton (2018) when she said that she was happy for Johnny Depp to be cast in the lead role in her *Fantastic Beasts and Where To Find Them* film franchise even though the actor had been issued with a restraining order after his ex-wife, Amber Heard, accused him of acts of domestic violence. Wooton describes Rowling as 'a holier-than-thou Twitterati preacher', 'the worst type of Hollywood Hypocrite' and someone 'who likes to slaughter anyone who dares publicly question her morals or decisions'. On this occasion, it was not Rowling but Johnny Depp who decided to sue, and at the time of writing Wooton's column can still be retrieved from the *Sun*'s archive but it concludes with a note stating that, following a complaint from Depp, the article is subject to legal proceedings. In February 2019, an attempt by News Group Newspapers and Dan Wooton to have the case halted was rejected in the High Court (PA Mediapoint 2019). An article that was essentially written to discredit J.K. Rowling has landed the *Sun* in a legal battle with a Hollywood star who doubtless has access to lawyers with a good track record in libel cases.

Jan Moir and Dan Wooton's vitriolic attacks on J.K. Rowling are politically motivated. She is an extraordinarily generous philanthropist but for the right-wing tabloids the vast sums she has donated to various charities are of far less importance than the £1 million she once gave the Labour Party. In addition, during the Brexit referendum of 2016 she supported Remain, something that the *Mail* and the *Sun* will neither forgive nor forget.

Another Hollywood actor chose not to sue but to post an open editorial on the website of a well-known America publication. In 2014, shortly after the announcement of George Clooney's engagement to Amal Alamuddin, the *Daily Mail* reported that his fiancée's mother was opposed to the match because her Druze religion did not permit inter-faith marriage, and that she had made her view clear in Beirut. Furthermore, the *Mail* made tasteless and ill-informed comments about marriage traditions in Druze communities. In reality, Clooney's future mother-in-law was not against the marriage, was not even Druze and had not set foot in Beirut since her daughter and the actor had started dating, so libel action was more than justified. However, the actor chose a faster way to shame the *Daily Mail* by writing a hard-hitting piece for *USA Today* in which he explained that while he didn't lose sleep over tabloid gossip that regarded him personally, the *Mail* had overstepped the mark by telling lies that concerned an entire community and risked stirring up religious tensions. He concluded: 'And when they put my family and my friends in harm's way, they cross far beyond just a laughable tabloid and into the arena of inciting violence. They must be so very proud' (Clooney 2014).

It worked. Within hours, the offending article was removed from *MailOnline* and an apology was posted. The headline to an article by Emily Yahr (2014) for *The Washington Post* summed up reaction within the newspaper world: 'George Clooney proves why shaming the tabloids is more effective than suing them'. Yahr makes the valid point that reputable outlets that had cited the *Daily Mail*'s article would be wary of trusting such a source again, which is 'far more damaging than a lawsuit'. Quite simply, the *Daily Mail* had published something offered to them without carrying out elementary fact-checking, and such negligence does not inspire confidence. As noted in Chapter 4 with regard to the reporting of immigration into Britain, three years after the wholly inaccurate article about Clooney's future mother-in-law, the editors of *Wikipedia* decided that the *Daily Mail* was too unreliable to be used as a reference.

One person who no longer sues the tabloids despite the great number of decidedly unflattering articles about her is Katie Price, who earlier in her career was known by the professional name Jordan (in 2008 she did, in fact, sue the *News of the World* but for reasons explained below has not had recourse to legal action since then). The papers tend to refer to her as a glamour model, but she has also been a reality TV star, a pop singer, a novelist (thanks to a ghostwriter) and a promoter of nutritional products of dubious efficacy. Her varied and paparazzi-pursued love life has so far involved three husbands, a string of lovers and five children. At the time of writing she is 41, her modelling days are nearly over, her ghostwriter has passed away and in November 2019 she was declared bankrupt, but tabloid readers continue to consume news about her breast implants, her publicly conducted 'private' life and her verbal intemperance. In short, Katie Price perfectly fits the definition of a celebrity as 'a person known for his [or her] well-knownness' (Boorstin 1961: 57, cited by Allan 2004:

204), and as such exemplifies the symbiotic relationship between those who are famous because they are famous and the media. The tabloids pry into her not-so-private life, thus satisfying their readers' prurience, an invasion of privacy that Ms. Price cannot object to since—to complete the pr- alliterative chain—she profits from the publicity that sustains her marketability.

When a marriage is breaking down the two parties' respective friends often find themselves, willingly or despite themselves, taking sides. If those two parties are famous, huge numbers of people take part in the exercise of pointing the finger of blame at one or the other. It is noted above that the *Star* got away with its 'Boring old gits to wed' headline because the targets were the two people widely held to be responsible for the much-photographed unhappiness of Diana, the people's princess. In the summer of 2009, the marriage of Katie Price and the pop singer Peter André had effectively collapsed, and the former gave the tabloids sensational material on a daily basis as she publicly and immodestly enjoyed the company of Alex Reid, her new lover, whose extraordinary muscles were indicative of his unusual career as a cage-fighter. Since Peter André appeared to conduct himself with greater decorum and seemed to be the more responsible parent of the couple's two children (Price also had another child from an earlier relationship), there was never any doubt as to which party the tabloids would attack. Neither was there any question that Price might seek legal recourse to prevent the intrusion into her theoretically private life.

When Price and Reid went off on holiday to Marbella, leaving André to look after the children (including his stepson), the *Daily Mirror*'s headline was 'Lewd Jordan and new lover Alex Reid in sick show', while the paper's official Head of Showbiz, Tom Bryant (2009), seemed strangely shockable before evidence of the indecorous behaviour of certain celebrities when they know there are paparazzi in the vicinity:

> Shameless Katie Price shocked family holidaymakers with a brazen X-rated public display with her new boyfriend Alex Reid. The glamour model, 31, raunchily cavorted with the semi-naked, muscular cagefighter in the grounds of an exclusive golf resort in Spain as young children innocently looked on.

*Shameless* and *brazen* are two of the tabloids' preferred judgemental adjectives to censure stars who do exactly what the papers want them to do. In the headline and two sentences cited above, we also have *X-rated* and *raunchily cavorted*, and in stark contrast there are references to *shocked family holidaymakers* and *young children*. The narrative is very clear: Katie Price is a lousy mother who offends common decency with a public display of her lasciviousness.

On the same day, the *Daily Mail* published similar photos and neatly summed up the situation in the opening sentence: 'With her estranged husband Peter Andre looking after the children, Katie Price has once again resumed her shameless antics' (Daily Mail Reporter 2009). The use of the expression *once again* indicates that Price's flagrant exhibitionism at the Spanish resort was not an aberration but habitual behaviour, while the adjective *shameless* is almost obligatory. Other lexical similarities with the *Daily Mirror*'s report are 'cavorting' in the second sentence and 'brazen' in the third.

A significant difference from the *Mirror*'s treatment, however, is the use of intertextuality, including a reference to a rival tabloid as we learn that '[a] source close to Jordan told the Sun' that Katie and her new lover 'are just all over each other all day long'. Unidentified experts suggest that the photos taken in Spain will be damaging to Price if the divorce goes to court, her own tweets are cited and a 'spokesman' comments on rumours that she has had health problems. Finally, beneath a photo of the saintly Peter André with his son, Junior, the singer's column in *New!* magazine is quoted to inform us that he is moving on from the trauma of the separation. There is also uncontrolled intertextuality in the form of readers' feedback, however, and this article generated 137 comments. The majority agreed that Katie Price was the villain of the piece but a significant minority of posters found André's posing as the doting father abandoned by his selfish, insensitive wife unconvincing, or worse.

Ten days later, the *Mirror* reported that: 'Horrified Peter Andre accused Katie Price of being a "despicable mother" during an expletive-filled row witnessed by the Mirror' (Moodie 2009). The row was actually conducted on the phone when Price called her husband to let him talk to the children. As they spoke the children's mother could be heard in the background using pretty earthy language, till she took the phone herself to inform André that his manager (and formerly her own) was a 'fat, ugly, evil c\*\*\*'. Just why the *Daily Mirror* was present and remained present, during this theoretically private conversation is not immediately clear. As the article proceeds, however, it emerges that an ITV2 camera crew also witnessed the scene since preparations were being made for a 90-minute TV special about Peter André called *Going It Alone*. Exchanges of a highly personal nature involving a husband and wife and their young children had not only been observed by a tabloid journalist but also caught on camera, but there would be no complaints about invasion of privacy. Katie Price may not be the most cerebral of people but she understands perfectly that bad publicity can never harm her as much as being boycotted by the tabloids, a fate that would certainly befall her were she to make a habit of taking the red-tops to court and winning substantial damages. Similarly, a man preparing to boost his career by making himself the subject of a TV programme can hardly complain if a camera crew obtain some unexpected footage.

Although Katie Price would never sue a journalist, she is quite happy to subject an inquisitive reporter to her repertoire of monosyllabic lexemes that denote orifices of various kinds, as Gemma Wheatley of the *Daily Star* discovered when she went to the airport to welcome home Price and her cage-fighter after their holiday in Spain. Wheatley wanted to know whether it was true that the couple were going to get married, only to be asked a syntactically similar question herself: 'Is it true that you take it up the a\*\*\*?', an enquiry made when 'dozens of youngsters' were within earshot (Wheatley 2009). The question is not uttered or asked or posed but 'screeched', a reporting verb that dehumanises the speaker, as does the expression 'Snarling Katie Price' that begins the article. As regards Price's mental state, we are told that she is 'crazed' and 'in meltdown'.

A celebrity who behaves and speaks as Katie Price does, craves publicity of any kind and never sues is a precious commodity for the tabloids. Since August 2009 when the articles cited above were published, she has rarely been out of the news. Ten years, two other marriages, a series of lovers and two more children later, she was still inspiring lurid headlines. On 10 October 2019, it was her sixth driving ban that prompted *MailOnline* to detail her long history of motoring offences, and also to report on her battle to avoid bankruptcy (Gordon 2019). The article generated 866 readers' comments, nearly all of which were highly critical of her lifestyle, but the mere fact that they had been posted at all was indicative of her continued power to be a somewhat shop-soiled object of interest.

On 24 October, the *Sun Online* published some of Katie Price's text messages, reproducing them verbatim and thus demonstrating that her eleven novels and six autobiographies were ghostwritten (Capon 2019). Once again, this blatant invasion of her privacy did not persuade her to seek redress through the courts. The article concerned the 22-year-old builder, Charles Drury, who had briefly been Price's lover. When the relationship came to an end he cashed in on his affair with a celebrity by selling a sex-and-drugs account to the *Sun Online*, and Price reacted, somewhat bizarrely, by sending indignant text messages not to Drury, but to his mother. The recipient of the messages also elected not to make an issue of the invasion of her privacy, and Price made no comment upon a headline that included the expressions 'toyboy fury', 'ranting texts' and 'coke-fuelled romp revelations'.

At the beginning of November, the *Mirror Online* did her a favour by posting photos of her in the streets of Dublin modelling a brand of hot pants in her efforts to claw her way back from the brink of bankruptcy. She wore an open jacket, which afforded now-you-see-them-now you-don't peeks at her surgically enhanced breasts and rather distracted attention from the red hot pants she was modelling. More significantly, since public nudity is banned in Ireland she was also risking prosecution and a fine (Randell 2019). The brief article and five photos attracted 220 readers' comments, the recurrent themes being uncomplimentary evaluations of her 41-year-old body, concerns about the mental health of someone who could not look in the mirror and see herself as others saw her, and criticism of the *Daily Mirror* for continuing to give her so much attention. When someone is known for her well-knownness to the extent that she must remain in the public eye even if it means attracting brutal comments on her appearance and emotional equanimity, the celebrity lifestyle loses its glamour and the tabloids' persistence in documenting a star's decline begins to take on a ghoulish quality.

Three days later, the *Sun Online* posted photos of Price in a London street with her youngest children, Jett and Bunny. Jessica Gibb's article (2019) begins with an attack on Katie Price the mother: 'The mum of five was dressed head-to-toe in Gucci and carried TWO Louis Vuitton bags while her daughter Bunny went barefoot on the cold November day'. In reality, the photos show that both children were underdressed for an autumn day but the four-year-old girl's shoeless state invites comparisons with her mother's spotless new trainers. The headline includes the expression 'feral family' while in the article Price's luxury home is described as a 'mucky mansion', a reference to previous reports of the filthy state of the house. The article then goes on to the decision by the Advertising Standards Authority to ban Price and other celebrities from posting irresponsible testimonials on Instagram for certain diet products, which meant that she was losing her main source of income precisely when she was struggling to avoid bankruptcy. Finally, her eight convictions for driving offences are listed, along with a ninth for abusive and threatening behaviour. Although photographing other people's children is not in itself an offence in the UK, when a national daily does this an ethical issue is raised, and the mother of those children has a case for complaining to the Independent Press Standards Organisation. No such complaint was lodged about this intrusion, nor about the depiction of those children as wild and their home as a tip. It is difficult to pity a narcissist who had it all but chucked it away through her own extravagance and debauchery, but a tabloid's detailed chronicling of an unstable woman's various problems, followed by the gleeful comments of 129 readers, makes one think of circling vultures.

The tabloids may give unnecessary emphasis to the more unwholesome aspects of the woes of George Michael and Katie Price, but they do not actively seek to add to the harm that such celebrities inflict upon themselves; on the contrary, in the case of the latter, they doubtless hope that she will thrive and grow old disgracefully for decades to come. *The Daily Mail*'s treatment of J.K. Rowling is a little different because the novelist's support for adequate welfare benefits is anathema to such an uncritically right-wing paper, although there is little it can do to damage the reputation of a genuinely talented writer who keeps her private life private. The main political targets for the pro-Conservative tabloids, the people who have right-wing hacks reaching for a broken bottle, are the most prominent Labour MPs. In 2019, that meant Party leader Jeremy Corbyn, Shadow Chancellor of the Exchequer John McDonnell and Shadow Home Secretary Diane Abbott. In April 2019, the *Sun* and the *Mail* thought they had a story that would greatly embarrass Diane Abbot and possibly force Corbyn to fire her from the Shadow Cabinet.

We have already seen that in the digital age a "journalist" can cobble together a story from the internet, perhaps from a rival paper's website, without moving from their desk. Today millions of people have a device in their pocket or handbag that enables them to photograph anything that takes their fancy, and then send it to others. Given the well-documented phenomenon of certain tweets spreading like a contagion, it may happen that something that was only intended to amuse friends gets seen by vast numbers of people and eventually reaches someone who has a mischievous purpose for it. Such was the case of the young Londoner who photographed Abbot on public transport, tweeted the image to a handful of friends, then forgot all about the incident until he discovered that the *Sun* had used the photo to try to discredit the politician.

A by-law prohibits the consumption of alcohol on all Transport for London trains. No such ban exists in most parts of Britain; indeed, many rail companies sell alcoholic drinks on board. When Pollard et al. (2019) for the *Sun* reported that the Shadow Home Secretary had been seen drinking a can of 8% proof mojito on a London train, the photograph their newspaper published was the one tweeted to friends by the young man mentioned above. Permission to use the image had not been requested. The tone of the article was stern and judgemental:

> The outspoken Labour MP stunned fellow passengers by swigging a £2 can of Marks and Spencer mojito on an Overground service.
> Ms Abbott – who has campaigned to end the sale of cheap alcohol – downed the rum cocktail on a journey through her constituency in North London last Saturday.

Normally one *sips* or *drinks* a cocktail, but the authors of this article write that she was 'swigging', which suggests taking large draughts of a liquid, while their claim that she 'downed' the mojito goes further in that it implies that she finished the drink very quickly, perhaps with single, unladylike gulp. Users of public transport are not that easily shocked, so the claim that other passengers were 'stunned' stretches credibility, and in any case they would have had very little time to become outraged if Abbot had really finished the 25cl can as quickly as is implied here. Later in the article an unnamed passenger is quoted saying that the MP 'kept slurping', which suggests noisy, ill-mannered drinking but the *keep* + *_ing* construction indicates a repeated action, not one-gulp consumption of a drink. Another unnamed passenger is cited, but it is difficult to see how the *Sun* managed to trace people who had witnessed Diane Abbott's reprehensible act committed a week earlier. Since the three "authors" of this piece lifted their photo from Twitter, it is not unreasonable to suspect that unattributed quotes were also taken from the same source. They did go to the trouble of contacting two individuals prepared to make on-the-record comments, but chose a member of the London Assembly's Police and Crime Committee and a retired Scotland Yard detective, both people who were duty-bound to adopt a zero-tolerance stance.

Nine days later, the *Mail on Sunday*'s political gossip column poked fun at 'Comrade Diane Abbott' and claimed that she had been the object of 'merciless mockery' by colleagues in the Shadow Cabinet (Black Dog 2019). The *Sun* and the *Mail* hoped to make a great scandal over law-breaking by a politician who aspired to become Home Secretary, but they had miscalculated the public's attitude towards a Member of Parliament who used public transport and shopped at Marks & Spencer. After the article in the *Sun* Diane Abbot immediately tweeted an apology, and by way of reply received many messages of solidarity plus appreciation of the fact that she did such thoroughly normal things, which made her constituents feel that they were actually represented by their MP. Levine (2019) concludes his summary of supportive tweets by noting that since becoming Britain's first black female MP in 1987 Abbott had been subject to racist and sexist abuse on a daily basis, '[s]o if she fancies a few swigs of mojito on the way home, well, who are any of us to judge?'. The hashtag #CansForDiane started trending as people defiantly sipped alcoholic drinks on Transport for London, partly out of solidarity with Abbott, but also to expose the practical impossibility of enforcing a ban that was originally intended to target groups of rowdy boozers, not 65-year-old women minding their own business. It was not a merely virtual protest; five days after the *Sun*'s article, Hansen (2019) reported that the 'flood of supportive emulation for the Labour MP – including variations on the "I've never felt more represented" theme' had resulted in Marks & Spencer stores in London running out of their mojito cocktail.

*Vice.com* managed to trace the young man who took the photo of Abbott and he agreed to be interviewed provided that his identity was not revealed. He stated that he thought Diane Abbot was 'a great politician and person', said that all the friends to whom he had sent the image denied that they had passed it on to the *Sun*, and felt ashamed that he had inadvertently provided a weapon for those who subject her to 'vitriolic racist and sexist abuse all the time' (Long 2019).

That the *Sun*'s attempt to discredit Diane Abbott backfired so spectacularly should give fair-minded people, conservative voters included, some satisfaction. It was a serious misjudgement to think that a can of mojito could damage a political career, but it should be noted that the right-wing press has a long and dishonourable record of smearing Labour leaders with far more serious (and entirely untruthful) allegations. In the 1980s and early '90s, Neil Kinnock was portrayed as an incompetent muddler in thrall to the Trotskyite wing of his party; in 1995, the former Labour leader Michael Foot sued the *Sunday Times* for accusing him of having been a KGB agent; the *Daily Mail* claimed that Ed Miliband ('Red Ed') had had a hard-left agenda instilled into him by a Marxist father who hated the Britain that had taken him in when he fled from Nazi-occupied Belgium (Levy 2013); in 2018, the *Sun* alleged that 'Jeremy Corbyn met a communist spy at the height of the Cold War and warned him of a clampdown by British intelligence' (Ryan 2018).

In reality, the hysterical reds-under-the-bed stories have always been a pretext to disguise the fact that newspaper proprietors have had a far more pragmatic, self-serving motive for fearing a Labour government under a certain type of leader. For years the Labour Party's manifesto included a commitment to have the Monopolies and Mergers Commission investigate the issue of media concentration, and it was this that spooked Rupert Murdoch and ensured that it was the *Sun* wot won the

1992 election for the Tories after a sustained campaign of demonisation of Neil Kinnock.

When Tony Blair took over the party leadership, he got rid of this potential threat to media giants like Murdoch's News Corporation (now News Corp), and it is no coincidence that he was never attacked by the right-wing tabloids with the vehemence reserved for other Labour leaders (Freedman 2015). What Miliband and Corbyn have in common is that they both believe that the recommendations of the Leveson Inquiry that investigated the *News of the World*'s phone-hacking scandal should have been implemented in full with the establishment of a genuinely independent press regulator and then a second Leveson II Inquiry into relations between the media and the police. The Cameron and May governments declined to do anything of the kind, but Corbyn's enthusiasm for enacting the recommendations of an independent inquiry into press ethics worries certain tabloids, worries them enough to tempt them to invent ludicrous stories about his past as a spy for the Soviet bloc. For Ivor Gaber (2018), professor of journalism at the University of Sussex, the right-wing papers are 'playing a dangerous game' because 'through their antics they undermine trust in both politics and the media'.

Can the tabloids still condition an election? The evidence of the 2017 and 2019 general elections is contradictory. In 2017, the *Mail, Express* and *Sun* relentlessly hammered away at Loony-Left Corbyn and his bunch of Marxist zealots, IRA sympathisers, soft-on-immigration blunderers and economic ignoramuses. The Conservative Party was not alone in believing that Corbyn had shifted his party so far to the left that it had become unelectable and was possibly heading for extinction. Indeed, the front cover of the April 2017 edition of *Prospect* magazine featured a tombstone bearing the inscription 'THE LABOUR PARTY 1900-2020', and the editor, Tom Clark (2017: 1), wrote in his Foreword '[…] we can't help but observe the evidence that Jeremy Corbyn is leading the party towards a crushing defeat'. As it happened Labour gained thirty seats and Theresa May lost her majority in the Commons. Hardly anyone had predicted this resurgence of support for an unapologetically socialist Labour Party and one of the reasons was the use Corbyn's team had made of social media. Gaber (2019: positions 7238–7247) notes that in the last three days of the campaign Labour spent £100,000 on

Snapchat, the social media platform preferred by young people, and showed little interest in Twitter, which political commentators favoured, and as a consequence 'much of the ferment taking place within public opinion, particularly among younger voters, went largely unobserved by Westminster-based journalists'.

Over the next two years, the Conservative Party became much savvier in the use of social media and Labour tied itself into knots over Brexit, but one thing that did not change in the slightest was the pro-Tory tabloids' cold dread at the thought of the 'Corbynistas' wielding power. A month before the December 2019 general election, Gary Younge (2019) noted that the Tory-supporting newspapers had resumed their vitriolic attacks on Corbyn because 'the rightwing press fear his premiership as they have feared no other Labour leader before'. The prospect of a government led by someone committed to both media pluralism and redistributive taxation left the *Sun*, *Mail* and *Express* with little doubt as to where their interests lay: the same pro-Brexit tabloids that had poohpoohed concerns about the economic consequences of leaving the EU now screamed hysterically (and untruthfully) that Corbyn's manifesto would cost a trillion pounds to implement, with the result that the Conservatives won handsomely and gained seats that Labour had held for decades.

## References

Allan, Stuart. 2004. *News Culture*. Maidenhead, UK: Open University Press.

Black Dog. 2019. Comrade Diane Abbott earns merciless mockery from Shadow Cabinet colleagues over M&S she was spotted drinking on a train. *MailOnline*, April 28. https://www.dailymail.co.uk/debate/article-6967759/BLACK-DOG-Diane-Abbott-mocked-colleagues-M-S-mojito-spotted-drinking-train.html#comments. Accessed 14 November 2019.

Boorstin, D.J. 1961. *The Image: A Guide to Pseudo-Events in America*. New York: Vintage.

Boyle, Darren. 2014. Harry Potter author JK Rowling sues Daily Mail over article about her 'sob story past as single mother. *Pressgazette.co.uk*, January 30. https://www.pressgazette.co.uk/daily-mail-sued-harry-potter-author-jk-rowling-over-single-mother-past-claims/. Accessed 28 October 2019.

Bryant, Tom. 2009. Lewd Jordan and new lover Alex Reid in sick show. *Daily Mirror*, August 5. http://www.mirror.co.uk/celebs/news/2009/08/05/lewd-jordan-and-new-lover-alex-reid-in-sick-show-115875-21571673/. Accessed 7 November 2019.

Capon, Tom. 2019. Toyboy fury. Katie Price bombards ex Charles Drury's mum with ranting texts about her 'cruel' son after coke-fuelled romp revelations. *Sun Online*, October 24. https://www.thesun.co.uk/tvandshowbiz/10205440/katie-price-charles-drury-ex-texts/. Accessed 9 November 2019.

Cares, Hugh. 2005. Boring old gits to wed. *Daily Star*, February 11.

Clark, Tom. 2017. Labour looks death in the eye. *Prospect*, April.

Clooney, George. 2014. Exclusive: Clooney responds to 'Daily Mail' report. *USA Today*, July 9. https://eu.usatoday.com/story/life/people/2014/07/08/george-clooney-daily-mail-exclusive-statement-response/12368061/. Accessed 29 October 2019.

Daily Mail Reporter. 2009. Peter Andre's despair as shameless Katie Price cavorts around Spanish resort with cage-fighter boyfriend. *MailOnline*, August 5. https://www.dailymail.co.uk/tvshowbiz/article-1204374/Katie-Price-cavorts-topless-cage-fighter-boyfriend.html#comments. Accessed 7 November 2019.

Duncan, Pamela, and Polly Bindman. 2020. Meghan gets twice as many negative headlines as positive, analysis finds. *Guardian Online*, January 18. https://www.theguardian.com/global/2020/jan/18/meghan-gets-more-than-twice-as-many-negative-headlines-as-positive. Accessed 19 January 2020.

Freedman, Des. 2015. Was it 'the Sun wot won it'? Lessons from the 1995 and 2015 elections. *OpenDemocracy.net*, May 12. https://www.opendemocracy.net/en/opendemocracyuk/was-it-sun-wot-won-it-press-influence-in-1992-and-2015-elections/. Accessed 15 November 2019.

Gaber, Ivor. 2018. 'Corbyn the Commie' smear is all about tabloid press fear of regulation. *Theconversation.com*, February 23. https://theconversation.com/corbyn-the-commie-smear-is-all-about-tabloid-press-fear-of-regulation-92301. Accessed 15 November 2019.

Gaber, Ivor. 2019. What goes around comes around. In *Culture Wars*, ed. James Curran, Ivor Graber and Julian Petley, positions 7019–7418, Kindle edition. Abingdon, Oxon and New York: Routledge.

Gibb, Jessica. 2019. Feral Family. Skint Katie Price dresses in Louis Vuitton and Gucci while her daughter Bunny goes barefoot as they walk the dog. *Sun Online*, November 4. https://www.thesun.co.uk/tvandshowbiz/10277971/katie-price-designer-clothes-bankrupt-bunny-barefoot/. Accessed 11 November 2019.

Gordon, Amie. 2019. Katie Price is banned from driving for two years after refusing to tell police who was behind the wheel when her pink Range Rover was in crash last year. *MailOnline*, October 10. https://www.dailymail.co.uk/news/article-7558813/Katie-Price-BANNED-driving-two-years.html#comments. Accessed 9 November 2019.

Graham, Caroline. 1998. Zip me up before you go go. *Sun*, April 9.

Hansen, James. 2019. Diane Abbott's Tube Tinny inspires Londoners to Drink (M&S) Mojitos. *London.eater.com*, April 24. https://london.eater.com/2019/4/24/18512416/diane-abbott-mojito-can-marks-spencer-labour-mp. Accessed 14 November 2019.

Levine, Nick. 2019. The best Twitter responses to Diane Abbott's already Legendary Tube Mojito. *Refinery29.com*, April 20. https://www.refinery29.com/en-gb/2019/04/230429/diane-abbott-mojito-apologies-tweets. Accessed 14 November 2019.

Levy, Geoffrey. 2013. The man who hated Britain: Red Ed's pledge to bring back socialism is a homage to his Marxist father. So what did Miliband Snr really believe in? The answer should disturb anyone who loves this country. *MailOnline*, September 27. https://www.dailymail.co.uk/news/article-2435751/Red-Eds-pledge-bring-socialism-homage-Marxist-father-Ralph-Miliband-says-GEOFFREY-LEVY.html. Accessed 15 November 2019.

Long, Jonny. 2019. 'I'm sorry, Diane'—We spoke to the guy who photographed MP Abbott's Train Tinny. *Vice.com*, April 30. https://www.vice.com/en_uk/article/9kxbye/im-sorry-diane-regret-of-the-guy-who-photographed-mp-abbots-train-tinny. Accessed 14 November 2019.

Moir, Jan. 2012. Where's the magic in this tale of middle-class monsters? First review of J.K. Rowling's very grown-up book. *MailOnline*, September 30. https://www.dailymail.co.uk/debate/article-2209165/J-K-Rowlings-The-Casual-Vacancy-review-Wheres-magic-tale-middle-class-monsters.html. Accessed 28 October 2019.

Moir, Jan. 2015. Nasty nimby toffs and typical Tory-bashing from the Beeb. *MailOnline*, February 16. https://www.dailymail.co.uk/debate/article-2954947/Nasty-nimby-toffs-typical-Tory-bashing-Beeb-JAN-MOIR-reviews-Casual-Vacancy.html. Accessed 28 October 2019.

Moodie, Clemmie. 2009. Katie Price branded a "despicable mother" by Peter Andre. *Mirror Online*, August 15. https://www.mirror.co.uk/3am/celebrity-news/katie-price-branded-a-despicable-mother-412690. Accessed 8 November 2019.

Nicks, Gary. 2005. Disrespectful, treacherous & bloody funny… that's the Daily Star. *Daily Star*, February 12.

PA Mediapoint. 2019. Sun fails in bid to halt Johnny Depp libel action over 'wife-beater' claim. *Pressgazette.co.uk*, 1 March. https://www.pressgazette.co.uk/sun-fails-in-bid-to-halt-johnny-depp-libel-action-over-wife-beater-claim/. Accessed 28 October 2019.

Parsons, Tony. 2016. Pop legend George Michael's 'voice poured out of every radio… but he'd never felt lower' as troubled star 'faced adulation and anguish' in his rise to fame. *Sun Online*, December 27. https://www.thesun.co.uk/news/2482187/george-michael-tribute-sun-writers-tony-parsons/. Accessed 9 January 2020.

Pollard, Chris, Tom Wells, and Chloe Kerr. 2019. Cocktail Party. Labour's Diane Abbott breaks the law by swigging a can of mojito on the train home. *Sun Online*, April 19. https://www.thesun.co.uk/news/8901060/labour-diane-abbott-drinking-on-train-illegal/. Accessed 14 November 2019.

Randell, Louise. 2019. Katie Price flashes her boobs in the street and risks another run-in with the law. *Mirror Online*, November 1. https://www.mirror.co.uk/3am/celebrity-news/katie-price-flashes-boobs-street-20790427. Accessed 10 November 2019.

Ryan, Jake. 2018. Corbyn and the Commie Spy. Jeremy Corbyn met a Communist spy during the Cold War and 'briefed' evil regime of clampdown by British intelligence. *Sun Online*, February 14. https://www.thesun.co.uk/news/5581166/jeremy-corbyn-communist-spy-cold-war-briefings/. Accessed 15 November 2019.

Thorne, Tony. 2014. *Dictionary of Contemporary Slang*. London: Bloomsbury.

Wheatley, Gemma. 2009. Jordan's foul rant at Star girl. *Daily Star*, August 7.

Wooton, Dan. 2018. Gone potty. How can JK Rowling be 'genuinely happy' casting Johnny Depp in the new Fantastic Beasts film after assault claim? *Sun Online*, June 12. https://www.thesun.co.uk/tvandshowbiz/6159182/jk-rowling-genuinely-happy-johnny-depp-fantastic-beasts/. Accessed 28 October 2019.

Yahr, Emily. 2014. George Clooney proves why shaming the tabloids is more effective than suing them. *The Washington Post*, July 9. https://www.washingtonpost.com/news/arts-and-entertainment/wp/2014/07/09/george-clooney-proves-why-shaming-the-tabloids-is-more-effective-than-suing-them/. Accessed 29 October 2019.

Younge, Gary. 2019. The Tories can't win without the press. This isn't how democracy works. *Guardian Online*, November 15. https://www.theguardian.com/commentisfree/2019/nov/15/tories-rightwing-press#comment-135488410. Accessed 26 November 2019.

# 9

# 'Bonkers Bruno Locked Up' and 'Under the Carapace of Glittering, Hedonistic Celebrity': When the Tabloids Misread the Public Mood

The tabloids like to think that they are in tune with the beliefs, values and aspirations of ordinary men and women, unlike the chattering classes, showbiz luvvies and far too many politicians. At fairly regular intervals, however, a paper will totally misread the public mood, and not just about something as trivial as drinking a can of mojito on a Transport for London train.

During the phone-hacking trial at the Old Bailey, Rebekah Brooks admitted that during her time as a tabloid editor she had made many mistakes, one of the worst of which was to authorise a front-page splash in the *Sun* on 23 September 2003. The story concerned the former heavyweight boxer and popular TV personality, Frank Bruno, who had been admitted to a psychiatric hospital under a section of the Mental Health Act. The headline 'Bonkers Bruno Locked Up' sparked an immediate public outcry and a string of protests from mental health charities, which convinced the editor, who was still called Rebekah Wade, to switch the headline in later editions to 'Sad Bruno in Mental Home'. She explained that the original headline only appeared in 15,000 of the four million copies distributed that day but confessed that she had made 'a terrible mistake' (Press Association 2014).

Quite simply, the *Sun* had failed to grasp that in 2003 mental illness did not carry the stigma that it once had, sufferers were no longer hidden from view in asylums, often shunned by their own families, and that a large section of the public had ceased to be amused by jokes about people who are nuts, loony, screwy, bonkers, cuckoo or, worse still, psycho or schizo. Frank Bruno was not 'bonkers' but had suffered a mental breakdown, a condition than an enormous number of families in twenty-first-century Britain know something about. He had been admitted to hospital, not 'locked up', but the original headline implies that a powerful man who twice fought Mike Tyson had been taken into custody because he represented a danger to the public. The second headline is less tasteless but as Raj Persaud (2014), a consultant psychiatrist, noted in the *British Medical Journal*: '[…] it was still sobering to mental health professionals that Goodmayes Psychiatric Hospital, the institution to which Bruno was admitted, should be referred to as a "mental home" *after* the *Sun* had thought long and hard about trying not to offend' (original italics). The term *home* implies an institution that people are unlikely to leave, such as an old people's home or care home, while a hospital aims to cure people and send them back into the world as soon as possible.

Although the *Sun* rarely does self-criticism or apologies, fallout from the ill-informed and insensitive depiction of Bruno's illness was so toxic that attempts to make amends were immediate. The next day a tactic examined in Chapter 6 was employed with the launch of the *Fund for Frank* to raise money to help people with mental health problems, and Wade got things started with a donation of £10,000. In addition, the charity SANE (Schizophrenia a National Emergency) was granted 500 words to inform *Sun* readers about mental illnesses and treatments. The quest for redemption continued over the following weeks; indeed, an article by Ian Cook (2003) detailing subsequent developments has become a document for academic study downloadable from the website of the Open University (and is no longer available on the BBC's site, where it was originally published). Cook reports that a few days after the launch of the *Fund for Frank* Rebekah Wade invited Marjorie Wallace, chief executive of SANE, to meet her for lunch to discuss language that was acceptable and unacceptable to describe the mentally ill. Wallace did not merely offer informal advice but proposed a comprehensive style guide for the *Sun*'s reporters. Furthermore, the newspaper's health editor signed up for a 72-hour mental health training course organised by SANE, and Wade herself was expected to attend at least part of it.

The punctuation of the headline to Cook's article—'The Sun: no longer bonkers?'—indicates a certain scepticism regarding the *Sun*'s commitment to using more politically correct language. That scepticism is made explicit in his penultimate paragraph: 'The habits of a lifetime may, however, prove hard to break. *The Sun* has won Mind's *Bigot of the Year* award more often than any other paper. And the Frank Bruno story was hardly a one-off'.

In February 2008, the former footballer Paul Gascoigne—whose nickname, Gazza, was invariably used by the tabloids—was sectioned under the Mental Health Act after the management of the hotel he was staying at alerted the police to their famous guest's disturbing behaviour. Kevin Mitchell (2008) for the *Guardian* identified parallels between the cases of two immensely popular sporting heroes, Bruno and Gascoigne, and also between the *Sun*'s reporting of the two men's mental health problems. Nearly five years after the Bonkers Bruno controversy, and despite the style guide supplied by SANE, the *Sun*'s headline to its report of the ex-footballer's crisis was '"Mad" Gazza on Suicide Watch'. The expression *suicide watch* is not used by medical staff working in the field of mental health (*close observation* is the less sensational but more precise wording), while the placing of the word *mad* between inverted commas was explained in the report of what triggered the hotel's decision to contact the police: 'Coke-crazed ace Paul Gascoigne stunned hotel staff before being sent to a psychiatric unit by answering his door in the buff – with "MAD" scrawled on his forehead'. The word *mad* was a quotation, so the *Sun* could argue that it was all right to use it in the headline, although it is less clear how the embarrassing details of Gascoigne's breakdown were something the public had a right or a need to know.

It was no doubt a simple matter to persuade poorly paid hotel staff to talk of what they had seen. It is difficult, and not entirely desirable, to try to stop chequebook journalism. Between 2011 and 2015, Operation Elvedon saw thirty *Sun* and *News of the World* journalists prosecuted for having offered cash for information to public officials, but after investigations costing £30 million only one was convicted. Keiligh Baker (2015) for *MailOnline*, and indeed her readers who posted comments, felt that a great deal of money had been wasted on prosecuting people who had merely been doing their job of raking through the muck.

The second quotation in the chapter title is taken from the concluding paragraph of an article by the *Daily Mail* columnist Jan Moir (2009a) about the singer Stephen Gately of the pop group Byzone, who had died suddenly at the age of 33 at the apartment in Mallorca he shared with his male partner. No apologies for turning to Jan Moir a fourth time having previously investigated her insightful views on feminism, environmental activists and J.K. Rowling's depiction of council tenants as human beings; she just seems to have a peculiar gift for outraging great numbers of people. Her column on Stephen Gately prompted 25,000 people to report her to the Press Complaints Commission and her views, or prejudices, were attacked on social media and severely criticised by commentators in other newspapers. The first accusation was that of having written 'a gratuitous piece of gay-bashing' (Brooker 2009) since she linked the singer's premature death to his homosexuality. To the chagrin of his many female fans, Gately had gone public about being gay in 1999 (in part because he knew the *Sun* was planning to out him), and in 2006 entered into a civil union with his partner, Andrew Cowles. On 10 October 2009, the couple returned to their apartment after a night out clubbing, Gately went to sleep on the sofa, and never woke up. To Moir the circumstances of the singer's death were 'more than a little sleazy', a judgement reached because there was a third man in the apartment on the day Gately failed to wake up. When heterosexual couples join dating sites for swingers to meet singles or other couples, the tabloids tend to refer to their activities with lexemes suggesting fun and naughty games: *frolics, erotic, libidinous, kinky, sensual, adventurous* and the like, plus the usual *romps* and *bonking*. For Moir, the fact that Cowles and Gately had brought someone home—for what purpose was, quite rightly, not specified in most reports—merits the adjective *sleazy*, which suggests something that is decidedly unpleasant, immoral and possibly dishonest, and certainly an activity that respectable people are constrained to condemn.

That was not the worst of it, however: the real sadness of Gately's sudden death, according to Moir, was that 'it strikes another blow to the happy-ever-after myth of civil partnerships'. Conventional marriages between a man and a woman are seldom, if ever, happy-ever-after experiences, and there is no reason to suggest that this fairy-tale expression is any more of a myth with regard to same-sex marriages. More egregiously deceptive is the use of the adjective *another*, which establishes the presupposition that there have been previous, perhaps many previous, blows to the institution of civil partnerships. She provides no statistical evidence to demonstrate that same-sex unions are more likely to end badly than traditional male-female marriages other than to cite a single parallel incident of a partner in a civil union dying prematurely.

The second accusation against her is that of breathtaking presumptuousness as she pursues her thesis that Gately's demise was linked to his debauched, drug-abusing lifestyle despite a post-mortem that revealed that the cause of death was a congenital heart defect and a toxicology report that showed that drugs were not a factor. Undeterred by her lack of medical training, she casts doubts upon the findings of a qualified pathologist, stating that official investigations had, in effect, done nothing more than rule out murder as the cause of death (although she does not indicate what might have triggered acute pulmonary oedema if not the Gately family's hereditary heart condition). She concludes with a literary flourish preceded by a second expression that suggests that the singer's death is a familiar story for young men who have, or had, a similar lifestyle: '[…] once again, under the carapace of glittering, hedonistic celebrity, the ooze of a very different and more dangerous lifestyle has seeped out for all to see'.

Jan Moir had clearly misjudged the mood of the nation concerning homosexuality and same-sex civil unions, and her insistence that Stephen Gately's death must have been linked to the immorality of how he had lived was deeply offensive to the singer's family and friends. The timing was also extraordinarily insensitive given that the column was published the day before Gately's funeral. After concluding its investigations, the Press Complaints Commission decided that the article was 'extremely distasteful' but 'just failed to cross the line' (BBC News, 18 February 2010) leading to disciplinary action. As we saw with the issue of race relations legislation examined in Chapter 3, tabloid journalists are generally adept at getting very close to the mark but not quite overstepping it.

The following week Jan Moir (2009b) used her column to apologise to Gately's family for the timing of her comments but strongly denied that she was homophobic or disapproved of civil partnerships. However, she defended her use of the word *sleazy*; indeed, she renewed her suspicions that drugs may have been involved and insisted that reports that there was another man in the bedroom with Gately's partner while the pop star himself slept on the sofa suggested '[…] a louche lifestyle; one that raised questions about health and personal safety'. She also felt that there had been 'a hysterical overreaction' to her earlier column.

Those of us old enough to remember when jokes about nutcases and poofters were part of many stand-up comics' repertoire can appreciate the change in attitudes that has occurred over the last fifty years. Another category of people who were once derided is that of the chronically overweight, but here too things are changing and the prime reason is mathematical. When obese people were a small minority of the population they were figures of fun, or contempt, or sometimes both, but in the last two or three decades there has been a sharp increase in the percentage of seriously overweight adults and children in the population, and as obesity has become more 'normal', perceptions of the condition have started to change. That is not to say that the popular media have ceased to poke fun at fatties or wag an admonishing finger at couch potatoes and junk food addicts, but there is also the realisation that our society has a health crisis on its hands and many, often very young lives are being ruined by disabling overweight.

One person who has not yet assumed a more compassionate approach towards the obese is Katie Hopkins, who stops short of using a metaphor comparable with cockroaches but is proud to be known as a fat-shamer. In her view, overweight adults are simply too lazy to take enough exercise and lack the willpower to ditch their fat- and sugar-rich diets, while feckless parents who allow their children to become dangerously fat are complicit in the ruined health of their own offspring. Not even the case of the youngest Briton to die of morbid obesity, 20-year-old and 40-stone (254 kg) Samantha Packham, softened her condemnatory attitude: 'I met her parents and challenged them on their care for their daughter. They allowed her to take taxis to get more food. I believe they fed their daughter to death – a view they would undoubtedly reject' (Hopkins 2015).

When one is aching with grief, Katie Hopkins is not the most comforting person to have at one's side. However, it must also be said that she conducted an interesting experiment to demonstrate that losing weight is really not that difficult at all. First she put herself on a high-calorie diet in order to gain three stone (19 kg), then she reverted to her usual eating habits to slim down again: 'My point was to prove what I've always told fat people – just eat less, move more, and those repulsive rolls of blubber will go away' (Hopkins 2016).

Hopkins insists that chronically overweight people not only ruin their own lives but also represent an unsustainable burden for the National Health Service, a point taken up by Henry Holloway (2018) for the *Daily Star* in the story of Matthew Crawford, a young man weighing 55 stone (349 kg) said to have cost the NHS £250,000 since being admitted to a hospital in Nottinghamshire six months earlier. Crawford is accused of 'bed-blocking' (in his case, of blocking the four beds required to support his exceptional bulk) since he is 'medically fit to be discharged into social care'. The article depends heavily upon the testimonies of unnamed 'sources' and 'insiders', while the passive voice in constructions involving the verb *claim* is frequently used. Perhaps the least credible thing claimed about him is that from his four-bed suite he orders pizzas to supplement the food the hospital gives him; an NHS hospital would surely turn away a pizza delivery ordered by any patient, never mind a patient disabled by obesity. In addition to the absence of named sources, another feature to make readers question the reliability of this report is the clear evidence of a cut-and-paste approach given that the three photos of Matthew Crawford are taken from his own Facebook account. Holloway gives the impression that Crawford is living quite comfortably thank you courtesy of UK taxpayers but there is no evidence that the reporter has ever met the subject of his article. Had he done so he might have discovered that a 33-year-old immobilised by his own body weight actually has a pretty wretched existence.

There is no shortage of studies linking unhealthy diets and obesity with low incomes. On the question of childhood obesity, Public Health England (www.gov.uk 2017) notes that 'prevalence in the most deprived 10% of children is approximately twice that of the least deprived 10%', while 'there are more fast food outlets in deprived areas than in more affluent areas'. For adults working long hours in a soul-destroying job for low wages the notion of shopping for high-quality ingredients and cooking healthy meals is something for which they have neither time nor money. When the journalist James Bloodworth went undercover to work in an Amazon warehouse, he and his mostly East European colleagues would have given short shrift to anyone who had attempted to chide them for buying a burger and chips instead of preparing a ratatouille (2018: 52): 'Regularity of dietary habit is simply incompatible with irregularity of work and income. As far as we were concerned the 'foodies' – those who appear on television to fetishise the over-intricacy of food made with expensive ingredients – could go to hell'. Cheap, high-fat fast food had a measurable impact on his health. Although his work in the warehouse involved walking an average of ten miles each shift, he gained a stone (6.35 kg) in weight (ibid.: 70).

In 2019, the outgoing Chief Medical Officer, Dame Sally Davies, proposed the following measures to combat the epidemic of obesity: a ban on the consumption of food and drink on public transport, plain packaging for biscuits and other sugar-rich products, the extension of sugar tax to milkshakes and coffees, an end to the marketing and sale of junk food at sporting events and concerts, new taxes on fast food and limits on the size of restaurant and takeaway meals. For Tanya Gold (2019) in the *Sun* Dame Sally, who had just become Master of Trinity College, Cambridge, clearly had no understanding of how millions of people live on low incomes. Two of the proposals—increased tax on fast food and a ban on eating on public transport—are seen as attacks on the poor and prompt Gold to ask two rhetorical questions about the former Chief Medical Officer: 'Who is she to place cheap food beyond people's reach with tax rises? [...] Who is she to tell a low-waged person working miles from home, who has possibly worked a 12-hour day, they cannot eat chips on the bus?' Although Gold does not absolve irresponsible parents who allow their children to stuff themselves with sweets, she understands perfectly why so many tired, demoralised and poorly paid people go to McDonald's, where the food is unhealthy but, crucially, is also cheap. The change in attitudes towards the chronically overweight consists in the acceptance of two facts about obesity: it is a medical crisis that often—though certainly not always—has economic causes, and it is a condition that blights and ultimately shortens lives, particularly the lives of the most disadvantaged members of society. The tabloids continue to mock individual celebrities who have put on a lot of weight, but since they like to see themselves as the voice of ordinary men and women, they are nowadays wary of making condescending or snide comments about the millions of dangerously fat Britons.

Where minorities are concerned, it is very much the case that familiarity breeds understanding and solidarity. Contempt, on the other hand, thrives on lack of familiarity. In 1968, when trade unionists marched to express their support for Enoch Powell, millions of white Britons had never exchanged two words with a Caribbean or Asian person. Half a century later most white city-dwellers have Black and Asian workmates and/or friends, classes in state schools are multiethnic, the casts of TV soaps more accurately reflect demographic reality, young Londoners speak Multicultural London English rather than Cockney, mixed-race couples raise no eyebrows and the tabloids believe black footballers are right to walk off the field if they are racially abused by spectators. Frankly, it is difficult to disparage an ethnic group if you work alongside, drink with or make love to someone from that community, and popular newspapers know that.

The first openly homosexual entertainers—such as the actor John Inman and the comedian Larry Grayson—played on their campness to raise a laugh, but they were groundbreakers who helped change perceptions of gay people. Over the decades, increased familiarity generated acceptance until *MailOnline* used the expression 'vile homophobic abuse' to refer to a woman's vulgar upbraiding of a homosexual couple guilty of kissing at a bus stop (Ardehali 2019).

The deinstitutionalisation of mental health services began in the 1960s, accelerated in the 1970s, and the switch to community-based solutions has made the mentally ill much more visible, and once again greater familiarity has bred understanding. Few families do not have someone who is subject to bouts of depression, or has suffered from PTSD, or has anxiety attacks, and with the removal of the stigma associated with mental illness no tabloid is likely to repeat the *Sun*'s Bonkers Bruno mistake.

The obese are still a minority, albeit a rapidly growing (in every sense) minority, and precisely because they are now so numerous, tabloid writers (Katie Hopkins excepted) tend not to be excessively judgemental, although as we see in the *Star*'s depiction of the unfortunate Matthew Crawford, individual cases may still be treated in a rather more sanctimonious manner. At the societal level, widespread obesity and the related issue of diabetes is now recognised as a very serious problem, although to announce an otherwise sensible and factually accurate article on the doubling of obesity levels in England over the last twenty years, the *Sun* still cannot resist using a punning headline that does not rank among its best: 'The Achocalypse' (Woller 2019).

# References

Ardehali, Rod. 2019. Shocking moment a mother hurled vile homophobic abuse at gay couple who were kissing at a London bus stop and told them to only show affection 'behind closed doors'. *MailOnline*, October 21. https://www.dailymail.co.uk/news/article-7596843/Shocking-moment-mother-hurled-vile-homophobic-abuse-gay-couple.html. Accessed 2 December 2019.

Baker, Keiligh. 2015. Last Sun journalists prosecuted for cash-for-stories probe are cleared: Lawyer slams 'monumental error of judgment' as four-year ordeal draws to a close. *MailOnline*, October 15. https://www.dailymail.co.uk/news/article-3274079/Sun-journalists-cleared-following-cash-stories-probe.html. Accessed 24 November 2019.

BBC News. 2010. Stephen Gately PCC complaint rejected. *BBC Online*, February 18. http://news.bbc.co.uk/2/hi/entertainment/8521105.stm. Accessed 28 November 2019.

Bloodworth, James. 2018. *Hired: Six Months Undercover in Low-Wage Britain*. London: Atlantic Books.

Brooker, Charlie. 2009. Why there was nothing 'human' about Jan Moir's column on the death of Stephen Gately. *Guardian Online*, October 16. https://www.theguardian.com/commentisfree/2009/oct/16/stephen-gately-jan-moir. Accessed 26 November 2019.

Cook, Ian. 2003. The Sun: No longer bonkers? *The Open University* (open.ac.uk).

Gold, Tanya. 2019. Raising taxes on fast food and banning eating on public transport is bullying the poor. *Sun Online*, October 11. https://www.thesun.co.uk/news/10110778/fast-food-eating-public-bullying-poor/. Accessed 1 December 2019.

Holloway, Henry. 2018. Obese lad weighing 55 STONE taking up four NHS beds 'costs taxpayers £250,000 in six months'. *Daily Star Online*, November 17. https://www.dailystar.co.uk/news/latest-news/obese-nhs-hospital-matthew-crawford-16819120. Accessed 30 November 2019.

Hopkins, Katie. 2015. This Christmas give a fat person you know the greatest gift of all—some brutal honesty! *MailOnline*, December 17. https://www.dailymail.co.uk/debate/article-3364239/KATIE-HOPKINS-Christmas-fat-person-know-greatest-gift-brutal-honesty.html. Accessed 30 November 2019.

Hopkins, Katie. 2016. Katie Hopkins changed our lives. *Sun Online*, April 5. https://www.thesun.co.uk/archives/news/212761/katie-hopkins-changed-our-lives/. Accessed 30 November 2019.

Mitchell, Kevin. 2008. Fears for Gazza as he faces up to Frank truth. *Guardian Online*, February 24. https://www.theguardian.com/sport/blog/2008/feb/23/fearsforgazzaashefacesup. Accessed 24 November 2019.

Moir, Jan. 2009a. A strange, lonely and troubling death…. *MailOnline*, November 16. https://www.dailymail.co.uk/debate/article-1220756/A-strange-lonely-troubling-death–.html. Accessed 28 November 2019.

Moir, Jan. 2009b. The truth about my views on the tragic death of Stephen Gately. *MailOnline*, November 16. https://www.dailymail.co.uk/debate/article-1222246/The-truth-views-tragic-death-Stephen-Gately.html. Accessed 28 November 2019.

Persaud, Raj. 2014. Knocking Bruno when he is down. *British Medical Journal* 327 (7418): 816, October 4. https://www.ncbi.nlm.nih.gov/pmc/articles/PMC214144/ (Accessed 23 November 2019).

Press Association. 2014. Rebekah admits 'terrible mistake' over Bonkers Bruno locked up headline, court told. *PressGazette*, February 27. https://www.pressgazette.co.uk/rebekah-admits-terrible-mistake-over-bonkers-bruno-locked-headline-court-told. Accessed 23 November 2019.

Public Health England. 2017. Health matters: Obesity and the food environment. *www.gov.uk*, March 31. https://www.gov.uk/government/publications/health-matters-obesity-and-the-food-environment/health-matters-obesity-and-the-food-environment–2. Accessed 30 November 2019.

Wooller, Shaun. 2019. The Achocalypse: Fears of diabetes epidemic as obesity levels in England almost double to 13 million in 20 years. *Sun Online*, November 14. https://www.thesun.co.uk/news/10342497/diabetes-obesity-epidemic-england/. Accessed 2 December 2019.

# 10

# 'Parents' Car Hid a Corpse' and 'Terror as Plane Hits Ash Cloud': Lies and Distortions in the Tabloids

The Introduction to this book concluded with Oscar Wilde's observation, 'The truth is rarely pure, and never simple'. Usually, it is not an unadulterated entity with clearly defined contours but a messy skein of tangled threads perforated by crannies and boreholes. As a consequence, there is great potential for judicious selection, exaggeration or minimisation, sensationalisation and distortion—that is, of employing all the techniques of tabloiding the truth—but in most cases some element of veracity remains. Even the infamous *Sun* headline 'Freddie Starr Ate My Hamster' was not entirely invented. The article began: 'ZANY comic Freddie Starr put a live hamster in a sandwich and ATE it, model girl Lea La Salle claimed yesterday' (Saxty 1986). La Salle is quoted saying that she was 'sickened and horrified' while the comedian 'thought it was hilarious' and 'fell about laughing'.

For years neither Starr nor his manager denied the incident, which was unsurprising given that a gesture of that nature was entirely in keeping with the image the comic cultivated as an uncontrollable madcap figure who boosted a chat show's ratings but represented an enormous risk for chat show hosts. Given the *Sun*'s reputation, most people assumed that the story was made up to provide a front-page splash on a day when there was nothing more newsworthy to prioritise. However, following

Starr's death in 2019 the *Sun* and Lea La Salle came clean about what had really happened. When La Salle refused to make Starr a sandwich, he did indeed butter two slices of bread, place her hamster between them and open his mouth as if to take a bite of rodent sarnie. Where Dick Saxty's article diverged from the truth was in the claim that Starr went on to devour the unfortunate hamster. In reality, he sank his teeth into the bread but not the animal, and La Salle was upset 'because the hamster was covered in butter, which took two days for it to lick off' (Sun Reporter 2019). That the comic had made himself a hamster sandwich was true, that he had actually eaten it was false and actionable, but there was never any danger that Saxty and his editor would be sued.

Not all victims of the *Sun*'s lying can grin and elect to do nothing. The worst disaster in the history of British sport occurred at a football match at the Hillsborough Stadium in Sheffield on 15 April 1989, and 23 years later the *Sun* admitted that its front-page splash four days after the horrific event was 'without doubt the blackest day in this newspaper's history' (*Sun Online* 2012, updated 2016). The official apology also acknowledged that '[t]he people of Liverpool may never forgive us for the injustice we did them'. The long and disturbing history of the Hillsborough disaster and subsequent investigations and court cases is well documented; the essential facts are that 96 Liverpool fans were crushed to death and many others injured owing to errors committed by South Yorkshire Police who, to cover up their incompetence, fed false information to the media shifting the blame onto the fans themselves by claiming that it was their own drunken, loutish behaviour that led to the tragedy. The *Sun*'s editor at the time, Kelvin MacKenzie, had no time to waste on verifying the accuracy of the information he had received, and on 19 April opted for the egregiously false headline 'THE TRUTH' for an article by Harry Arnold (1989) on accusations against the Liverpool supporters that had not been substantiated by sources other than South Yorkshire Police. Chippindale and Horrie (2013: position 4960) report that Arnold tried to impress upon his editor the need to handle carefully what were mere allegations, not verified facts. MacKenzie patiently listened to the reporter's misgivings, then decided to follow his headline with three subheadings: '•Some fans picked pockets of victims •Some fans urinated on the brave cops •Some fans beat up PC giving kiss of life'. Apparently, he believed that using the expression 'some fans' exculpated the Currant Bun from charges of smearing all Liverpool fans and justified the publication of atrocious and entirely unproven accusations against 'some'.

Fans of the city's other team, Everton, and Liverpudlians who were not remotely interested in football joined Liverpool fans in boycotting the *Sun*. Newsagents were contractually bound to display the paper but nobody bought it. It was not a short-lived protest and neither was it restricted to the half a million inhabitants of Liverpool since the boycott was also supported in surrounding towns. When a second inquest in 2016 ruled that the 96 victims had been unlawfully killed and that the police had been guilty of gross negligence (while the fans were entirely exonerated), the city's local newspaper, *The Liverpool Echo*, reported that Liverpool F.C. had decided to ban *Sun* journalists from the club's Anfield Road stadium and to deny them access to interview players and staff (Kay 2017, updated 2019). At the time of writing, thirty years after the tragedy, Merseyside remains a no-go area for the *Sun* and its sports reporters can only watch the European club champions on television.

The tabloids like news stories that allow their readers to take sides and apportion blame to one party or another, and that was certainly the case with regard to the 'Parents' car hid a corpse' quote in the title of this chapter. The parents in question were Kate and Gerry McCann and for many readers of the *Express* and the *Star* the corpse that had been hidden in their car was that of their daughter, Madeleine. People resident in the UK will remember the story of little Madeleine McCann's mysterious disappearance because over the last twelve years claims that her whereabouts have been discovered have periodically made the news, only to be quickly dismissed as unreliable or worse. The McCanns were on holiday with Madeleine, who was nearly four years old, and their two-year-old twins at Praia da Luz in the Algarve region of Portugal. On the evening of 3 May 2007, the parents left their three children sleeping in their holiday apartment and went to a nearby restaurant to have dinner with seven British friends. At frequent intervals during the meal, one of the party went back to the apartment to check that the children were all right. At about 22.00, Kate McCann found the twins sleeping soundly but Madeleine was missing. The Portuguese police immediately suspected that the parents (both doctors) had accidentally killed their daughter by giving her an overdose of sedatives and had then disposed of the body in some way. The McCanns vigorously denied that they had done anything of the kind and protested that the police were not doing enough to find Madeleine since they had jumped to the conclusion that she was dead. In September 2007, Gerry and Kate McCann were given *arguido* (suspect) status and the debate began in earnest. Were they living the nightmare of not knowing what had happened to their little girl while the police were not making much effort to find her? Or were they callous and calculating individuals who had sedated their children so that they could have a good time with their friends, and then had invented a tale of abduction as a cover-up?

All the tabloids devoted considerable attention to the disappearance of the pretty little blonde girl and the McCanns acknowledged the importance of the popular press in keeping the story, and particularly the photo of Madeleine, in the public eye. However, as the weeks passed the child's parents found the way things were reported in the *Express* and the *Star* increasingly hurtful. Both papers fluctuated between sympathy for the McCanns and uncritical promotion of the version promulgated by the Portuguese police and media. They were, of course, encouraging readers on both sides, those who empathised with Madeleine's parents and those who believed they had killed their daughter. Even when the police officer investigating Madeleine's disappearance was discredited and taken off the case, speculation about Gerry and Kate continued, and in the end they sued both newspapers. How the *Daily Express* and the *Sunday Express* reported the story is considered below, while the *Daily Star*'s relationship with the truth will later be examined with regard to two other stories.

For one hundred consecutive days, from 3 August to 10 November 2007, Madeleine's disappearance was on the front page of the *Express*. The texts investigated below start from 22 September, by which time regular readers were familiar with the Portuguese word *arguido*, could recognise Chief Inspector Gonçalvo Amaral of the *Polícia Judiciária* and had probably begun to envy the journalists David Pilditch and Martin Evans who had been dispatched to sunny Praia da Luz. When the police announced that their inquiries suggested that Madeleine had not been seen by anyone other than her parents in the seven hours before the McCanns met their friends for dinner, the headline in the *Daily Express*—'THE MISSING SEVEN HOURS' (Pilditch and Evans 2007a)—presents this as a fact.

As the story continues on page four, a 'source' is quoted saying that the police 'are very doubtful that Madeleine disappeared when the McCanns were at dinner', and it is implied that something happened to her—an overdose of sleeping pills, for instance—earlier in the day and her parents had already hidden her body when they joined their friends in the evening. This was pure speculation and as Pilditch and Evans note, the hypothesis of seven missing hours was contradicted by 'written records and witnesses' proving that Madeleine had spent the afternoon at the crèche of the Ocean Club holiday resort while her parents played tennis. However, they also betrayed their willingness to give credence to the *Polícia Judiciária*'s version with a reference to 'the afternoon Madeleine disappeared' using the indicative mood of the verb, 'the one characteristically used in factual assertions' (Huddlestone 1984: 78). Since the McCanns and their friends maintained that the little girl was fine until shortly before 22.00 when her mother discovered that she was no longer in their apartment, one might have expected the suggestion that she actually disappeared in the afternoon to be hedged in some way to acknowledge the contentious nature of the claim.

Two days later, there was no more talk of seven missing hours. Instead, the front-page splash focused on the McCanns' seven friends, four of whom were also doctors, who came to be referred to collectively as the 'Tapas Seven' owing to their preference for dining at the same tapas bar each evening. Again relying on unnamed sources, Pilditch and Evans (2007b) reported that the *Polícia Judiciária* now suspected that the McCanns' friends were complicit in the cover-up and therefore risked being declared *arguidos* along with Madeleine's parents. Rather than the text, on the front page it was one of the two photographs that seemed carefully chosen to discredit Kate McCann. She and her husband were practising Catholics, and despite their very limited knowledge of Portuguese, the couple had attended mass in Praia da Luz the previous day. The same photo of Madeleine appeared on page one of the *Express* practically every day during the period investigated, but on Monday 24 September there was also a photograph of her mother with the caption

'SMILING: Kate McCann leaving church yesterday'. The image plus the use of capital letters for emphasis invite readers to focus on the discrepancy between Kate McCann's expression and the grief she was supposed to be suffering, while those who were already convinced that she had killed her daughter were bound to see her going to mass as shameless hypocrisy.

The article continued with a headline that straddled pages four and five: 'Kidnap? We just don't believe it'. That headline is necessarily in quote marks here but it appeared without inverted commas in the newspaper, which misleadingly gave the impression that it was the *Daily Express* that did not believe Madeleine had been kidnapped when, in reality, Pilditch and Evans were still reporting the view of the Portuguese police. More mysterious sources testified to inconsistencies and contradictions in the Tapas Seven's responses to police questioning, and one of the group was suspected of inventing a tale about seeing a man carrying a child wrapped in a blanket on the evening of Madeleine's disappearance. On page four, it was also noted that in an opinion poll more than 60% of respondents thought that the McCanns were in some way involved in the disappearance of their daughter, which was symptomatic of how a child's disappearance was polarising public opinion, generating positions for or against Madeleine's parents based on inadequate information and highly subjective assessments.

On page five, beneath a photo of Gerry and Kate McCann (both smiling!) with their twins walking to church the previous day, a short unsigned piece (Daily Express 2007) bore the headline 'WHEN KATE WAS HOT LIPS HEALY'. Healy was Kate McCann's maiden name and the article was based on unnamed former friends of hers at Dundee University who remembered an undergraduate who partied enthusiastically, enjoyed a drink and was nicknamed after the character of Hot Lips Houlihan in the American comedy series M*A*S*H. Few of us do not cringe when we recall certain things we did as undergraduates, and the disloyalty of former friends is something we all learn to half expect, but that the *Express* had researched Kate McCann's past and come up with something not wholly commendable was particularly mischievous. The juxtaposition of the photo of the respectable Catholic family on their way to church and the recollections of the single woman living for fun at university inevitably generated a measure of diffidence regarding Madeleine's mother. Gerry McCann did not escape criticism, but during the period under investigation it was Kate who was more frequently depicted as unconvincing in her grief.

On the question of smiling, it is not unreasonable to suppose that a couple anguished by the loss of one child would put on a brave face, even smile, for the benefit of the two who remain. Judging from Kate's coat collar and necklace, it is clear that the close-up of her on page one is taken from the family portrait on page five when she was with her twins, who could still make her smile despite everything.

Pilditch and Evans (2007c) were rather more sceptical when the *Polícia Judiciária* suddenly declared that Madeleine had not died of an accidental overdose but instead had fallen and hit her head on a tiled staircase. Their theory was that she had woken up and gone in search of her parents, but had tripped and died 'due to a traumatic shock to the back of the head'. On this occasion, the reporters wrote of 'new smears', quoted one of the Tapas Seven pointing out that such a precise description of the cause of death was plainly absurd in the absence of a body and also cited Sir Richard Branson, who had donated £100,000 to the McCanns' legal costs, as he attacked both the Portuguese press and the police for spreading stories that 'all turned out to be a lot of garbage'. Suddenly, the *Express* was firmly behind Kate and Gerry.

Two days later, their diffidence with regard to the Portuguese police was seen to be justified when Chief Inspector Gonçalvo Amaral was taken off the case, demoted to the rank of inspector and transferred to another town in the Algarve. The primary reason for his abrupt removal was his allegation that Leicestershire Police, who had been liaising with the *Polícia Judiciária*, were protecting the McCanns, but it also emerged that he had been spending insufficient time on investigating Madeleine's disappearance and was known to enjoy leisurely and rather boozy lunches. Furthermore, he was himself an *arguido* under investigation for allegedly concealing evidence regarding three colleagues accused of having extracted a confession through torture. The case concerned a woman who in September 2004 had reported the disappearance of her eight-year-old daughter but had been persuaded to confess that she had killed the child (Pilditch and Evans 2007d).

Five days after Amaral's removal the *Express* appeared to have arrived at the definitive conclusion that the McCanns were entirely innocent and that the *Polícia Judiciária*'s case against them had been full of holes from the beginning. Beneath the headline 'MADELEINE PARENTS IN THE CLEAR' Martin Evans (2007a) wrote: 'The case against Kate and Gerry McCann lay in tatters last night after DNA evidence was found to be inconclusive'. On page nine, he explained that traces of Madeleine's DNA found in the boot of the car her parents had rented twenty-five days after her disappearance could be explained by the fact that her used clothes had been transported in the vehicle. Sniffer dogs had also indicated that a corpse had been placed in the boot but this was explained by the fact that the McCanns had used the car to transport food waste, including meat, to the rubbish tip.

A lot can happen in 24 hours. After announcing that the McCanns were in the clear, Martin Evans (2007b) completely contradicted his article of the previous day with the headline 'DNA PUTS PARENTS IN FRAME' and the insistence of a 'source' representing Forensic Science Service, the laboratory in Birmingham that was analysing the DNA traces, that the evidence was not inconclusive. On the contrary, (s)he stated that '[t]he new material adds to the existing picture that has been built up by police and fills in a few more pieces of the jigsaw'. The doctors McCann were again under suspicion and the *Polícia Judiciária* had suddenly regained credibility. To rub it in, on the same day another article reported that the Portuguese police had stopped looking for Madeleine three months earlier and that the search for her was now entirely in the hands of the private security firm Control Risks Group, which was staffed by former MI5 and MI6 officers and was paid from funds raised by the *Find Madeleine Campaign* (Bonnici 2007). Oscillation of this kind kept both the McCanns-are-guilty and McCanns-are-innocent parties supplied with ammunition and ensured that public interest, or ghoulishness, did not fade.

The 'PARENTS' CAR HID A CORPSE' headline of the chapter title appeared in the *Daily Express* on 17 October to announce the news that bodily fluids found in the boot of the car the McCanns had hired 'could only have come from a corpse' (Pilditch 2007a). Once again a headline was used that should have been in inverted commas since it did not refer to a fact established by the Forensic Science Service laboratory (definitive results were not yet ready), but to what 'a Portuguese police source alleged'. A mere claim was misrepresented as an objective truth but it was also counter-balanced by references to the McCanns' conviction that they were 'being framed by police desperate to close a case they have bungled'. Madeleine's parents had by this stage returned to England, and on the same day the *Express* published a piece in which Kate McCann's parents described the enormous pressure their daughter was under. Her mother quoted Kate giving her own explanation for the treatment she was receiving in the Portuguese and, to a lesser extent, the British media: 'Kate said last night, "If I weighed another two stone, had a bigger bosom and looked more maternal, people would be more sympathetic." [...] She does feel persecuted, not by the general public who have been extremely supportive, but by some sections of the media [...]' (Riches 2007).

If Kate McCann's slim figure counted against her, aspects of her behaviour also attracted suspicion, and once Forensic Science Service declared that nothing had been found that would be acceptable evidence in a court of law, coverage of the case became increasingly gossipy. Hotel and restaurant staff can be useful sources of gossip, and since they are poorly paid it is not difficult to persuade them to talk to the press. On 23 October, the front-page headline in the *Express*—'McCANNS OR A FRIEND MUST BE TO BLAME'—was at least placed inside inverted commas in an article based on the observations of José Batista, the waiter who had served the doctors McCann and the Tapas Seven on the evening of Madeleine's disappearance (Pilditch 2007b). Batista revealed that he had told the police that at the time of Madeleine's disappearance the streets were deserted, so it would have been very difficult for a stranger to observe the McCanns' apartment without attracting suspicion. For this reason, he believed that only the child's parents or one of their friends could have taken her away. He was surprised that neither the McCanns nor their friends elected to use the resort's babysitting service but confirmed that one of the party went to check on the children at frequent intervals. What was damaging to Kate McCann's credibility, however, was his claim that it was always one of the men who went to see that everything was OK, never Kate or any of the other women. The only time Kate went to check was when she discovered that Madeleine was gone: 'It didn't really mean anything at the time, but after all that happened I did begin to think that it was slightly strange. Why had Kate suddenly gone to check on the children that time, when she never had before?' Ex-Chief Inspector Gonçalvo Amaral would doubtless maintain that Kate McCann's anomalous behaviour was only to be expected given that earlier in the day she had killed her daughter and hidden the body, and he would explain her decision to check on the children herself as the first move in the carefully planned cover-up. Those *Express* readers who had always been in the McCanns-are-guilty camp probably interpreted José Batista's recollections as further evidence that there was something decidedly fishy about the abduction claim.

More of José Batista's reflections were published the next day, including the staff's surprise that Gerry McCann played tennis days after Madeleine's disappearance and neither he nor his wife showed a great deal of emotion (Pilditch 2007c). The following day the allegedly unemotional McCanns were interviewed on Spain's Antena 3 channel and the crew had to stop filming four times because Kate kept breaking down into tears. This display of grief did not entirely convince Spanish viewers since a telephone poll immediately after the broadcast found that 70% believed that the McCanns were hiding something: 'Public opinion in Spain appears to be mirroring the shift that occurred in Portugal, where many people have turned against the couple' (Flanagan 2007a).

In the final days of October, the *Express* seemed to become increasingly desperate to keep the story alive despite the absence of anything genuinely newsworthy. A Spanish psychiatrist wrote in a Portuguese newspaper that Kate McCann had a personality disorder, an extraordinary diagnosis given that he had not actually met her, much less examined her. The *Express* focused on Susan Healey's insistence that her daughter was under enormous stress but was not mentally ill (Stote and Flanagan 2007). The next day the *Sunday Express* published an exclusive by the former Deputy Chief Constable of Greater Manchester Police. While admitting that he had been 'horrified by the abject failure of Portuguese detectives to adhere to basic principles of policing', he also felt that the McCanns and their friends were withholding something:

'My gut instinct is that some big secret is probably being covered up' (Stalker 2007). It may be supposed that all experienced detectives sometimes follow lines of inquiry based on their gut instincts but they also know—or should know—that gut instincts are not proof, or even evidence, just as a psychiatrist's impression after watching a televised interview is not a proper diagnosis.

After all the insinuations that the McCanns were in some way involved in their daughter's disappearance and/or death, they then had to deal with allegations that they had misused the vast sums of money raised to help the search for Madeleine. In order to prolong their stay in Praia da Luz for a considerable period after Madeleine's disappearance, Gerry and Kate McCann took unpaid leave from their respective posts as hospital consultant and general practitioner, which obviously created difficulties for them. On 30 October, the front-page splash in the *Express* featured a photo of Gerry McCann carrying his golf clubs (with the caption 'RELAXED: Gerry McCann out on the golf course yesterday'), the headline 'McCANNS USE FUND TO PAY MORTGAGE' and an opening sentence in bold print: 'KATE and Gerry McCann have paid their mortgage with some of the £1million donated to help find Madeleine, it emerged yesterday' (Stote 2007). In addition, we learn that their house is valued at £600,000 and that Gerry McCann is about to return to work, and his salary of £75,000. Both the headline and the initial sentence are ambiguous in that they could be interpreted as stating that the McCanns have dipped into the Find Madeleine Fund to pay *off*, i.e. settle their mortgage rather than just to cover the monthly repayments during the period in which they were earning nothing. The overall impression is of someone fortunate enough to have a salary and a home beyond the dreams of many *Express* readers who enjoys himself on the golf course while funds donated to find his daughter are instead used to extinguish his mortgage.

The story continues on page five with the outraged comments of three unnamed donors and another photo of Gerry McCann playing golf. Only at the end of the article is a director of the Find Madeleine Fund quoted clarifying three points: when the fund was set up an explicit aim was to help the family financially if it became necessary; only the monthly mortgage repayments while the McCanns were not drawing their salaries were paid from the fund; the McCanns had not used money from the fund for any other purpose. Of course, readers who had merely glanced at the front page were left with the impression that Kate and Gerry McCann had misappropriated funds that ordinary men and women had generously donated to assist the search for their daughter.

Back in Praia da Luz more details emerged of the basic errors committed by the Portuguese police on the evening of Madeleine's disappearance, including the failure to release an accurate description of Madeleine, not conducting house-to-house inquiries early enough, not closing the border with Spain and, worst of all, rendering scientific evidence useless by allowing the McCanns' apartment to be contaminated. However, suspicions regarding the McCanns and their friends were renewed when two of the uniformed police officers who responded to the original 112 emergency call spoke (on condition of anonymity) to the *Express* and, while scathing about their superiors responsible for the investigations, described the behaviour of the McCanns and the Tapas Seven as follows: 'They were scared, and not the usual scared. They were jumpy and nervous. [...] it wasn't normal. None of it was normal and hasn't been right the way through' (Flanagan 2007b).

When the McCanns decided to sue the *Daily Express*, the *Daily Star* and their Sunday sister papers it was because of the relentless campaign of innuendo conducted day after day over several months. Although the incompetence of the *Polícia Judiciária* and of Chief Inspector Gonçalvo Amaral in particular was established at an early stage, anonymous police sources were still cited even when there was no hard evidence to support their often bizarre theories as to what happened on the evening of 3 May 2007 (how they could attribute the cause of death to either an overdose or a fall when there was no body to examine remains a mystery). Every time something was published that conveyed some empathy with the McCanns, it was counterbalanced by insinuations regarding Kate's failure to weep, her continued ability to smile in the presence of her twins or her undergraduate days as Hot Lips Healy. Readers were called up to a kind of tabloid-centred jury service as the McCanns-are-guilty v. the McCanns-are-innocent trial was conducted with little consideration of the fact that the McCanns were grief-stricken.

In March 2008, the four newspapers were successfully sued for having published defamatory stories about the McCanns and were ordered to publish apologies on their front pages. On 19 March, one of the front-page headlines in the *Express* was 'Kate and Gerry McCann: Sorry', and in addition to the apology the text included the announcement that '[a]s an expression of its regret the Daily Express has now paid a very substantial sum into the Madeleine Fund and we promise to do all in our power to help efforts to find her' (Daily Express 2008). Four days later, the *Sunday Express* followed suit.

So had a contrite *Daily Express* learnt its lesson and was now resolved never again to turn its front page into a kangaroo court? Not really. Its other front-page headline on the day the apology was published was 'JUDGE SAVAGES FANTASIST HEATHER', the Heather in question being Heather Mills and the judge Mr. Justice Bennett, who the previous day had given his ruling on the divorce settlement between Mills and Paul McCartney (Reynolds 2008). In the preceding weeks, *Express* readers had been invited to take sides in this rancorous separation and divorce, although there was never any doubt as to which of the two would be favoured given that Mills was consistently depicted as a foul-mouthed opportunist while Sir Paul was a national treasure.

The second quotation in the chapter title—'Terror as plane hits ash cloud'—refers to a front-page splash in the *Daily Star*. For six days in April 2010, UK airspace was closed because of an enormous cloud of volcanic ash caused by the eruption of the Eyjafjallajökull volcano in Iceland. This left many thousands of Britons stranded abroad and prompted the government to deploy three Royal Navy warships to repatriate holidaymakers and business travellers from various ports in France and Spain. On 20 April, it was announced that the ash cloud had dispersed sufficiently to allow the re-opening of British airspace the following day, so the *Daily Star* (2010a) helpfully published 'THE BLOW BY BLOW GUIDE TO THE VOLCANO!' plus an editorial comment the title of which was shortly to be seen as ironic: 'Find truth in the ash' (*Daily Star* 2010b). The editorial acknowledged the role of the Royal Navy in helping to get people home and also informed readers that '[…] your ever-caring Daily Star has chartered coaches to start the flow of people back to the UK'. The next day the *Star* showed just how much it cared and demonstrated its somewhat idiosyncratic approach to finding the truth in the ash.

The 'TERROR AS PLANE HITS ASH CLOUD' headline was superimposed upon a photograph of a British Airways 747 with all four engines on fire, along with the subhead 'Dramatic pictures as jets get OK to defy volcano' (Wall 2010). What the *Star* neglected to clarify on the front page was that the 'dramatic pictures' published with the report had nothing whatsoever to do with the Eyjafjallajökull eruption, but were computer-generated images taken from a TV reconstruction of an incident when a BA 747 had indeed flown into an ash cloud, but eighteen years earlier. On another page, it was explained that the pictures related to 'a near disaster' in 1982, but people who did not read beyond the first page naturally assumed that the report was about a full disaster on 21 April 2010 and must have felt decidedly uneasy about having to board a plane that same day.

This misleading and—for people flying that day—deeply distressing front-page splash had an immediate consequence in that Manchester, Gatwick, Leeds-Bradford, Bristol and Liverpool airports responded to travellers' complaints by removing from sale that day's edition of the *Daily Star*. Unlike the boycotting of the *Sun* in Liverpool following the Hillsborough scandal, however, the ban was temporary and brief. Naturally, the incident was reported to the Press Complaints Commission and three months later, on 17 July, a not particularly penitent *Star* published a half-hearted page-2 rectification that made conspicuous use of the epistemic modal verb *may* to acknowledge that the controversial front-page image 'may have wrongly suggested to readers that the photograph depicted a recent event' and to make an unconvincing apology 'for any misunderstanding which may have been caused by the use of the image' (Daily Star 2010c).

Unlike the authors of academic or technical reports, newspaper journalists are permitted to apply a little spin; indeed, their readers expect them to put a certain slant on things and might even be disappointed if they are excessively even-handed. If they overstep the mark and publish plain falsehoods, the victims of their defamation sue them and often receive generous compensation. It should be remembered, however, that not everyone who sues a tabloid does so in good faith. In 1987, the former Deputy Chairman of the Conservative Party and best-selling novelist, Jeffrey Archer, successfully sued the *News of the World* and the *Daily Star* after they had published stories claiming that he had paid a prostitute for sex. Both papers were found guilty of libel and the *Star* was obliged to pay £500,000 in damages. Fourteen years later, it emerged that the two tabloids had told the truth and that Archer had not only lied in court but had also asked others to lie in his support. The day after he was sentenced to four years in jail for perjury and perverting the course of justice, the *Daily Star* dedicated pages 1, 2, 3, 4, 5, 6, 7, 8, 9, 32 and 33 to the tale of hubris followed by nemesis that was Archer's life. Its headline on 20 July 2001 was 'PAY US £2.2M' with the subhead 'NOT A PENNY MORE NOT A PENNY LESS', which was the title of the first of Archer's novels. The *Star*'s legal team acted swiftly: 'A writ for fraud was given a High Court stamp just 69 minutes after Archer headed for the court cells to begin his sentence. We then hammered on the door of his solicitors Mishcon de Reya to serve them the demand for our money' (Paul 2001).

The Archer case serves to remind us that the same papers that sometimes go too far in tabloiding the truth occasionally do the public the immense service of exposing dishonesty, hypocrisy or just plain humbug. Archer had been an MP, was a peer of the realm and was the Conservative candidate for the London mayoral election of 2000 until the *News of the World*'s allegations that he had committed perjury in the 1987 libel case obliged him to withdraw his candidature. After his conviction and imprisonment in 2001, the nation knew that he was manifestly unfit to hold political office, but that truth only emerged because fourteen years earlier two grubby tabloids got wind of his seedier side and decided to publish and be damned. And damned they were, but their subsequent vindication gave them good cause to gloat over the disgrace of a man who lied more outrageously than any tabloid hack would ever do.

# References

Arnold, Harry. 1989. The Truth. *Sun*, April 19.

Bonnici, Tony. 2007. How the hunt was called off three months ago. *Daily Express*, October 9.

Chippindale, Peter, and Chris Horrie. 2013. *Stick It Up Your Punter!* London: Faber and Faber ebook.

Daily Express. 2007. When Kate Was Hot Lips Healy. *Daily Express*, September 24.

Daily Express. 2008. Kate and Gerry McCann: Sorry. *Daily Express*, March 19.

Daily Star. 2010a. The blow by blow guide to the volcano! *Daily Star*, April 20.

Daily Star. 2010b. Find truth in the ash. *Daily Star*, April 21.

Daily Star. 2010c. Terror plane picture. *Daily Star*, July 17.

Evans, Martin. 2007a. Parents in the clear. *Daily Express*, October 8.

Evans, Martin. 2007b. DNA puts parents in frame. *Daily Express*, October 9.

Flanagan, Padraic. 2007a. 70% don't believe McCanns. *Daily Express*, October 26.

Flanagan, Padraic. 2007b. McCanns and friends 'jumpy and nervous'. *Daily Express*, November 6.

Huddlestone, Rod. 1984. *Introduction to the Grammar of English*. Cambridge: Cambridge University Press.

Kay, Dan. 2017/2019. LFC finally bans The S*n: The history of the boycott. *Liverpool Echo Online*. https://www.liverpoolecho.co.uk/news/liverpool-news/lfc-finally-bans-sn-history-12589119. Accessed 8 December 2019.

Paul, David. 2001. Pay us £2.2m. *Daily Star*, July 20.

Pilditch, David. 2007a. Parents' car hid a corpse. *Daily Express*, October 17.

Pilditch, David. 2007b. McCanns or a friend must be to blame. *Daily Express*, October 23.

Pilditch, David. 2007c. Father played tennis after she vanished. *Daily Express*, October 24.

Pilditch, David, and Martin Evans. 2007a. The Missing Seven Hours. *Daily Express*, September 22.

Pilditch, David, and Martin Evans. 2007b. McCanns are lying. *Daily Express*, September 24.

Pilditch, David, and Martin Evans. 2007c. Now police say she fell down the steps. *Daily Express*, October 1.

Pilditch, David, and Martin Evans. 2007d. Madeleine detective kicked off case after blasting British police. *Daily Express*, October 3.

Reynolds, Mark. 2008. Judge Savages Fantasist Heather. *Daily Express*, March 19.

Riches, Chris. 2007. Madeleine's mother: People would show more sympathy if I had a bigger bosom. *Daily Express*, October 17.

Saxty, Dick. 1986. Freddie Star Ate My Hamster. *Sun*, March 13.

Stalker, John. 2007. McCanns 'are hiding a big secret'. *Sunday Express*, October 28.

Stote, Martin. 2007. McCanns used fund to pay mortgage. *Daily Express*, October 30.

Stote, Martin, and Padraic Flanagan. 2007. Be kind to Kate. *Daily Express*, October 27.

Sun Reporter. 2019. Goodnight Starr: Who was comedian Freddie Starr and did the I'm a Celebrity star really eat a hamster? *Sun Online*, May 14. https://www.thesun.co.uk/tvandshowbiz/9042426/freddie-starr-dead-hamster/. Accessed 7 December 2019.

The Sun. 2012/2016. We are sorry for our gravest error. *Sun Online*, April 6. https://www.thesun.co.uk/archives/news/919113/we-are-sorry-for-our-gravest-error/. Accessed 8 December 2019.

Wall, Emma. 2010. Terror as plane hits ash cloud. *Daily Star*, April 21.

# 11

# Conclusions

The Introduction to this volume makes the case that the press of no other country combines in a single format a heady mix of real information and lowbrow entertainment, sensationalism and genuine investigative journalism, trashy gossip and well-informed analyses, political partisanship and the self-confidence to cock a snook at the rich and powerful, plus, of course, the willingness to tell their readers both uncomfortable truths and copious quantities of bovine faeces. In the digital age, we can add the function of providing a platform for readers to air their unexpurgated views and sometimes engage with one another in what is euphemistically called banter.

The eclectic nature of tabloid content is demonstrated below by looking at the three most prominent stories in the digital editions of the *Sun*, *Star*, *Mirror*, *Mail* and *Express* between 16.30 and 17.30 UK time on Friday 24 January 2020. That date was not cherry-picked; it was quite simply the afternoon when I started work on these concluding remarks. For Reuters, the most important items of world news that afternoon were the Chinese government's emergency measures to deal with the outbreak of the coronavirus in the city of Wuhan, President Trump's decision to host Israeli leaders to discuss a Middle East peace plan, and breaking news of a shooting incident in the German town of

© The Author(s) 2020
S. Buckledee, *Tabloiding the Truth*,
https://doi.org/10.1007/978-3-030-47276-4_11

Rot am See. As regards British news, Reuters UK prioritised the view of the Metropolitan Police that live facial recognition cameras should be installed in London, the improved performance of UK businesses and the consequent unlikelihood of a cut in interest rates, and Boris Johnson's decision to convene a COBRA[1] meeting to discuss appropriate responses to the coronavirus emergency. In its 170-year history, the Reuters news agency has always sought to inform, not to amuse or titillate, and no one expects similar evaluations of newsworthiness in the tabloids.

That said, all five of the papers considered here made the coronavirus one of their most prominent news stories. That was somewhat surprising because on 24 January 2020, when we were all cramming into tube trains and meeting friends in pubs, restaurants, gyms and football grounds, we could not imagine the extent to which a mysterious illness in a faraway land would shortly have an enormous impact on our daily lives.

It has already been noted that the right-wing tabloids will not defend a conservative politician is he/she appears to have let the public down, and on the day in question the *Sun*, which a few weeks earlier had worked energetically for a Boris Johnson victory in the December 2019 election, pulled no punches in its headline: 'TOO LITTLE TOO LATE Fury at government "inaction" over deadly coronavirus hitting Britain putting thousands of lives at risk' (Matthews 2020). The article reported that fourteen Britons had been hospitalised while tests were conducted to see if they had contracted the virus, and was highly critical of the government, particularly of the Health Secretary, Matt Hancock, for having waited until earlier that day before chairing the emergency COBRA meeting. The *Sun, which* had regularly attacked the Liberal Democrats for their anti-Brexit stance, now backed the Lib Dems' acting leader, Ed Davey, who was quoted stating that '[i]t's time Matt Hancock pulled his finger out'. It was classic tabloid stuff: exaggeration of the health risk (there were at that time no confirmed cases of the coronavirus in Britain), the *Sun* standing up for the public and attacking ministerial incompetence, the colloquial language of ordinary people.

*Daily Star Online* managed to interview (by telephone, presumably) Josh Nielsen, a young Australian trapped in Wuhan after the government effectively sealed off the city of eleven million inhabitants in an attempt to prevent the virus from spreading. Instructed just three days earlier to stock up with food and wear a face mask, he did not know if he had been infected because the symptoms did not manifest themselves for ten days. In addition, he was quoted stating that the full extent of the pandemic had only become evident when the emergency became global news that the Chinese authorities could no longer censor (O'Donoghue and Parker 2020). Another of the *Star*'s most prominent stories that afternoon—a round-up of the weirdest or most disgusting dishes eaten in various parts of the world (Livesy 2020)—also established a connection to Wuhan since one of the hypotheses concerning the origin of the coronavirus linked it to the local delicacy of bat soup. A medical emergency that looked sure to worsen considerably was thus associated with a piece intended primarily to entertain.

*Mirror Online* focused on the inability of medical staff in Wuhan's overstretched hospitals to cope with the numbers of people requiring tests and/or treatment, and the Chinese government's extraordinary plan to build a new 1000-bed hospital in just five days (Kitching and Blanchard 2020). The authors note that the Chinese authorities had learnt valuable lessons during the Severe Acute Respiratory Syndrome (SARS) epidemic in Beijing in 2003, but they also point out that to get the bad news that the government tries to hide they rely on videos posted on social media.

Blanchard et al. (2020) for *MailOnline* focused on the foreigners unable to leave Wuhan and quoted an unnamed man who claimed to have many contacts among the international community in the city and reported that, 'Everyone is panicked and wants to leave the [*sic*] China and go back to their countries or at least move to a safer city in China'. A biostatistics researcher at Lancaster University was quoted saying that his calculations indicated that over the following two weeks the number of infected people in Wuhan alone would rise to around 250,000, and possibly to 350,000.

State-controlled Chinese television is hardly a reliable source of information and *Express Online* surprised no one by reporting that, 'China has been accused of covering up the true scale of the coronavirus crisis, which has already affected a suspected 1000 people across the globe' (Anderson 2020). Western journalists who, even if they wished to go to Wuhan, could not do so had to seek news from whatever sources they could find.

*Sina Weibo*, a Chinese microblogging site, is also subject to censorship but it seems that footage critical of government policy can be posted and will survive for a short period. While the government insisted that the city had been swiftly quarantined, Claire Anderson for the *Express* quoted the *Washington Post*, which had discovered that Wuhan Railway had posted on *Sina Weibo*, and then deleted, a report that 300,000 people had taken trains out of the city before the travel ban became effective.

Given the difficulty in obtaining credible news from Wuhan, the five tabloids considered here chose four distinct strategies: the *Star* and the *Mail* each managed to communicate with a foreigner living in the city; the *Mirror* focused less on the clinical aspects of the virus than on the plan to build a new hospital in under a week, a subject on which State television did not need to be treated with the same diffidence; the *Express* trawled Western and Chinese social media as well as American newspapers to create a coherent whole from a collection of fragments; the *Sun* got round the problem by concentrating on the British government's response to the emergency.

If all five tabloids gave prominence to one of the main news items identified by Reuters, they obviously did not neglect trivia, sex and gossip. Chapter 8 investigated the way the tabloids gleefully report the fall from grace of celebrities they themselves had helped to elevate to fame and fortune, while in Chapter 5 we saw how papers full of photos of young and nearly naked women are implacable in their condemnation of sex offenders, and on 24 January these characteristics were evident in reports in the *Mirror* and the *Sun* of the nine-year sentence handed to the singer Danny Tetley. He had shot to fame in 2018 following his appearances on ITV's musical talent show *X Factor*, but after his conviction for paying teenage boys to send him indecent photos of themselves the judge observed that his celebrity status was 'gone, tarnished and destroyed' (Saunders 2020) and that his former fans would see him as 'a despicable creature' (Christodoulou and Vonow 2020).

*MailOnline*'s celebrity gossip story concerned Meghan Markle and her decision to be interviewed on American TV by the comedian and chat show host Ellen DeGeneres, which represented 'a snub to BFF[2] Oprah' (Roundtree 2020).

For sex, the *Star* turned to Adult Video News (AVN), the trade magazine of the adult video industry, and the awards ceremony (Adult Entertainment Expo) that it has organised every January since 1984. While the 2020 edition was in progress in Las Vegas, a female journalist for *Star Online* interviewed the porn star Lexi Lore, who explained that, 'The unique aspect of AVN Expo is that our industry has created a body-positive, liberating experience where performers and fans can join together in a safe, controlled environment' (Roberts 2020). Pornography is presented as a perfectly legitimate business and there is no suggestion that it might be degrading for women.

*Mirror Online* had a second article about a minor celebrity's fall from grace with a piece on the former footballer, Jermain Pennant, who had been removed from the Sky Sports News programme after appearing to be drunk on-air (Prenderville 2020), while the *Sun* matched the *Star*'s post on strange and/or revolting dishes from around the world with a survey of the fifteen best fish and chip shops in Britain (Coyle 2020).

By far the most surprising of the fifteen articles given prominence on the afternoon of 24 January was one on the *MailOnline* site that was clearly sympathetic towards a French national whose application for permanent UK residency had been rejected by the Home Office. The *Daily Mail* had campaigned vigorously and with more than a touch of xenophobia for the Leave campaign during the months leading up to the Brexit referendum of 23 June 2016, and under Paul Dacre's long editorship it was never particularly concerned about unhelpful officialdom when the victims of unnecessary rigidity were foreigners. In September 2018, Dacre stepped down and was replaced by Geordie Greig, who had been editor of the sister paper *Mail on Sunday* and in 2016 had been in favour of Britain's remaining in the EU. On 24 January 2020, the influence of the new editor was plain to see. The first two sentences made it abundantly clear that the French citizen concerned had an impeccable case for permanent UK residency based on his professional expertise, his years living in Britain and his marital circumstances:

> A French super-chef whose food has wowed the country for two decades today slammed the Home Office after he was denied permanent UK residency despite living in the country for 23 years.

Claude Bosi, who has won two Michelin stars at his London restaurants, has lived in England for more than 20 years alongside his wife Lucy, who is believed to be British. (Robinson 2020)

Later in the article, it emerged that Bosi had filled in the wrong form—he should have applied for EU Settled Status—and that the Home Office had contacted him to explain the correct procedure. Before September 2018, he might well have been described as a thick Frog who in twenty-three years had not learnt enough English to understand clear instructions on the Home Office's website, but under Geordie Greig's editorship being French was no longer enough in itself to provoke hostility.

In 2016, the *Express* had also been tenacious in urging the public to vote to leave the EU, and eight days before Brexit became a reality *Express Online* looked forward to Britain's imminent freedom to negotiate trade deals and invited readers to vote in a poll on whether Boris Johnson should prioritise a deal with the USA, the EU, Japan, Australia or some other country[3] (Mowat 2020). That Brexit was now unstoppable did not mean that the *Express* had softened its attitude towards the European Union: on the same afternoon, an interview with Daniel Hannan, Conservative MEP from 1999 to the UK's last day as a member of the EU on 31 January 2020, focused on his claim that the European Parliament routinely breaks its own rules to discriminate against Eurosceptic parties and individuals (Bet 2020).

From this very small sample of articles given prominence during a one-hour period one afternoon, several of the positive and negative characteristics of the tabloids are evident. Two Conservative-supporting papers took to task a Conservative government, and although in both cases the criticism was somewhat unfair—Health Secretary Matt Hancock was urged to pull his finger out when there were as yet no confirmed cases of the coronavirus in the UK, while to secure his settled status in the UK Monsieur Bosi only needed to go back to the Home Office's website and do things properly—the fact that those tabloids were so obviously not in thrall to power was no bad thing. Mercenary sex, with images of a young porn star revealing quite a lot of herself, earned no hint of disapproval from a female journalist, while a celebrity's voyeuristic obsession with underage boys and consequent imprisonment was reported with some relish. Megan Markle's preference for one chat-show host over another was given far more importance than it merited. A survey of the appalling things that only foreigners would be able to eat was contrasted with a celebration of good old British fish and chips. And although it was clear to even the most ardent opponent of Brexit that at 11.00 p.m. GMT on Friday 31 January Britain would be out of the EU, the *Express* could not resist a parting shot at the European Parliament.

Previous predictions of the imminent demise of this most British of institutions proved to be mistaken, and today it would be unwise to claim that social media are ringing the death knell for the popular press now that the digital versions of the tabloids are compensating for reduced sales of the paper editions. There are people who never have a good word to say about them but nevertheless read them online, while the more discerning understand that tabloid hacks, for all their questionable taste and sometimes dodgy practices, have the great virtue of being entirely traceable. Of course, they tabloid the truth, but because we know the business interests and political bias of their employers, we understand how and why they misreport things and can therefore read between the lines. This makes them rather predictable, as is evinced by the fact it is very easy to parody the style of individual titles and produce spoof headlines. 'Single mum of 12 pregnant with QUADS rehoused in MANSION, and YOU are paying for it!' could only be the *Daily Mail* giving a characteristically enlightened depiction of benefits claimants. Similarly, 'WORSE-OFFSTADT Glum Guy admits EU feeling the pinch after Bo Jo turns off dough flow' features the *Sun*'s typical use of puns, rhyme and colloquial language to deride that paper's least favourite European. Both of these spoof headlines are offensive: the first denies the tough reality of most single mothers' lives and the second mocks a perfectly decent man whose only crime is to be a Belgian who can pick holes in the case for sovereignism in very effective English. But if the papers responsible for such headlines were no longer around, I think we would miss them.

## Notes

1. Meetings of the Cabinet Office Briefing Rooms (COBR) are usually held in briefing room A, hence the acronym COBRA.
2. Presumably, the initials BFF are used in the sense of Best Friend Forever rather than the alternative of Big Fat Fuck.
3. When the poll closed 7078 people had voted, 66% of whom indicated a deal with the USA as the top priority.

## References

Anderson, Claire. 2020. Coronavirus patients treated next to dead bodies as Wuhan hospitals reach breaking point. *Express Online*, January 24. https://www.express.co.uk/news/world/1232877/Coronavirus-china-video-wuhan-hospital-uk-virus-symptoms-cases-bat-soup-death-toll. Accessed 25 January 2020.

Bet, Martina. 2020. Brexit Farce: Daniel Hannan exposes three times EU has 'made up rules as they go along'. *Express Online*, January 24. https://www.express.co.uk/news/uk/1233072/brexit-news-eu-bill-boris-johnson-deal-daniel-hannan-mep-brussels-spt. Accessed 26 January 2020.

Blanchard, Sam, Vanessa Chalmers, and Stephen Matthews. 2020. 'We're all trapped now': Wuhan residents say they have all been left to catch China's deadly coronavirus as city orders total lockdown—As country reports 41 people have died and more than 1,200 infected. *MailOnline*, January 24. https://www.dailymail.co.uk/health/article-7923913/Shanghai-Disney-closed-Saturday-help-prevent-spread-virus.html. Accessed 25 January 2020.

Christodoulou, Holly, and Brittany Vonow. 2020. Sick singer X Factor star Danny Tetley, 39, jailed for 9 years for exploiting kids after begging children to send him indecent pics. *Sun Online*, January 24. https://www.thesun.co.uk/news/10812735/x-factor-danny-tetley-exploiting-kids/. Accessed 26 January 2020.

Coyle, Matt. 2020. First Plaice: Britain's 15 best fish and chip shops revealed—Does your local make the cut? *Sun Online*, January 24. https://www.thesun.co.uk/news/10807957/britains-15-best-fish-and-chip-shops-revealed-does-your-local-make-the-cut/. Accessed 26 January 2020.

Kitching, Chris, and Ben Blanchard. 2020. Coronavirus epicentre Wuhan building new 1,000-bed hospital in just five days. *Mirror Online*, January 24. https://www.mirror.co.uk/news/world-news/coronavirus-epicentre-wuhan-building-new-21349881. Accessed 25 January 2020.

Livesy, Jon. 2020. Wackiest foods sampled by Daily Star writer as bat soup is linked to China coronavirus. *Daily Star Online*, January 24. https://www.dailystar.co.uk/news/latest-news/wackiest-foods-sampled-daily-star-21343774. Accessed 25 January 2020.

Matthews, Alex. 2020. Too little too late: Fury at government 'inaction' over deadly coronavirus hitting Britain putting thousands of lives at risk. *Sun Online*, January 24. https://www.thesun.co.uk/news/uknews/10812271/fury-at-government-inaction-over-coronavirus/. Accessed 25 January 2020.

Mowat, Laura. 2020. Brexit poll: Which trade deal should Boris Johnson prioritise? Vote here. *Express Online*, January 24. https://www.express.co.uk/news/politics/1232998/brexit-latest-news-trade-deals-boris-johnson-donald-trump-japan-australia. Accessed 26 January 2020.

O'Donoghue, Rachel, and Emma Parker. 2020. The last tourist in Wuhan: 'We were told to stockpile food and stay inside'. *Daily Star Online*, January 24. https://www.dailystar.co.uk/news/world-news/wuhan-virus-china-tourist-travel-21352993. Accessed 25 January 2020.

Prenderville, Liam. 2020. Jermaine Pennant taken off air by Sky Sports News for 'failing to meet standards'. *Mirror Online*, January 24. https://www.mirror.co.uk/sport/football/news/jermaine-pennant-taken-air-sky-21351684. Accessed 26 January 2020.

Roberts, Sophie. 2020. AVN Expo porn star lifts lid on kinky event—Including 'surreal' moments with fans. *Daily Star Online*, January 24. https://www.dailystar.co.uk/love-sex/avn-expo-porn-star-lifts-21349008. Accessed 26 January 2020.

Robinson, Martin. 2020. 'Am I not good enough to stay?': Two-Michelin-starred French chef Claude Bosi who ran top restaurant Hibiscus and cooked for the Royals is DENIED permanent UK residency despite having lived here for 23 years. *MailOnline*, January 24. https://www.dailymail.co.uk/news/article-7925459/Two-Michelin-starred-French-chef-Claude-Bosi-DENIED-permanent-UK-residency.html. Accessed 26 January 2020.

Roundtree, Cheyenne. 2020. Meghan Markle is planning to give her first interview to Ellen because they are 'kindred spirits and host understands her pain and suffering'—A snub to BFF Oprah. *MailOnline*, January 24. https://www.dailymail.co.uk/news/article-7917487/Meghan-Markle-plans-interview-Ellen-understands-pain.html. Accessed 26 January 2020.

Saunders, Emmeline. 2020. X Factor's Danny Tetley jailed for nine years after begging underage boys for explicit snaps. *Mirror Online*, January 24. https://www.mirror.co.uk/3am/celebrity-news/breaking-x-factors-danny-tetley-21351150. Accessed 26 January 2020.

# Index

## A
Abbott, Diane 143–145
Adams, Gerry 31
Alliteration 78
Alliterative headlines 77, 81
Audience Measurement for Publishers 6

## B
Barroso, Manuel 101
Beckett, Charlie 1–3, 8
Bedroom tax 118
Blair, Tony 32, 35, 37, 39, 43, 45, 46, 83, 100, 117
Bovine spongiform encephalopathy (BSE) 113–115
Brexit 82, 83, 98, 103–106, 124, 125, 147
Brexiteers 97, 103
Brexit referendum 64, 136
British Union of Fascists 51, 73
Brooks, Rebekah 86, 120, 123, 151–153
Brown, Gordon 45
Bruno, Frank 151
Bush, George W. 35, 36, 41, 46

## C
Calais Jungle 58, 64
Callaghan, Jim 27
Cameron-Clegg government 56
Cameron, David 57, 103, 104
Cameron government 56
Chilcot Inquiry 39, 43, 45
Chilcot, Sir John 45
Child sex grooming 121
Clinton, Bill 32, 34, 84
Clooney, George 136

Colloquial substitutes 79
Connotations 77
Corbyn, Jeremy 143, 145–147
Coronavirus 181–183

D

Dacre, Paul 71, 72
Delors, Jacques 98, 101, 106
Depp, Johnny 136

E

Elite 103, 104, 125
Elitists 105
Emotive language 31
English, David 14
Euphemistic substitutions 78
European Commission 100, 105
European Community 99
European Economic Community (EEC) 99, 102
European Union (EU) 56, 99, 101, 102, 113

F

Falklands 20
Falklands War 19, 24, 41
Farage, Nigel 73, 105
Fein, Sinn 31
*Femail* 14
Figurative language 31
Foot, Michael 28, 145
France 38, 58

G

Gascoigne, Paul 153

Gately, Stephen 154
Germany 38
Good Friday Agreement 29, 31, 32, 46
Goody, Jade 134
Gove, Michael 44
Greenslade, Roy 3, 22

H

Harman, Harriet 86
Harmsworth, Harold 51
Heath, Edward 54
Hillsborough disaster 164
Homosexuality 13, 83
Hussein, Saddam 35–37, 43

I

Idioms 17
Immigration 52, 55, 61
*Implicature* 13
Independent Press Standards Organisation (IPSO) 8, 65, 69, 73, 83, 142
Intertextuality 139
Iraq 35, 38
Iraq War 19, 25, 41, 45
Irish Republican Army (IRA) 27, 28, 31, 34
ISIS/Daesh 56
Islamophobia 56, 67

J

Johnson, Boris 104, 124
Jordan 137
Juncker, Jean-Claude 102, 103, 105

## K

Kennedy, Charles 39
Kinnock, Neil 28, 29, 145, 146
Kohl, Helmut 97

## L

Lamb, Larry 11, 12, 19, 82
Lawrence, Stephen 70–72
Leavers 103
Leveson Inquiry 146
Leyen, Ursula von der 105

## M

Maastricht Treaty 99, 100
MacKenzie, Kelvin 20–25, 81, 98, 164
Mad cow 113–115
Major, John 99
Maxwell, Robert 3
May government 56
May, Theresa 82, 104, 146
McCann, Madeleine 165
McGuinness, Martin 31–34
Merkel, Angela 98
Metaphor 55, 69, 97, 103
Michael, George 131, 132
Miliband, Ed 145, 146
Mogg, Jacob Rees 104
Monopolies and Mergers Commission 145
Morgan, Piers 41, 43, 95
Mosley, Oswald 51, 73
Murdoch, Rupert 3, 5, 11, 15, 19, 123, 145

## N

National Health Service (NHS) 113, 157
National Union of Mineworkers (NUM) 20, 29
Neesom, Dawn 86
Neologism 23
News Corporation (News Corp) 146
Nicknames 17
Northern & Shell 5
Northern Ireland 19, 46
Northern Island 26

## O

Onomatopoeic 23

## P

Page-3 girls 12, 13, 80, 82, 86
Paisley, Ian 34
PAMCo 6
Parker-Bowles, Camilla 132, 133
Payne, Sarah 120
Paywalls 5
Permissive Society 11
*Polis* 1
Powell, Enoch 52–54
Press Complaints Commission 154, 155, 176
Presupposition 155
Price, Katie 137
Prince Charles 13, 132, 133
Princess Diana 133
Prodi, Romano 101
Provisional IRA 27, 31
Punning headline 78, 95, 160
Puns 17, 78, 79

**R**
Race Relations Bill 53, 54
Reach plc 5
Remainers 103, 104
Remaniacs 103
Remoaners 103
Rhyme 78
Rhyming headlines 95
Ridley, Nicholas 97, 104
Rothermere, Viscount 51, 73
Rowling, J.K. 134–136, 142
Royal family 13
Royal Ulster Constabulary (RUC) 27, 29

**S**
Santer, Jacques 100, 102
Sarah's Law 120, 123
Scargill, Arthur 20, 29
Scottish independence 82, 83
Short, Clare 80
Simile 69
Slang 17, 78, 79
Starr, Freddie 163, 164

Sturgeon, Nicola 82

**T**
Thalidomide 112
Thatcher, Margaret 19, 20, 24, 25, 27, 28, 97–99, 117
Tory sleaze 119
Treaty of Lisbon 101
Trinity Mirror 5
Troubles 19, 26, 29
Trump, Donald 181

**V**
Variant Creutzfeldt-Jakob disease (vCJD) 113–115
Verhofstadt, Guy 106

**W**
Wade, Rebekah. *See* Brooks, Rebekah above
*Wikipedia* 137
Wilson, Harold 53

Printed by Printforce, United Kingdom